D1426894

Deleuze and the Naming of God

Plateaus – New Directions in Deleuze Studies

'It's not a matter of bringing all sorts of things together under a single concept but rather of relating each concept to variables that explain its mutations.'
Gilles Deleuze, *Negotiations*

Series Editors

Ian Buchanan, Cardiff University
Claire Colebrook, Penn State University

Editorial Advisory Board

Keith Ansell Pearson
Ronald Bogue
Constantin V. Boundas
Rosi Braidotti
Eugene Holland
Gregg Lambert
Dorothea Olkowski
Paul Patton
Daniel Smith
James Williams

Titles available in the series

Forthcoming volumes:

Visit the Plateaus website at www.euppublishing.com/series/plat

DELEUZE AND THE NAMING OF GOD
Post-Secularism and the Future of Immanence

Daniel Colucciello Barber

EDINBURGH
University Press

© Daniel Colucciello Barber, 2014

Edinburgh University Press Ltd
22 George Square, Edinburgh EH8 9LF

www.euppublishing.com

Typeset in Sabon by
Servis Filmsetting Ltd, Stockport, Cheshire,
and printed and bound in Great Britain by
CPI Group (UK) Ltd, Croydon CR0 4YY

A CIP record for this book is available from the British Library

ISBN 978 0 7486 8636 0 (hardback)
ISBN 978 0 7486 8637 7 (webready PDF)

Contents

Acknowledgements

The writing of this book depends on so many others. Its impetus emerged from a reading group on Deleuze, one with great intensity, and I intensely thank my collaborators: Michelle Koerner, Alvaro Reyes, and Erin Yerby. I am also especially grateful to Philip Goodchild and Ken Surin, who have been insightful and encouraging throughout my work on this book, and to Stanley Hauerwas, for pushing me to value the act of writing. I am able to write, to sign anything at all, only because of a multitude of relations. The fact that we cannot count a multitude does not keep me from acknowledging some of those on whom I have counted in making this book what it is: Michael Hardt, J. Kameron Carter, Anthony Paul Smith, Joshua Ramey, Brian Goldstone, Nathaniel Cunningham, Davis Rhodes, Zeynep Bulut, David Kishik, Vincent DeLuca, Rocky Gangle, Jason Smick, Joe Winters, Adam Kotsko, David Liu, Clayton Crockett, Creston Davis, Wendy Lochner, and Jeff Robbins. Additionally, I thank the anonymous reviewers of this book for their comments.

I am very grateful to Carol Macdonald, of Edinburgh University Press, and to Ian Buchanan and Claire Colebrook, editors of the Plateaus series, for their support of this project. I would also like to express my gratitude to the ICI Berlin Institute for Cultural Inquiry, where I was a fellow while finishing the editing of this book.

Much of Chapter 1 appeared, in a previous iteration, as 'On Post-Heideggerean Difference: Derrida and Deleuze', *Southern Journal of Philosophy* 47.2 (2009), pp. 113–29. Chapter 4 is an expanded and revised version of a previous article, 'The Particularity of Jesus and the Time of the Kingdom: Philosophy and Theology in Yoder', *Modern Theology* 23.1 (2007), pp. 63–89. Also, at several points in this book I have drawn on selections from my article, 'Immanence and Creation', *Political Theology* 10.1 (2009), pp. 131–41. I would like to thank these journals for permission to make use of this material.

Introduction

A Proclamation

It's been awhile since Nietzsche's madman passed through the marketplace, proclaiming 'God is dead!'[1] Should we imagine that we have, by now, taken his proclamation to heart? A look at the contemporary marketplace shows that we still imagine quite a few things. Some imagine that a world without God has been achieved. Such a world includes exceptions, of course, but they are imagined as survivals, antiquarian curiosities bound to be swept away as secularisation advances. Alongside such confident ones there are more polemical advocates of Enlightenment, who imagine that a world without belief in God will emerge only by taking the fight against religion more seriously. Belief in God, say such polemicists, will go away only when we push it out the door. On the other side, however, there are those who contest Nietzsche's proclamation by continuing to imagine God's existence, or by doing so in a new manner. Sometimes this takes the form of an imagination of God that sees itself as having accounted for Nietzsche's proclamation, such that we might speak of a post-Nietzschean image of God. At other times, this imagination of God's existence is discursively linked to a so-called 'return of religion'.

All of this is to say that the imagination is profligate. Such profligacy exceeds the limits that are imposed when we attempt to frame responses to Nietzsche's proclamation in terms of direct affirmation and negation. This, however, seems to be something Nietzsche already understood, for his proclamation is meant primarily not as a denotative claim, but rather as an invocation of the imagination and its power. To proclaim the death of God is to proclaim that God belongs to the imagination, it is to proclaim that the imagination is capable of creating something so powerful that it can be recognised as the essence of all existence. Nietzsche, of course, is calling for a liberation of existence from this divine essence. Yet such existence is inseparable from its imagination as that which is liberated from something else (God), which is also being imagined. We are always

1

imagining, even when we seek to liberate ourselves from what has been imagined.

It is along these lines that we can understand Nietzsche's proclamation to be concerned not just with God but also with the power of the imagination – that is, with the imagination's productivity, its profligacy, its capacity to generate a world. In fact, Nietzsche's proclamation presumes that there is no world without the imagination of that world, and that the world that exists is the world we have imagined. To imagine is to make the world; to call for a different imagination, or to imagine differently, is to make a different world. We should, in virtue of these claims, interpret Nietzsche's proclamation as having less to do with God's existence than with the world produced by the imagination of God's existence. It is a proclamation that concerns theology, but it is just as much one that concerns what is at stake in making a world. And to be concerned with the making of a world is to be concerned with the political. Nietzsche's proclamation, then, is a theopolitical proclamation, one that concerns both God and the task of making the world, but one that always and only does so by way of the imagination.

To invoke Nietzsche's proclamation in the way that I am doing is to read it squarely as being about the theopolitical, but in such a way that attention[2] is directed not to the specific claim about God's death so much as to the fact that God's death, as well as God's life, stands or falls on the power of the imagination. In other words, what is at issue here is not just a Nietzschean version of an already settled theopolitical imagination, but also, and more so, an instance in which the *act* of imagining the theopolitical is brought to the fore. To be even more precise, this is an instance in which the act of imagining God – or of naming God, that is, theology – is brought into relation with the act of imagining and making the world. Theology is at issue insofar as this act of imagination addresses itself to the purportedly highest value, the value that is imagined to give value to the world. The political, on the other hand, is at issue insofar as this act of imagination wants to evaluate the name of God in virtue of the world that the imagination of God brings into being, and in virtue of the world that might be brought into being through a different imagination.

When we keep in mind this aspect of Nietzsche's proclamation – that is, the way that it raises the question of world-making – it becomes a bit clearer why we are today able to find a variety of responses, a variety that does not correspond to anything like a straightforwardly affirmative or negative position on the proclamation. If there are a variety of positions on 'the death of God', this is not because it is hard to decide one way or the other, to agree or disagree, but rather because such a proclamation is not ultimately about responding with a yes or a no. What is ultimately put forth by this proclamation is the task of imagining a world, the task of world-making. If Nietzsche's proclamation has charged us with a demand, then it is not a demand to say yes or no to God, it is instead a demand to say yes or no to the world we find ourselves always already imagining – and there are, I think it is clear, very many ways of imagining and making a world. The variety of responses to the death of God, then, correspond to the variety of ways that the world may be imagined, or to the variety of worlds that could be made. This is also to say that disagreement about the death of God emerges from disagreement about the political, where the political is broadly understood in terms of the decision or decisions made about the world that is to be made. If God is important here – and I believe God, or at least the name of God, most definitely is – then this is because it is with God that the stakes of world-making are pushed to the highest degree.

But why is this the case? Why is it that God plays such a special role in the act of world-making? The most direct answer is that God names the value of values, or the value in terms of which the world is evaluated. Consequently, if what is in play is the evaluation of the given world, then this cannot take place without addressing the given world's axis of evaluation. Whether this *has* to be the case – that is, whether it is somehow necessary to begin by thinking of the highest value in terms of God – is, in the end, a scholastic preoccupation. For it is, *in fact*, the case that the world that is presently given, at least for Nietzsche, is a world in which this is the case. There can be no evaluation of the world, therefore, without an encounter with and evaluation of the name of God. Pushing this point a bit further, we can observe that any attempt to evaluate the world, or to imagine another one, that does not encounter the name of God, or that attempts to bracket the name of God out of the discussion, is going to have a hard time accomplishing its purposes. For this reason, the question of the political will have to be, at least for the time being, a question of the theopolitical. For the same reason, secularisation – insofar as it tries to define the political in such a way that the name of God is put to the side – will fail to encounter the political at its broadest level. This broadest level is the imagination of the world, a world that has, for a very long time, been associated with God. If such a world is to be changed, then the name of God must be encountered rather than bracketed.

There is another – though not unrelated – answer that may be given to the question of why God plays such a special role in the act of world-making, and this is that the name of God has a tendency to subsume within itself the act by which God is named. Put otherwise, this is to say that God, imagined as the value of all values, subordinates imagination to itself. The production of God is the production of a value that devalorises the act by which value is produced; the God that is imagined captures and imposes itself on imagination. This is the meaning of the transcendent, of what Nietzsche has in mind when he tells us: 'do not believe those who speak to you of otherworldly hopes!'[3] God here names the otherworldly – that is, the value that takes one away from the world, that takes one away from the act of imagining the world. Of course, even when we name God, even when we invest ourselves in a hope that is otherworldly, we are still imagining the world, which is to say that the link between imagination and world-making does not go away. It is just that this link is obscured, it is subordinated to the form of evaluation named by God, as if this God somehow pre-existed the act of imagination. Along these lines, we can say that Nietzsche's antagonism toward God, or the otherworldly, stems not from something else that he wants to imagine, but rather from the indissoluble link between imagination and its world. In short, the reason that the name of God plays a special role in the act of world-making is because it is with God that the act of world-making becomes separated from its power.

This power is that of immanence. If God here names the transcendent, then the imaginative productivity of world-making names immanence. More exactly, immanence refers to the relation between the act of imagination and the making of the world. The relation between imagination and world is an immanent one, which means that to speak of the world is to speak of imagination and to speak of imagination is to speak of the world. If God is transcendent, then it is precisely because God interrupts this immanent relation, because God makes both imagination and the world into God's subordinates.

Three Trajectories for Deleuze's Immanence

To transpose Nietzsche's proclamation into the terms of an opposition between transcendence and immanence is to link the milieu of problems addressed and produced by this proclamation to Gilles

Deleuze's philosophy of immanence, which is the central interest of this book.[4] I will not speak of immanence in general, such that Nietzsche and Deleuze could appear as differing instances of the same immanent philosophy. In fact, there will be no analysis of Nietzsche's thought, much less a survey of various thinkers of immanence. The aim is much more exact, namely to think immanence in Deleuze, or to use the question of immanence to think Deleuze. In commencing with Nietzsche, then, I am retroactively summoning a precursor to Deleuze. I am introducing, through retroactive philosophical figuration, a problematic field that makes the work of Deleuze possible, even as this work proceeds in a register of philosophical prose that may seem to depart from the manifestly rhetorical and interpellative character of Nietzsche's proclamation. The aim, in other words, is to use Nietzsche's forceful language, his intensified call, as a contextualisation, and as a reminder in advance, of what is at stake in the more serene, arid, and conceptual work of Deleuze. Accordingly, before turning more explicitly to Deleuze and to a description of the work this book will do with, from, on, and against him, it will be beneficial to reflect a bit further on the context that emerges from Nietzsche's proclamation and for Deleuze's immanence. This reflection can be articulated along three trajectories, each of which poses a task for Deleuze's immanence.

First of all, it is important to observe a slippage between 'God' and 'otherworldliness'. They appear to be interchangeable, or at least mutually supportive, in the proclamation: to remove God from the picture is to refuse otherworldly hope, and the reason otherworldly hope is bankrupt is because God is dead. Still, they do not immediately signify the same thing, and so we must ask what binds them together, or what makes them part of a common project. In fact, as long as we lack a sense of what renders God and otherworldliness interchangeable, we will remain uncertain of what it is, exactly, that is being opposed. More to the point, we will remain uncertain of why, and even whether, they really do entail one another.

The question, we could say, is whether the naming of God *must* be linked with an otherworldly investment. Nietzsche's proclamation seems to presume that this is the case. It is as if Nietzsche, having proclaimed the death of God, felt the need to elaborate just what is so valuable about affirming this death, about becoming finished with God, and responded to this need by observing that the imagination of God produces otherworldly hopes. What is wrong with the imagination of God's existence, then, is that it enables our attention to become affixed to and captured by the otherworldly. In this sense, the obstacle that the proclamation ultimately seeks to destroy would be not God but otherworldliness. For my own part, this is a compelling way to put the issue, and it is for this reason that I have already introduced and given centrality to the opposition between transcendence and immanence. What is felicitous about these terms is their ability to characterise, respectively, the obstacle that is otherworldliness and the promise that belongs to the link between the imagination and the world. To take up Nietzsche's proclamation is thus to take up the opposition of transcendence and immanence.[5] But is it also to take up the opposition of God and immanence? Is it possible, for instance, to name God while affirming immanence, or to refuse God while remaining caught up in the transcendent? These are the kind of questions left unaddressed by Nietzsche's proclamation. They are also the kind of questions that need to be addressed by Deleuze's immanence.

Second, we should take note of the way that Nietzsche's proclamation is unthinkable apart from the question of change. The death of God is proclaimed because of, and is evaluated in relation to, a dissatisfaction with the presently given, or with what is taken to be given in the present. It is issued in response to a dissatisfaction with the way things are, and to a demand to produce a state of affairs, a future, that would be different. This is what I mean when I speak of change. One might also speak of this in terms of transformation or emergence, although these terms tend to have more specific connotations than those carried by change in general. If this means, on the other hand, that change remains too vague and refers to more modalities of development than are implied by Nietzsche's proclamation, then it seems best, when speaking of change, to speak of it as the constitution of a break. What the proclamation desires, after all, is not just any old change, but a change in relation to which we could mark a before and an after. The change at stake is one that could not be imagined in terms of a development of what is already given. Much better is the imagination of a breakdown of the present, one in which the future rests on a destructive rather than developmental relation to given forms of the world.

When we articulate this sensibility in terms of the proclamation, we see that the death of God serves as the hinge for the creation of a future that breaks with the given. The death of God becomes the condition of possibility for the production of new possibilities. If Nietzsche's proclamation is charged with tension, with the intensification of dissatisfaction, hope, and the relation between them, then this is because in this way it poses quite directly the demand to make a different world, and to do so by encountering the axis around which present imagination revolves, which is the naming of God. The need to force this encounter makes perfect sense when we take into account that the proclamation wants to produce a genuine break. There can be no break with the present if the essence of the present is not directly approached.

This, however, produces an interesting juxtaposition, namely that of the demand for a break, for something new, and the discarding of the name of God as the necessary condition for such a break. I say this is interesting simply because for some, if not for all, the demand for a genuine break can only be fulfilled *by* some manner of relation to the name of God. This is certainly the case for those who adhere to a 'religious' transcendence, but it is also present in – and could be proposed as the motivation for – the recent turn, amongst various 'secular' continental philosophers, to the figure of Paul. Though such philosophers will make this Pauline turn in a way that cannot be identified simply as religious, it is no doubt the case that their appropriation of Paul is bound up with a political aim. They appropriate Pauline theology, even while secularising it, so as to articulate the possibility of another world, of a world that is other insofar as it is born of an event that does not belong to the present situation.[6] From the vantage of the Pauline philosopher, if God is the name that secures the world as it is given, then God – or at least the act of naming God – is also that by which one might turn against the given world. The task is thus to name God otherwise, or to make the naming of God, of that which gives value to the order of the world, into a means of breaking with this order.

Simply put, the presupposition of 'religious' and 'secular' theologians – where theology is understood, quite literally, as any thought concerned with the naming of God – raises a challenge: Does not the demand for a break undermine itself when it makes the refusal of God into a condition of possibility for this break? Does not the very desire for such a break require, contrary to Nietzsche's proclamation, some affirmation of thought that finds itself invoking the name of God, if only in a secularised manner? These questions, along with the fundamental challenge they present, must be addressed by any account of Deleuze's immanence; the force of their challenge is a force that motivates this book.

Finally, we should note the significant degree to which questions of temporality are at issue in Nietzsche's proclamation. This is the case, first of all, because it is not possible to talk about change, much less a break, without talking about structures of temporality. Such change can have no sense apart from its narration, in some way or another, in terms of a before and an after. But there are larger issues raised when we raise the question of temporality, and we can see this by focusing on the notion of the new, or on the production of the novel. When we talk about a break with the present we will likely find ourselves talking about what emerges after the break, or what is made possible by the break, in terms of the new. It would be right, in fact, to say that Nietzsche's proclamation is ultimately concerned with the production of a future that, in order truly to be a future, would have to be capable of being named as new. Yet this presses us to reflect more broadly on what is implied, or what is invoked, by a discourse of the new.

Such a discourse, it must not be forgotten, may be found at work in colonisation, where the coloniser, eager to find some point of evaluation that would be able to transcend the manifest incommensurability between the cultures of the coloniser and the colonised, will often present colonisation as a moment of modernisation and progression, as a chance to do something new. Even if the content of the coloniser's culture may be resisted – so the logic seems to go – surely the opportunity to advance into the future cannot be gainsaid? And beyond the issue of the coloniser's own appeal to a discourse of the new, there is the fact that the colonial encounter is by and large narrated in terms of novelty. Consider, for instance, how normalised it is to think of colonial encounters in terms of beginnings and of new relationships. Consider, furthermore, the very image of a 'new world', which is intrinsic to colonisation but is certainly inherited in some manner from Christianity's sense of itself as the medium of a new humanity. In fact, to attend to this developmental narrative is to discern an imaginary shared not just by Christianity and colonisation, but likewise by the secular – for the secular also presents itself as the medium by or in which difference is overcome and a better, more peaceable, and truly human future is produced.

Should we add Nietzsche's proclamation to all of these, insofar as it too invokes a discourse of the new? And if we should not, then by what means are we able to distinguish its discourse of the new from the one presented by Christianity, colonisation, and the secular? To find an answer to these questions, or at least to find a better way of framing the problem they pose, it is useful to observe the relationship between Christianity and the secular. This is not to leave colonisation to the side, but rather to focus on the imaginaries that have made the world in which colonisation exists.

It is my contention that the opposition between Christianity and the secular, or more broadly between religion and the secular, is epiphenomenal. In other words, despite the differences between them – and there are certainly differences – these differences are less significant than the commonalities.[7] One key commonality, as I have just mentioned, is found in the discourse of the new. On this point, then, the task for Deleuze's immanence is to articulate a discourse of the new that would be different from both the Christian and the secular, which is also to say that there is nothing to be gained by allying such a discourse with the secular and against the Christian. In this sense, a discourse of the new that is proper to immanence should not be aligned with any project of secularisation (much less with any project of Christianisation). Furthermore, as a means of developing its separation from these, it will be important to show how Deleuze's immanence gives rise to a perspective – regarding the discourse of the new, but also, with the previous two points in mind, regarding the relationship between God and world – that is indifferent to the distinction between the Christian and the secular.

Deleuze and Philosophy of Religion

I have begun a book on Deleuze – or, more precisely, on Deleuze's account of immanence and its relation to questions treated under the heading of philosophy of religion – by reflecting on a proclamation belonging to Nietzsche. As long as we recall Deleuze's own stated affinity for Nietzsche's thought, this appears quite commonsensical. Yet the commonsensical connection between Nietzsche and Deleuze tends to include a resolutely anti-theological dimension, whereas I have used Nietzsche's proclamation as a means of stirring up – rather than discarding or overcoming – questions surrounding the naming of God, as it is conjoined with the demand for a break with the presently imagined world. My approach to Deleuze, concomitantly, is one in which such questions are at issue. In fact, these questions indicate for me the problematic field in which Deleuze's work should be read. What, then, is gained by reading it in this manner?

Above all, I believe that to read Deleuze's work in this manner is to emphasise the investment it has in change, understood in terms of a break. Deleuze's philosophy, in this sense, is an attempt to think what it means to break with the given form of the present. To insist on the centrality of an investment in the task of a break is to insist on the fundamentally political character of Deleuze's work. Such a politics may not be recognisable insofar as we think of the political in terms of representation or the public; it will likely not be recognised as politics as long as we think of politics in terms of recognition. But Nietzsche's proclamation is useful here, for it allows us to keep in mind the essentially political character of the act of imagination. If politics involves, and even begins with, the making of the world, and if this world-making is linked to imagination, then the act of imagination is ineluctably political. Against this background, we can see that though Deleuze's philosophy is political, this is not because it thinks 'about' politics. One certainly will not find much of this sort of thinking about politics in his work – but the way to interpret this fact is not to say that the political is something distinct from Deleuze's philosophy. No, the proper interpretation is to say that Deleuze's philosophy is political through and through, because whenever it insists on immanence it is insisting on the link between, the immanence of, imagination and world. The fact that Deleuze's work has a very high degree of complexity and philosophical precision does not signal an abandonment of immanence's political character. Instead, it should be understood as an attempt to extend the more explicit, but less elaborate, politics of world-making set forth in Nietzsche's proclamation.

Yet this still does not address the issue of the naming of God. Even when we grant that Nietzsche's proclamation helps foreground the importance of change to Deleuze's philosophy, that it makes more manifest Deleuze's investment in the task of making the world, we have still not taken up the question of the theological. In order to do this, we can recall what I identified as the theopolitical nature of Nietzsche's proclamation. For better or worse, it is necessary, when charged by the demand for a break with the present, to encounter that by which the present is made possible. The present is made possible, I have said, by the imagination, but more specifically by the imagination of God, or the imagination of the otherworldly. There will be no break with this present unless there is also a break with that which conditions this present. What Nietzsche's proclamation makes clear, then, is that if Deleuze's philosophy is concerned with change, then it must likewise be concerned with God – or, again, with the otherworldly. This is also to say that it must be concerned with, or put in connection with, the task of discerning the obstacle to change. It is certainly the transcendent, but is it also God? And if immanence discards God, is it discarding the order of the present or is it discarding a means by which present may be discarded? None of these questions disappear when we are talking about immanence. On the contrary, to talk about immanence – especially when we talk about it in relation to the matter of understanding what it means and what it would take to make a world that differs from the one presently given – is to feel the pressure of such questions.

Feeling this pressure also makes it much more difficult to conflate immanence with the secular, given that the latter does not stage so much as defer, prophylacticise, and disavow the encounter with the name of God. Whatever Deleuzian immanence may be, it cannot be simply secular. This is a very important point, especially when viewed from the perspective of the political, as I have defined it. What is the secular, after all, if not a dominant formation of the present? Even when the secular finds itself encountering resistance, it tends to frame this resistance in secular terms. This is to say that the secular is a dominant formation at the level of the imagination, and thus a dominant formation of the given world. So if Deleuze's philosophy is concerned with a break from the present, how can it be allied with something that is essential to the imagination of the present? This problem, I think it is fair to say, is one not generally addressed in readings of Deleuze. Far more common is the easy equation of immanence with a secular sensibility. It is precisely such an equation that needs to be made not just difficult, but impermissible. If this creates a problem for the interpretation of Deleuze, if it leaves us without a way of fitting his immanence into the imagination we presently possess, then all the better, since such a problem is the kind one should want to have when one takes as one's aim the production of the new.

Although it is implicit in virtually everything I have thus far said, it should nonetheless be made explicit: to approach Deleuze's immanence in this way is to address it in its intersection with the philosophy of religion.[8] The term 'intersection' is important. Deleuze was not a philosopher of religion, at least not in any standard sense of the appellation. There is little in his work that leads one to recognise an attempt to speak directly *about* religion, at least not in the manner one finds in certain instances of phenomenology, which in their desire to account for experience may find themselves addressing 'religious' experience, or even claiming that experience as such points to a donation that is divine in nature. The difficulty that this latter sort of philosophy of religion encounters, in my view, is its presupposition of a certain separation between philosophy and religion. Such an approach engages religion, but it does so in a manner that seems to presume that religion is already established in terms of a bounded object or field. It is thus a virtue of Deleuze's work, when considered from this vantage, that it does not attempt to apply the philosophy it develops to a settled domain called religion. As I will argue in the course of this book, the concept of the problem is essential to Deleuze's differential immanence. A problem is not the same as an obstacle or a difficulty, for a problem refers to something that is intrinsically open or undecidable. My strategy, then, is to understand the intersection between Deleuze and the philosophy of religion as a problem, as something undecidable, to which this writing is a response. Such an approach, in seizing on this undecidability, also depends on and takes advantage of the fact that Deleuze, by refusing to apply his philosophy to something called religion, allows us to take religion itself as a problematic term.

Religion is, after all, a term deployed as if it had a certainty that it certainly does not have. Its undecidability is too often ignored – or, even worse, presumed not to exist. There is a great deal that could be said about the problems involved in the discourse of religion, far too much for us to take up in this moment. It will have to suffice to recall that when religion is discussed, it is initially and for the most part imagined in such a way that Christianity remains the primary analogate amongst religions. Or perhaps religion will be imagined, from a post-Christian, secular (but still European or neo-European) vantage, as that which is practised – and too often simply 'believed' – by those who have not achieved what those who were once Christian have achieved.[9] The point of all this is to point out what is usually left unaddressed, and unchallenged, when philosophy of religion is practised as usual, namely the presumed equation of religion with Christianity.

My strategy, then, in addressing the *intersection* between Deleuze and the philosophy of religion, is to treat the lack of obvious relation, or the nonrelation, between these loci as a space of potentiality. This means, first of all, understanding the lack of any obvious connection between them as a potential resistance, on the part of Deleuzian immanence, to the still implicitly Christian discourse of religion. This discourse, I have already mentioned, is implicitly Christian both in the sense that religion is often linked to Christian thematics and in the sense that when it is avowedly secular it is assuming a logic that is more post-Christian than anti-Christian (since secularisation is here understood as participating in much of the same developmentalist logic that Christianity incarnates). From the perspective of my interpretation, Deleuze's relative silence on the task of philosophy of religion should be read as a mode of nonparticipation in this logic.

In order to fill out this interpretation, however, the mode of nonparticipation must become more explicit. This is also to say that such nonparticipation in Christian, or secular, logic must take on a more explicitly antagonistic modality. Putting it otherwise, this means that the intersection must itself be articulated, and in such a way that Deleuze's differential immanence converges with an expression of religion that would be indifferent to the discourse of, or between, Christianity and the secular. One way of doing this would be to argue that what appears in Deleuze's immanence resonates with religions that are not Christian. I have sympathy for this sort of project, and it is one I would not oppose, but it is nonetheless not the one that I take up. The reason I do not take up this project is that I am interested in understanding Deleuze's thought in relation to the rather explicitly Christian or secular milieu in which it emerges. While I take his philosophy to be basically antagonistic to this milieu, I simultaneously believe that the articulation of this antagonism benefits from contextualising it within the milieu being antagonised. In other words, if Deleuze's immanence is against Christianity, and is simultaneously not reducible to a post-Christian secular, then it will be quite useful to think of it in connection with both of these terms.

This is why, when I talk in this book about religion, I talk about Christianity. The point in doing so is not to presume that religion is reducible to Christianity but to take seriously the discourse of religion that shaped the milieu of Deleuze's antagonism. Furthermore, the point of talking about Christianity is not to reconcile Deleuzian immanence with Christianity but rather to understand how it is against Christianity, or what it is within Christianity that is the object of antagonism for Deleuze's immanence. In this sense, the emphasis on Christianity, or really on theology – as it is by way of the discourse of theology that Christianity establishes its religious status – has nothing to do with the investment in a future that will have 'worked through' Christianity.[10] On the contrary, the emphasis on Christianity, on theology, on the naming of God, is in service of a future that will have made a break with the dominant, transcendent implications of Christianity. It is in this sense that my emphasis on Christianity, when thinking the intersection between Deleuze's immanence and philosophy of religion, is in alliance with a dechristianisation of the discourse of religion.[11] To say it once again: there can be a break only where there is an encounter with what forecloses the possibility of a break.

One final remark should be made about my approach. Because it requires a reading of Deleuze in which the implications of his own reticence regarding the question of religion are made into a more explicit object of experimentation, I have at certain moments of this book made use of language – particularly language that carries religious connotations – that is more closely linked to philosophers he thought (and read and wrote) about than to his own philosophy. For example, I will make use of the term 'God', which appears in Spinoza and enters into Deleuze's philosophy by way of his interpretation of Spinoza, but which might be imagined as Spinoza's term, rather than Deleuze's. The same predicament may be found in Deleuze's relation to Nietzsche: the latter's concern with the death of God, and with the notion of affirmation, may be imagined as belonging to Deleuze's thought only by way of an 'artificial' graft. To mention all of this is to anticipate, and to address up front, the possible emergence of the suspicion I am now addressing.

My response, first of all, is to observe that even if such language is presumed to belong to Spinoza, or Nietzsche, rather than to Deleuze, we are still talking about philosophers whom Deleuze recognised as his own precursors, philosophers he imagined as belonging to the same trajectory to which he belonged. Any imagined differentiation would therefore fail to touch the question of a Deleuzian philosophy, broadly considered. I would, however, push even more strongly against the very notion of a hard and fast distinction between Deleuze's precursors and Deleuze himself. After all, it seems very difficult, if not impossible, to speak of any philosophy that could be defined independently of its inheritance of other philosophies. Furthermore, the inheritance of Spinoza and Nietzsche by Deleuze is one that Deleuze has not only foregrounded, it is one that he has shaped: as is well known, he quite consciously understood his accounts of such precursors as stemming just as much from his own, strong interventions or reformulations as from the precursors themselves.[12] So while I think it can be helpful to initially observe a certain distinction between Deleuze's own language and the language of the others – his precursors – I think this distinction is sustainable only in an ad hoc and basically fluid manner.

If my own reading has an ad hoc aspect, then the hoc is religion:

my use of Spinozian and Nietzschean language derives from the concern to make explicit the intersection of immanence and religion. This concern, in other words, benefits insofar as we are able to think of Deleuze's philosophy as including not only his own works but also those works in which his philosophy is inseparable from his own reading practice. This is especially the case where the production of Deleuze's philosophy depends on the practice of reading language that is inseparable from religion (such as with Spinoza and Nietzsche). If philosophy is inseparable from the practice of reading – of inheriting – philosophy, then the specific decisions, the cuts or recapitulations, made by a philosopher are especially indicative of what that philosopher's philosophy is actually doing with or against inheritance's unavoidability. (In fact, we might ask whether the tendency to leave 'religion' unthought is – given religion's association with figures of tradition and thus inheritance – linked to philosophy's own anxiety about itself as a practice of reading.) Furthermore, though we may argue about whether it is best to say that religion has been with us, is still with us, or is returning to us, there can be no argument that a reading of religion is necessarily practised. The intersection at stake in this book, then, belongs to the intersection between such a practice of reading religion and the practice of reading Deleuze. Reading practices are thus understood as constitutive of, rather than extraneous to, thought – and this likewise holds for the thought that is imagined as belonging to Deleuze.

This insistence on the inseparability of a philosophy from its inheritance, and from the reading practices that enact this inheritance, is what motivates my use, in this book, of the work of John Howard Yoder and Theodor Adorno. The argument is, and remains throughout, concerned with the philosophy of Deleuze, and specifically with Deleuze's understanding of immanence. However, in order to articulate this philosophy it is necessary to address the problems that it opens up and that intersect with it. And in order to address these matters it will be necessary, at various points, to draw on thought that does not belong to Deleuze but that enables the articulation of the thought that does belong to Deleuze. Accordingly, the role here played by Yoder and Adorno is supplemental. This means that Deleuze's work is central throughout, whereas the work of Yoder and Adorno is encountered occasionally and partially, and in such a manner that these occasions and parts are selected in virtue of their ability to help articulate Deleuze's work. In this sense, my approach takes Yoder and Adorno to be allies of Deleuze's thought – allies that make possible a practice of reading Deleuze in which the possibilities of Deleuze's own thought become better understood.

Surveying the Argument

My reading of Deleuze begins from an attempt to understand his philosophy in terms of differential immanence. Such a reading obviously insists on the centrality of immanence to Deleuze's thought – in doing so, however, it says not only that this thought is an articulation of immanence, but also that it is a thought that takes immanence as a constant problem. In other words, we should understand immanence not only as the effect of Deleuze's work, but also as the problem that motivates it. Furthermore, as the term 'differential immanence' implies, the immanence that is central to Deleuze is determined by its differential character. What does it mean to speak of an immanence that is differential? In essence, it means that immanence is without object. When we speak of Deleuzian immanence, we are not speaking of immanence to some object or thing, nor are we speaking of an immanence between two things. Immanence, because it is differential, can never be thought in terms of relations to or between things, because before there are things there are differences. In fact, it is even imprecise to speak of immanence itself as an object or thing – after all, difference is prior to things, and so wherever there is a thing, it is a thing that has been constituted by difference.

The concern of Chapters 1 and 2 is to explore how differential immanence is articulated. Because the more explicitly constructive moves that I will be making require a deployment of differential immanence, both as such and in terms of several of its conceptual elements, it is necessary to first devote relatively substantial space to the task of carefully detailing its character and function. These chapters provide this space, and so they tend to hew more closely to a traditional model of philosophical exposition than do the later four chapters. Through what concepts is differential immanence expressed, and how do these concepts interact? How does differential immanence depart from philosophical approaches that pursue the transcendent or leave in abeyance the force of difference? These are the kind of questions that direct Chapters 1 and 2.

The exposition of Deleuze's own philosophy takes place in Chapter 2, whereas Chapter 1 is concerned with something like a very short prehistory of Deleuze's differential immanence. I speak of a 'prehistory' so as to observe that the convergence of the two central themes of difference and immanence had already taken place prior to Deleuze's work. It is Deleuze who innovated these themes, who brought them together with the sort of creativity that allows us to say that differential immanence remained unthought until it was signed by him. Nonetheless, it is important to briefly look at the way these two themes first came together – in the work of Martin Heidegger – in order to understand the precise moves made by Deleuze. Chapter 1 thus begins by examining how the relation between immanence and difference emerges in Heidegger. It proceeds by tracking the problems produced by Heidegger's formulation of this relation, and it concludes by looking at how Jacques Derrida's work may be seen as an attempt to respond to these problems. The chapter thus provides a prehistory, but not without offering a narration of and argument about this prehistory, which is that the convergence between difference and immanence, though incredibly potent, is beset by numerous problems and difficulties – problems that make possible, along with difficulties that are resolved by, Deleuze's own philosophy of differential immanence.

The exact manner in which Deleuze's differential immanence responds to these problems and difficulties becomes evident only in Chapter 2. Here I develop his philosophy at length – working through a variety of its conceptual elements – in order to show how immanence, precisely because it is differential, is always in need of re-expression. There is, I argue, an irresolvable intensity at the essence of immanence's differential structure. While every expression of immanence is produced by this intensity, the intensity itself does not disappear but remains with the expression, and so each expression's intensity demands the production of further expression. This aspect of differential immanence is especially relevant for the larger aims of this book, such as the question of how to conceive change, or the related question of whether it is possible to conceive this change in terms of a break if one does not have reference to the transcendent. What emerges here is the capacity to imagine change without the transcendent: if immanence is differential, and thus requires re-expression, then immanence can alter itself intrinsically, it can change without having to relate to something outside of it. I emphasise the way that this account of immanent change is furthered by Deleuze's treatment of temporality, which culminates in a discussion of creation. The future, I argue, is expressed in terms of creation – that is, as a product that is in immanence with the past and present yet simultaneously brings about something genuinely new.

This, in any case, is the position made possible by my interpretation of Deleuze's immanence. Along these lines, we could say that the production of new possibilities of existence, of possibilities that are novel precisely insofar as they break with the present order of things, emerges in terms of immanence, or without reference to the transcendent. Many questions, however, still must be pursued. Above all, we have yet to address the question of theology, or of the role to be granted to the naming of God. Thus far we have an account of how Deleuzian immanence will attempt to articulate, via re-expression, the capacity for change, for the creation of new possibilities of existence. But this is only a beginning, for at this point we lack a sense of how it encounters the challenge presented by theology, which will stake out a position from which the change articulated by Deleuzian immanence appears to fall short of a genuine break with the present. From this theological vantage, such change amounts to a mere mutation of the given that is unable to essentially get out of the given's frame. Once again, regardless of whether this challenge holds up – I will argue that it does not – it remains extremely important to encounter it, for production of the new must include an encounter with whatever is imagined as foreclosing the new. Furthermore, if we do not take up the challenge posed by the naming of God, we will find ourselves in (at least implicit) agreement with the secular tendency to quarantine and evade, rather than to explicitly struggle with, this challenge.

These and other issues surrounding the relation between Deleuze's differential immanence and the naming of God are taken up in Chapters 3 and 4. Roughly speaking, my argument attempts to draw a line within theology, which allows me to argue that Deleuzian immanence responds not to theology as such but to two different modalities of theology. The purpose of such line-drawing, then, is to distinguish these two different modalities. The first modality of theology is the subject of Chapter 3, which attends to the rivalry that emerges between Deleuzian immanence and Christian theology's analogy of being (where analogy refers to a symbiotic relation between the world, or the immanent, and the divine, or the transcendent). Specifically, I look at this theological modality as it appears in its preeminent contemporary exponents, David Bentley Hart and John Milbank. Their account of analogy is of interest precisely because it is developed by means of a critique of the themes of difference and immanence that are so central to Deleuze's work. In fact, they contend that the political aim I locate in Deleuze cannot be accomplished from within his differential immanence. I argue that their critique of Deleuzian immanence does not succeed, and in doing so I find the opportunity to further articulate the significant contribution that themes of suffering and disaccord make to an account of immanent creation.

While Chapter 3 discusses the modality of theology in relation to which Deleuzian immanence adopts an antagonistic relation, Chapter 4 introduces an alternative theological modality – one that immanence is able to affirm. My aim in introducing this affirmative (or at least non-exclusive) relation between differential immanence and the naming of God is to show how the former's object of antagonism must be strictly understood as the transcendent. At times the naming of God belongs to the transcendent (as is the case with analogy), but this is not always the case. The subject of Chapter 4 is Yoder's theology, and I attend especially to his account of a politics of Jesus, which expresses God not in terms of a transcendent relation to the world, but on the contrary as the name of the world's resistance to domination and as the capacity to produce a world that departs from such domination. I argue that Yoder's theology – on this theme and others, including the theory of time and the notion of the minoritarian – resonates with Deleuze's differential immanence. Additionally, I show how in Yoder's thought the distinction between secular and Christian continually breaks down, such that what comes to matter is not this distinction but instead the act of immanent, differential construction. To ally Deleuze's philosophy with Yoder's theology is to push even further this breakdown and construction.

Chapters 3 and 4 thus establish the relation between Deleuze's differential immanence and the role of theology, but in doing so they bring to the fore another, and final, set of issues – this time surrounding the question of mediation. As long as one remains focused on the naming of God, the role of mediation remains quite clear: it concerns the relation between the divine and the world. Mediation thus refers to the task of bringing together the possibilities of existence set forth by the name of God and the conditions set forth by the given character of the world. This is an especially clear cut matter where the name of God indicates the transcendent, where mediation brings together the givenness of the thisworldly and the exteriority of the otherworldly. Yet, as I argue, such recourse to the transcendent must be excluded. How, then, might we understand mediation within immanence?

Such a question is too often left to the side, and this is because

19

of the strong link that is presumed between mediation and the transcendent. If we affirm immanence rather than transcendence, then why would we even need to speak of mediation? I argue that while there is evidently no need to mediate the transcendent and the world, it is still necessary to provide an account of mediation. Specifically, this would be a mediation between differential immanence's given expression and its re-expression. Such mediation, it should be noted, is a matter of the political character of immanence: if the concern is to break with the present, then this will happen by way of the re-expression of the present. Although my account of re-expression, in Chapter 2, developed the conceptual lineaments of the immanent creation that is here at stake, it left somewhat undefined what would need to be attended to in order to make sure that the re-expression actually breaks with the given expression. That account ensured only that there must be a re-expression, and that such re-expression is the place where new possibilities of existence could be created. What it did not do, however, is articulate what matters for the actual making of these possibilities. All of these issues, revolving around the theme of mediation, are the concern of Chapters 5 and 6.

Chapter 5 takes up this theme under the heading of the relation between the unconditioned and the conditioned. Deleuze's immanence is essentially unconditioned, for its differential intensity enables the production of new possibilities of existence, yet it must not be forgotten that such possibilities are produced only amidst determinate historical conditions. Where this is forgotten, immanence actually functions as a form of the transcendent – that is, it starts to be imagined as distinct from, or as above and beyond, the conditions of the present. Immanence, even as it opposes otherworldliness, must avoid being treated in an otherworldly manner, as if it existed apart from the conditions of its production. All this is to say that while Deleuzian immanence is never limited to the present, it will be able to break with the present only insofar as it becomes affected by the present. I argue, in fact, that Deleuze's own work, at certain points, falls short in this regard. In this chapter I contend, specifically, that Deleuze's thought is ultimately unable to conceive the relationship between the unconditioned nature of the future and the conditioned nature of the present. In order to resolve this problem I draw on the work of Adorno (as well as certain elements in Deleuze) so as to develop my own notion of metaphilosophy: the task of philosophically conceiving the ways in which philosophy has failed. I develop this notion by working on themes not often associated with the relatively affirmative connotations of creation, such as shame, animal suffering, depression, wretchedness, and senselessness. My argument, however, is that these conditions are not at odds with the demand for creation. Only if we think from such conditions will we be able to resist the present's tendency to continue into the future. There can, after all, be no break with the present unless there is also resistance to the present.

This problematic is further developed in Chapter 6, which begins with an account of immanent belief. Such a belief may be usefully distinguished from belief in the transcendent, which draws one's attention away from the world. Immanent belief is a means of insisting on the reality of the affection of dissatisfaction that metaphilosophy conceives. The political aim remains one of creating new possibilities of existence, but such possibilities belong to this world, the one that, as it is presently given, gives rise to a dissatisfaction that precludes any reconciliation with the given. It is exigent, then, to mediate – and thus precisely *not* to moderate – this dissonant affection, or sense of impossibility, with the creation of possibilities that would break with what is given. If immanent belief supplies this link, then the fabulation of icons – another concept that I develop in the wake of Deleuze's differential immanence – names the process by which the new is created. The future, or at least the future that would genuinely break with the past, must be produced. In order to be produced, it must have, or give to itself, a place – and it is exactly such a place that is produced by icons of immanence. Such icons, I argue, should be understood as real beings, beings that are produced by the re-expression of differential intensity. Re-expression, having now passed through a dissatisfaction that is utopic – that has no place of satisfaction and that remains senseless – is put in service of the production of new, iconic places. Immanence is thus differentially re-expressed as a polytopic future, given place through the imagination of icons, and in this way made real.

Notes

1. Friedrich Nietzsche, *The Gay Science*, trans. Walter Kaufmann (New York: Vintage, 1974), p. 181.
2. My dependence, here and throughout, on terms such as 'matter', 'attention', 'evaluation', and the 'value of values', is influenced by the work of Philip Goodchild, especially *Capitalism and Religion: the Price of Piety* (New York: Routledge, 2002), and *Theology of Money* (Durham, NC: Duke University Press, 2009).

3. Nietzsche, *Thus Spoke Zarathustra*, trans. Walter Kaufmann (New York: Penguin, 1975), p. 13.

4. Out of a concern for simplicity and continuity of citation and exegesis, I do not distinguish between the works authored solely by Gilles Deleuze and those works co-authored with Félix Guattari. This is, I confess, a rather problematic erasure, given my belief that Guattari's influence on Deleuze is substantial. In fact, my account of Deleuze relies heavily on their co-authored *What is Philosophy?*, trans. Hugh Tomlinson and Graham Burchell (New York: Columbia University Press, 1994). For an account of Guattari's work that helps counterbalance the common sublation of 'Guattari' into 'Deleuze', see Janell Watson, *Guattari's Diagrammatic Thought: Writing Between Lacan and Deleuze* (London: Continuum, 2009).

5. 'Transcendence', as I use the term here, and as I intend it throughout the book, refers to that which is made possible by, or which is descriptive of, the 'transcendent'. In other words, I intend transcendence to be understood as interchangeable with the transcendent, where the transcendent refers to any mode of being that belongs to a register or plane that goes beyond the register or plane of the world. Otherwise put, whenever we have more than one plane of being, we have the transcendent. I mention that I mean transcendence to be interchangeable with the transcendent simply because it might be possible to imagine a transcendence that does not come from the transcendent. For instance, if a given mode of existence were to become something else, something other than it is or was, then we might want to say that such a mode of existence has enacted a sort of transcendence. Such enactment, I believe, could be imagined as taking place within immanence, where there is no reference to the transcendent. It is therefore in order to avoid any ensuing terminological confusion that transcendence, in this text, is understood to refer not to the imagination of transcendence within immanence, but always to a transcendence made possible by *the* transcendent. Regarding these distinctions, I am deeply indebted to discussions with and the influence of Ken Surin.

6. Although the literature on this Pauline turn is rapidly growing, the foundational (trinity of) texts can be delineated as including: Alain Badiou, *Saint Paul: The Foundation of Universalism*, trans. Ray Brassier (Stanford: Stanford University Press, 2003); Slavoj Žižek, *The Fragile Absolute: Or, Why Is the Christian Legacy Worth Fighting For?* (London: Verso, 2000); and Giorgio Agamben, *The Time That Remains: A Commentary on the Letter to the Romans*, trans. Patricia Dailey (Stanford: Stanford University Press, 2005). This focus on the Pauline turn should be thought in connection with the Schmittian and Benjaminian trajectories that are usually categorised in terms of 'political theology', as well as with the more deconstructive approach to reli-

gion evident in the work of Jacques Derrida and Jean-Luc Nancy. Nor should we overlook the deployment of religious themes in the writings of Antonio Negri and Michael Hardt.

7. The argument behind this contention may be found in Daniel Colucciello Barber, *On Diaspora: Christianity, Religion, and Secularity* (Eugene, OR: Cascade, 2011).

8. For other treatments of Deleuze and the philosophy of religion that resonate with this 'intersectional' approach, see the work of Goodchild, whose pathbreaking approach is on display in *Capitalism and Religion* as well as in *Gilles Deleuze and the Question of Philosophy* (Madison, NJ: Farleigh Dickinson University Press, 1996). See also: Joshua Ramey, *The Hermetic Deleuze: Philosophy and Spiritual Ordeal* (Durham, NC: Duke University Press, 2012); Paul A. Harris and Joshua Ramey (eds), *Spiritual Politics After Deleuze, Substance* 39.1 (2010).

9. Though these points have emerged in various ways and from various perspectives, see especially the following texts: Talal Asad's *Genealogies of Religion: Discipline and Reasons of Power in Christianity and Islam* (Baltimore: Johns Hopkins University Press, 1993), and *Formations of the Secular: Christianity, Islam, Modernity* (Stanford: Stanford University Press, 2003); Tomoko Masuzawa, *The Invention of World Religions: Or, How European Universalism Was Preserved in the Language of Pluralism* (Chicago: University of Chicago Press, 2005); Saba Mahmood's *Politics of Piety: The Islamic Revival and the Feminist Subject* (Princeton: Princeton University Press, 2005), and, 'Secularism, Hermeneutics, and Empire: The Politics of Islamic Reformation', *Public Culture* 18.2 (2006), pp. 323–47; Gil Anidjar's *The Jew, the Arab: A History of the Enemy* (Stanford: Stanford University Press, 2003), and *Semites: Race, Religion, Literature* (Stanford: Stanford University Press, 2008). For my own approach to these issues, and specifically for a genealogy of religion as it emerges through the inventions of Christianity and the secular, see Barber, *On Diaspora*, pp. 88–114.

10. Instances of such investment are legion (and are often marked by some kind of relation to Hegelian developmentalism). It will have to suffice to note one especially succinct account of this working through, found in Santiago Zabala's 'Introduction' to Richard Rorty and Gianni Vattimo, *The Future of Religion*, ed. Zabala (New York: Columbia University Press, 2004), p. 2. According to Zabala, the motivation for the 'rebirth of religion in the third millennium' is to be located in 'the secularization of the sacred that has been at the center of the process by which the civilization of the western world developed'. Zabala affirms this 'rebirth', at least insofar as it is allied with secularisation, which itself is to be allied with themes of western civilisation and its development. In other words, 'secularization is the appropriate way of bearing witness to the attachment of modern European civilization

to its own religious past, a relationship consisting not of surpassing and emancipation alone, but conservation, too'. Secularisation – on Zabala's account, which unfortunately is the rule rather than the exception – thus becomes a way of inheriting or working through Christianity, where this working through is the very process of 'western civilization's' development. Such a process is precisely what I wish to oppose in my problematic of Deleuzian immanence and the question of religion.

11. Or, if we presume that the link between religion and Christianity is inescapable, what will be necessary here is not just a dechristianisation of the discourse of religion, but also an antagonistic undoing of religion as such. For more on dechristianisation, see Gil Anidjar, 'The Meaning of Life', *Critical Inquiry* 37.4 (2011), p. 720, where he foregrounds 'the persistence of the Christian question', remarking that, 'the critique of Christianity ... its decolonization, is still ahead of us'.

12. Here we might recall his well-known comment that he approached 'the history of philosophy as a sort of buggery or (it comes to the same thing) immaculate conception. I saw myself as taking an author from behind and giving him a child that would be his own offspring, yet monstrous.' See Gilles Deleuze, *Negotiations*, trans. Martin Joughin (New York: Columbia University Press, 1995), p. 6.

Beginning With Difference: Heidegger, Derrida, and the Time of Thought

Heidegger's Difference: A 'More Originary Way'?

The philosophical attempt to think immanence, to give it a high degree of determinacy, and to think it in connection with the theme of difference, begins with the work of Martin Heidegger. This is not because Heidegger spoke specifically of immanence – in fact, the term is foreign to his work. Nonetheless, the impulse behind immanence pervades his writing, most notably in one text, relatively late in his career, entitled *Identity and Difference*. The aim of my investigation has to do with the question of immanence as it is ultimately developed in Deleuze, rather than with the independent question of Heidegger interpretation. Accordingly, I will focus on the key theme of *Identity and Difference* – namely the relation between thought and being – and direct it toward the ensuing, and much more detailed, account of Deleuze's differential immanence.

It is precisely by addressing this relation between thought and being that Heidegger responds to the impulse behind immanence. This is because, for Heidegger, when thought thinks being, it never thinks something that is utterly beyond thought; being, or that which exists, is not something that transcends thought. At the same time, this does not mean that being is identical to thought, for when thought thinks being it does, in fact, think something that is different from thought. There is, then, a difference between thought and being, it is just that this difference is not articulated in terms of transcendence.[1] Heidegger thus distances himself from the classical discourses on being that are associated with Platonico-Aristotelian and theological traditions. In these discourses, the essence of that which exists (whether cast in terms of forms or of God) remains outside of thought; when thought thinks being, it thinks something that is not only different, but also transcendent. Heidegger, on the other hand, affirms being's difference from thought while denying its transcendence.

All of this, however, begins to sound like an attempt to define immanence merely in terms of what it is not. Such comparison can be useful, but only once immanence has been defined on its own, apart from its being simply a refusal of the transcendent. So we must ask: what can Heidegger contribute to an autonomously determined immanence? For an answer, we must look further into his account of the relation between thought and being. The task he gives himself is to think their difference without making being transcendent to thought, but also without claiming that being is simply identical to thought (perhaps the error of German Idealism). He does this by speaking of 'the Same': the non-transcendent relation of thought and being is not one of identity, it is instead one of sameness. This nonidentical sameness is derived from his idiosyncratic interpretation of Parmenides – 'for the same perceiving (thinking) as well as being' – and contrasted with what he calls the 'doctrine of metaphysics', which in Heidegger's nomenclature stands in for a relation of identity.[2] According to metaphysics, 'identity belongs to Being'; according to Heidegger's position, 'thinking and Being belong together in the Same and by virtue of this Same'.[3] What sameness opens up, then, is a relation of thought and being that does not bind them together in identity but that still maintains their mutuality, and in a non-hierarchical manner. Being does not transcend thought, nor does it melt together with thought into sheer simplicity. This means that even as being and thought differ, they always 'belong together'; difference does not compromise their mutuality, it constitutes it.

The Same, Heidegger says, is a 'belonging together' where *belonging* determines together. The benefit of this making belonging determine the meaning of together, he says, is that it opens 'the possibility of no longer representing belonging in the unity of the together, but rather of experiencing this together in terms of belonging'.[4] The Same, in other words, frees the sense of thought and being's belonging together from the presuppositions of identity. Identity would simply assert the togetherness of thought and being without letting the experience of their tension take place, it would sacrifice difference in order to secure unity beforehand. What Heidegger proposes, on the contrary, is to escape from the assumption that difference and sameness are inversely related or mutually exclusive. Difference may be denied by identity, but it is not denied by sameness. In fact, if thought and being *belong* together, then the meaning of this belonging must be allowed to emerge through the very experience of difference. It is thus the experience of difference – an experience for which identity does not grant the time and place – that makes the sameness of thought and being emerge.

A couple of aspects of Heidegger's thought should be emphasised. First, though it does not use the name of immanence, it is a response to the impulse behind immanence, and this response helps us determine immanence in an autonomous manner, apart from mere fact that it differs from notions of the transcendent. Such determinacy is provided by the sameness of the thought-being difference. What follows from sameness is an immanence of thought and being, for thought emerges in response to being, and whatever thought does to being affects the emergence of being. The point here is that the relation between thought and being goes in both directions, that neither one side nor the other, neither thought nor being, is ultimate. Each side, even as it is dependent on the other, also can impact and shape the other. This is what it means to say that they belong together, or to say, in the terms of our investigation, that they are immanent. What is ultimate, then, is neither one side nor the other, but rather the very relation; what is most basic is not thought, not even being, it is that which takes place between them. Any thought about being is also a thought about thought, and any thought about thought must be a thought about and of being. Thought and being relate immanently, and the direction this relation takes, whatever it may come to be, can never be found outside of the relation.[5]

The second aspect of the thought-being relation that needs to be emphasised is the essential role played by difference. What makes sameness superior to identity is that sameness is able to think the mutuality of thought and being without precluding difference. Yet difference does not just distinguish sameness from identity, it also provides a response to a challenge that will be brought – repeatedly, and not without reason – against immanence. This challenge is that immanence cannot maintain the possibility for essential change. To abandon the transcendent is – according to the logic behind this challenge – to abandon this possibility. In order to see the force of this challenge, we can begin by noting that there will always be an initially given relation between thought and being. This given relation governs the coordinates of reality, the coordinates in which the possibilities of existence are imagined. The challenge brought by advocates of the transcendent, then, is as follows: if there is no appeal to the transcendent, then a radical break with the given coordinates of reality is impossible; a new way of thinking, when it remains immanent, will amount to nothing more than a scrambling of the given, a rearrangement that plays with but ultimately accepts – and thus does not essentially transform – the coordinates of reality.

Let us give a bit more space to this challenge's logic. The transcendent, it should be noted, does provide something like a guarantee that the possibilities of existence are not exhausted by existence as it is given. Whatever may be presently given is not the final word, for what is given is set against a background that transcends the given. In this arrangement, the transcendent is presented as – and thus legitimated as – the condition of possibility *for* alternative possibilities. This seems to be the inestimable and irrefutable value of transcendence: to invoke the possibility of something that goes beyond and rises above the way we normally or presently imagine our existence. Presuming this value holds, it follows that if one wishes to bring about something genuinely different, something new, one should be committed to some form of the transcendent; transformation would be possible only insofar as it proceeds from a form of the transcendent. Does immanence, in rejecting the transcendent, thus reject the novel as such? Does immanence call for accommodation to what is presently given? My argument will be that it does not. Immanence, in refusing the transcendent, still enables the production of new relations. It is just that in order to do so it must find a new way of conceiving this production. Immanence must invent new means of producing alternative possibilities, new means of conceiving of such production – new means of the new.

In order to make an initial step toward imagining how this may be the case, we can return to the role of difference in Heidegger's thought, to the fact that the immanent relation of thought and being is driven by difference. Specifically, we should observe how difference might offer an answer to the challenge posed by advocates of the transcendent. The apparent problem with immanence, here represented by Heidegger, is that it cannot think the emergence of something genuinely different – but does not difference, in Heidegger, name that which is genuinely different? It is important here to do some parsing. There are two senses in which 'difference' is in play: (a) the difference between thought and being, which identity has denied but sameness now affirms; (b) the difference between the coordinates of reality that are given and the coordinates of reality that would be brought about by a radical change of coordinates. What advocates of transcendence claim is that immanence cannot provide difference (b); what we need to address is whether this claim holds once immanence is understood as turning on difference (a).

The claim does not hold, and this is because difference (a) serves as the catalyst for bringing about difference (b). It is able to serve as such a catalyst because the given coordinates are stabilised by the refusal to think, or to affirm, difference (a). In other words, the given coordinates are what they are, at least in part, because difference (a) is not affirmed. Accordingly, to affirm difference (a) is to push against the given coordinates, it is to destabilise the given coordinates. It is also, along these lines, to open a space for the emergence of new possibilities of existence, possibilities that do not belong to the given coordinates. Heidegger describes this process by using the term 'unthought'. The refusal to think, or to affirm, difference (a) means that difference (a) is the unthought.

The unthought, for Heidegger, does not name something that is strictly transcendent to thought, it names that which, within the thought-being relation, has not been thought. It names, in other words, an excess that is nonetheless immanent. The unthought is excessive insofar as it remains outside the given coordinates of the thought-being relation. Yet it is simultaneously immanent, for it names something that lies within the relation between thought and being, even if only as a possibility of relationality, and as a possibility that has been denied. The unthought is therefore of paramount importance for Heidegger, for it articulates the open relation between thought and being. It is what is exterior to thought, insofar as it has not been thought, yet it is simultaneously intrinsic to being. The unthought is immanent to the thought-being relation as such, but it is exterior to the presently given way we articulate this relation. In the instance that we are considering, what is unthought is the difference between thought and being. This means that to affirm the unthought is to affirm difference (a), that is, the difference within the thought-being relation. To affirm the unthought is thus to change the way we approach this relation, to make the thought-being relation move in a new direction. It is for this reason that difference (a), as the unthought that comes to be thought, can be proposed as a means of bringing about difference (b), which would here mark the difference between the thought-being relation before and after the unthought comes to be thought.

The possibility of a novel configuration between thought and being, in Heidegger, thus stands or falls on thought's endeavour to encounter the unthought. Such an endeavour can be understood as a dynamic of reduction and donation: reduction names the need to bracket the given thought-being relation, in order to discover what is unthought in this relation; donation names the sought-after, novel thought-being relation, the emergence of which depends on an encounter with the unthought. Reduction puts identity out of play in order to advance toward what Heidegger calls an 'event of appropriation' – an event in which thought encounters ontological difference and appropriates the new possibility of the belonging together of thought and being.[6] It is along these lines that the Heideggerean reduction opens 'a more originary way' – a way prior to the identity that is reduced – and donates 'the essential nature of metaphysics', an essence encountered through unthought difference.[7] The unthought thus has a negative and a positive significance: negatively, it stands as what thought has failed to think; positively, it may furnish, when encountered by way of reduction, the donation of a new relation between thought and being.

Don't Think Ahead of Time: From Heidegger to Derrida

We have seen, thus far, how Heidegger begins to give philosophical determinacy to immanence (the sameness of thought and being), and how in doing so he presents an initial response to the challenge of transcendence (the unthought, or difference). Nonetheless, this is only a beginning. In fact, Heidegger's advance founders on its ambiguous account of how, exactly, difference is bound up in sameness. We must ask: Is 'the Same' already there, *waiting* for thought to affirm it? Or is it the case that the sameness of thought and being emerges only *after* we have affirmed unthought difference?[8] The question, in other words, is whether sameness pre-exists thought's affirmation of difference, or whether, on the contrary, sameness is constituted by thought's affirmation of difference. This question of constitution is also a question of time: Does the affirmation of difference come before or after the constitution of sameness? More generally, what is the relation between the constitution of sameness and the temporality in which this constitution is accomplished?[9]

Our goal, let us recall, is to understand the intersection between immanence and difference. Heidegger provides a key advance, which is to show that the question of immanence pivots on the concept of unthought difference. But what remains is the problem of grasping the temporality by which this difference comes to be thought. Accordingly, our investigation now turns to the work of Jacques Derrida – a strange turn, no doubt, insofar as he professed confusion regarding the very meaning of immanence.[10] But in fact this turn is not strange, for immanence pivots on the question of difference, and Derrida was, above all, a philosopher of difference. In what follows, then, we will look at the way he takes up and expands upon the question of difference, paying particular attention to his ability to connect difference to the questions of constitution and time (or temporal constitution).

Derrida's treatment of difference has, like Heidegger's own thought, a phenomenological origin. Yet the similarity ends there. Heidegger moves directly from phenomenology to ontology (due to phenomenology's inability to answer the question of being, or the matter of ontology); Derrida, by contrast, seeks to delineate the exact degree to which phenomenology truly permits an opening onto being. In order to see how Derrida thus complicates Heidegger's discourse on being, let us look at Derrida's own approach to phenomenology.

Derrida argues that phenomenology, though it attempts to subject every presupposition of thought to the 'principle of principles' – the principle that evidence lies solely in the immediacy of lived experience – still remains caught up in presuppositions. Phenomenology, he claims, does not fulfil its desire to think *from* experience. And this is because it conceives lived experience according to a notion of 'presence'. Derrida argues that experience is more than presence. Indeed, he observes how presence can emerge only on the basis of what amounts to an 'absence'. An object can become present in our experience only insofar as it is contrasted to a prior absence from our experience. It comes into presence only as it comes away from absence. This means that absence is just as much a part of experience as is presence. Experience includes not just the presence or appearance of an object to the subject of experience, it also includes the absence of an object. Experience, considered in its entirety, thus means both presence and absence, fullness and emptiness, convergence and divergence. The upshot of all this is that phenomenology, because it thinks of experience in terms of presence, does not actually think experience. The very criterion that it uses in order to reveal real experience is revealed as stemming from a presupposition, rather than from the reality of experience. Phenomenology, because it is wedded to this idea that real experience is a matter of presence, cannot actually think the full reality of experience, which includes absence.

Let us call this absence, this experience in which presence is lacking, the inapparent. What Derrida is arguing, then, is that there is a layer of experience that is real, but that this is a reality of the inapparent. The inapparent is the lack of presence, but it is not the lack of reality. In fact, the inapparent – because it is that against which presence appears – is an inescapable aspect of reality. Experience of reality is thus no longer biased in favour of presence, rather it involves both presence and absence. Appearance becomes inseparable from the inapparent – and rightly so, for appearance and the inapparent are central to real experience. Phenomenology, once Derrida is done with it, undermines itself: it tried to think the presence of real experience, but Derrida showed that if it wants to think real experience, it cannot think presence alone, it must also think absence, or the inapparent. This means that phenomenology, in Derrida's hands, becomes 'undecidable' – that is, it cannot decide between presence and absence.

Derrida advances beyond phenomenology, addressing this fundamental undecidability between presence and absence, or appearance and the inapparent, through his well-known account of 'différance'. The aim of différance is to capture and think through the difference between presence and absence. Derrida speaks of this play of difference, this alternation of presence and absence, in terms of a 'polemical unity of appearing and disappearing'. This polemos, he continues, 'signifies the authenticity of phenomenological delay and limitation'.[11] Derrida's version of phenomenology thus makes valid the reality of the *between* of appearing and disappearing, a between that makes temporality and spatiality unavoidable. It is through this temporalisation and spatialisation that différance is articulated. The verb 'différer', Derrida points out, has two meanings: first, it indicates a deferring, 'the action of putting off until later', a delaying; second, it indicates a differing, a distance of separation.[12] The former meaning implies a temporalisation of difference, while the latter implies a spatialisation of difference. Therefore 'différ*ence*' is said in two valences – temporal and spatial – one of which must be foregrounded. However, 'différ*ance*', Derrida's neologism, advances both meanings at once by making them revolve around one another. It can do this because it adopts the middle voice (-ance), which refuses the choice between active and passive, and thus prevents a situation in which either spatial difference (separation) or temporal difference (delay) is the effect of the other. Différance affirms this middle voice by articulating 'the becoming-time of space and the becoming-space of time'.[13] Space is temporalised, and time is spatialised.

Derrida's différance, then, marks the play of appearance and the inapparent, and it does so in both a temporal and a spatial sense. There is a spatial difference between presence and absence (the simultaneous coming-into-appearance and rescinding-from-appearance of objects of experience), as well as a temporal difference between presence and absence (the simultaneous appearing and disappearing of the present moment). Furthermore, these two modes of difference – the spatial and the temporal – are themselves involved in a differential play, such that each shuttles back to the other. All of this makes up différance. While there is a relatively high degree of complexity here, the logic running throughout is quite direct: oppositions cannot be resolved in favour of one side, nor can they be utterly dissociated, and so we find ourselves in a dynamic of difference and mutuality. Indeed, this is the sense in which Derrida resonates with Heidegger: just as Heidegger thinks the sameness-difference, the belonging together, of thought and being, so Derrida thinks the belonging together of presence and absence. Yet if this points to their agreement, then where does the disagreement lie?

In order to get at the disagreement, we can observe the separation between Heidegger and Derrida on the move from phenomenology to the question of being. Heidegger makes this move directly, but Derrida remains sceptical. Derrida argues, in fact, that the question of being can never '*simply* precede transcendental phenomenology as its presupposition or latent ground'.[14] One *may* move from phenomenology to ontology – that is, from the question of presence and absence, or différance, to the question of being – but one must do so by following phenomenology all the way to the end, such that the 'question would mark within philosophy in general the moment wherein phenomenology terminates as the philosophical propaedeutic for every philosophical *decision*'.[15] What Derrida is claiming is that to jump straight to the question of being, or to the question of thought's relation to being, is to give rise to a kind of transcendence. More precisely, it is to transcend the way in which the question of being emerges – namely, it emerges through the play of presence and absence, through différance. Derrida wants a sense of finitude to cross-pollinate the question of the thought-being relation. This is why he speaks of the 'authenticity of phenomenological delay and limitation'. Such delay and limitation, far from being that which may finally be overcome by a decision to resolutely affirm sameness-difference, is that which itself must be affirmed.

We can, in fact, push a bit further into the disagreement between Heidegger and Derrida by observing how this is ultimately a disagreement about what it means to think difference. For Heidegger, it is by thinking difference that we achieve an awareness of the sameness of thought and being. Difference is what allows us to separate from identity and to move into 'the Same'. As we noted, however, the role of time in the constitution of this movement – from identity to the Same – remains confused. The Same is at once that which precedes the time of its thinking and that which is brought about as a result of the time of its thinking. When this is recalled, Derrida's disagreement becomes clearer. Derrida is proposing that it is not just difference that is unthought; time is also unthought. In other words, Heidegger rightly sees the need to think difference, but he does not completely take stock of the need to think time. More precisely, Heidegger does not quite grasp the way that the thought of time – as 'delay', as 'limitation', as finitude – shapes the thought of difference. To put it bluntly: différance is what you get when you combine Heideggerean difference with time. Heidegger seems to have presumed that by thinking difference one would achieve the Same. But this is to decide, *ahead of time*, what the process of thinking difference will donate. How could Heidegger know this? How could he know, prior to the process of thinking difference, what difference would donate?

To take time seriously is to see that one cannot know what will come from difference ahead of time. So, when Heidegger claims that thinking difference will bring about an awareness of the Same, he is not taking time seriously. He is – to borrow Derrida's terms – still caught up in presence: the presence of thought and being, the presence of the Same. That is, he is not addressing the role that absence plays in temporality, an absence that calls into question the presumption that the difference of thought and being will be resolved in terms of sameness. So even as Heidegger frees difference from identity, Derrida suggests this may still not be enough. Difference is, of course, liberated from identity, but it may also need to be liberated from sameness. Derrida rightly understands that the question of the direction in which difference takes us must remain open. The direction in which difference takes thought, once thought affirms difference, is *inapparent*. One can only find where difference goes by accepting, finitely, the delay and limitation of time; one can only *follow* difference – and this means affirming time – without presupposition or reservation. The affirmation of unthought difference requires, beyond Heidegger, the affirmation of unthought time. Only in this way is there a future.

What Comes After *Différance?*

Différance, for Derrida, names the double affirmation of difference and of the temporal process by which difference is thought. It names the condition under which the delay and limitation of time become fully operative, such that difference cannot be equated with the differentiation *of* an organic whole or the teleology of a dialectical negation of negation. Différance is anterior to these paradigms, which from its vantage are grasped as stoppages of differential play, as refusals to affirm the temporality by which difference is thought. In this sense, the movement of différance is irreducible and cannot be surpassed (although I will qualify this below). One could say that we find ourselves *in* the movement of différance. At the same time, the play of difference articulated by différance does not unfold according to an eternal law – on the contrary, it is historical. Derrida notes that 'if the word "history" did not in and of itself convey the motif of a final repression of difference, one could say that only differences can be "historical" from the outset and in each of their aspects'.[16] How, then, are we to negotiate différance's dual status as something akin to an essential condition for thinking time and difference, as well as something that is historical and contingent?

Différance names the movement that constitutes and temporalises the passage of reduction and donation – that is, the passage of thinking difference and thereby opening thought onto new directions. This movement of différance is thus the condition that enables us to think new possibilities of existence, for it is the dynamic by which the unthought – now including difference *and* time – emerges and enables a genuine break with the given coordinates of reality. But what, then, does it mean to say that this play of difference is itself '"historical" from the outset'? If différance is historical, then does this mean différance can be reduced to history? Certainly not, if this involves forgetting that différance is the condition for thinking history. History only emerges as history through différance; différance does not take place within history, it is rather that history, as we normally imagine it, emerges against the background of différance. In other words, différance is the condition for thinking history as genuinely historical, as the openness of difference. Différance is both that from which history emerges and that which renders historical development contingent, or subject to time and difference.

No history without différance, then, but where this is true it seems that différance need not be the final word. And this is actually quite literally true when Derrida remarks that différance is 'neither a word nor a concept', but a 'strategy'. He 'wish[es] to emphasize that the efficacy of the thematic of différance may very well, *indeed must*, one day be superseded, lending itself if not to its own replacement, at least to enmeshing itself in a chain that in truth it never will have commanded'.[17] The relation between the name 'différance' and the (historical) differential movement it marks out is thus determined by strategy. What I am emphasising, with my questions regarding the dual status of différance, is Derrida's evasiveness regarding the precise way in which a movement (the temporal play of difference) and the 'strategic' *naming* of this movement (as différance) are related. On the one hand, Derrida tells us we cannot think this movement apart from différance; différance is what protects this movement from having transcendent aims imposed upon its temporal dynamic. Yet on the other, Derrida insists that this name of différance is strategic, that the movement it names cannot be captured by the name, that this movement somehow exceeds the name of différance (hence the need, 'one day', to 'supersede' this name). Différance protects the excessive open-endedness of the temporal movement of difference, but the very excessiveness of this movement requires the surpassing of différance.

Of course, any replacement for différance cannot belong to a thought that would resolve differential play in virtue of a precon-ceived manner of identification. One cannot replace différance in the name of something transcendent, something that would cut off the temporal process of thinking difference. That said, it is clearly the case, for Derrida, that one can *pass through* différance, in virtue of the differential play that exceeds it. In this passage one may exceed différance not by way of identity, but rather by way of differential play. Putting this back in terms of the connection between différance and history, this means that a history conditioned by différance – a genuinely contingent history, one that, in the name of différance, affirms the open-ended temporality of thinking difference – may exceed différance.

The question is thus: *What comes after différance?* This question can be posed in two senses. First, we view it in the obvious relation to chronological position. If the name of différance will be replaced, then what replaces it? Yet what truly matters is a second, more fun-damental question concerning différance's role as a transcendental – that is, as the condition by which the movement or play of differ-ence is named. If différance must be replaced, then there is a condition belonging to differential play that exceeds différance. In other words, if différance can or must be replaced, then there is a capacity of differential play – which thought must encounter – that is not named by the transcendental condition of différance. The question of 'after-différance' would be not simply historically after, but transcendentally before. That which is donated in the movement named by différance may exceed, and thus cause us to replace, the reduction articulated by différance. There is, intrinsic to the passage of reduction and donation, an open relation between thought and difference – a relation indicated by the term 'immanence' – that *exceeds* the articulation of différance.

The point, then, is that différance articulates a strategic denial of any thought that would resolve and foreclose differential play, but it does not articulate the play of difference itself. Its strategy is to draw a border around differential play, such that differential play is secured against any resolution of difference from beyond. Différance serves as an incredibly effective prophylactic against the presuppositions and impositions of the transcendent. In serving this strategic function, however, différance itself remains extrinsic to the differential play it secures. This, after all, is why différance must be superseded.

Where does this initial foray into the attempt to think the intersection of difference and immanence, into the 'prehistory' of differential immanence, leave us? What we have been able to establish, thus far, can be summarised according to five theses:

1. An initial response to the impulse driving immanence emerges in Heidegger's desire to think the sameness of thought and being. If thought and being are 'the Same', then neither fully transcends the other. An immanent relation of thought and being is thus put in place.
2. This immanent relation of thought and being pivots on difference. Immanence is not identity, it is rather the affirmation of difference. The connection of immanence to difference as it is found in Heidegger, and the exploration of the temporality of this connection as it is found in Derrida, express problematic potentialities for the differential immanence that Deleuze articulates.
3. The centrality of difference to immanence provides a preliminary (though still insufficient or underarticulated) basis for responding to the challenge of transcendence, which is that immanence

cannot imagine the possibility for a radical break from the given. Immanence pushes back against this challenge through the affirmation of difference. According to this proposed reading, immanence would not entail acceptance of the given insofar as the affirmation of difference is the affirmation of what is unthought by the given.

4. To think immanence, to affirm difference, requires that we address the temporal constitution of this thought and affirmation. Différance, with all that it entails, serves to remind us of this requirement. It shows that whatever is to emerge from the affirmation of difference cannot be imagined ahead of time; the novel depends on the affirmation of difference, but it will emerge only insofar as we also affirm the thoroughly temporal nature of this affirmation.

5. Although différance successfully serves to remind us of the essentially temporal nature of thinking difference, it is not ultimately able to follow this process all the way. The affirmation of difference exceeds even the name of différance. Différance protects against transcendent impositions, but it does not provide an immanent relation to the temporal process it protects. Différance is like a fence that keeps out transcendence, but that in doing so always looks away from the very movement it defends – the temporal movement of difference.

It is in order to address the difficulties and potentialities stated by and implied in these theses that we now move from the prehistory of the intersection between immanence and difference to the elaboration of differential immanence as it is provided by Deleuze.

Notes

1. The difference between thought and being stems from ontological difference, or the difference between being and beings. The reality of a difference within being is what calls for thought, and so thought is at once distinct from being and involved in being's own difference.
2. Martin Heidegger, *Identity and Difference*, trans. Joan Stambaugh (New York: Harper & Row, 2002), p. 27.
3. Ibid.
4. Ibid., p. 39.
5. Heidegger delineates rather tersely the dynamic relation between the unthought, determined as difference, and the emergence of new possibilities that are immanent to the thought-being relation: 'We speak of

the *difference* between being and beings. The step back goes from what is unthought, from the difference as such, into what gives us thought [*Das zu-Denkende*]' (ibid., p. 50). But this movement, from unthought difference into a renewal of the thought-being relation, presupposes a prior movement into unthought difference. One must first encounter the unthought, and in order to do this one must undo the presently given manner of relation between thought and being, which Heidegger rather famously termed 'ontotheology'. If the difference between being and beings has remained unthought, this is because thought has been enveloped in an ontotheological framework. Ontotheology, according to Heidegger, names the tendency of thought that joins ontology (as science of being) and theology (as science of God, the ground of being) through a certain complicity between the grounded (*ontos*) and the ground (*theos*). In this ontotheological framework, one cannot think the difference between being and beings directly, for both being and beings are thinkable only by way of their inherence in God, the being that grounds being. Heidegger draws the evident conclusion that, in order for thought to encounter directly the *difference* of being and beings, the ontotheological, identitarian account of being, or the ontotheological tendency of thought – which effectively obscures difference, rendering it unthought – must be reduced.

6. Ibid., p. 39.
7. Ibid., pp. 40, 51.
8. Heidegger makes the vague claim that the event of appropriation moves us from (identity-based or ontotheological) metaphysics to the 'essential nature' of the metaphysical, yet this 'essential nature' is indeterminate. A thinking of the Same, by way of unthought difference, seems both to open a new thought-being relation and to return to a yet more primordial and originary metaphysics. Take, for instance, his claim 'that we do not reside sufficiently as yet where in reality we already are' (ibid., p. 31). The 'not as yet' and 'already are' blend together.
9. Heidegger implies, on one hand, that sameness is already available when he says it arrives 'neither incidentally nor only on rare occasions' (ibid., p. 31); on the other, he indicates that it has not yet arrived when he remarks that the donation of sameness is not something that 'could be achieved in a day . . . it must take its time, the time of thinking' (ibid., p. 41).
10. Jacques Derrida remarked that he would like to 'question' Deleuze further regarding 'the word "immanence" on which he always insisted'. See *The Work of Mourning*, trans. Pascal-Anne Brault and Michael Nass (Chicago: University of Chicago Press, 2003), p. 195.
11. Jacques Derrida, *Edmund Husserl's 'Origin of Geometry': An Introduction*, trans. John P. Leavey, Jr. (Lincoln, NE: University of Nebraska Press, 1989), p. 153.

12. Jacques Derrida, *Margins of Philosophy*, trans. Alan Bass (Chicago: University of Chicago Press, 1982), p. 8.
13. Ibid.
14. Derrida, *Edmund Husserl's 'Origin of Geometry'*, p. 150. Emphasis in original. All emphases are in original unless otherwise noted.
15. Ibid.
16. Derrida, *Margins*, p. 11.
17. Ibid., p. 7; my emphasis.

2

Deleuze: The Difference Immanence Makes

The Architecture of Immanence

Deleuze's account of immanence begins with his interpretation of Spinoza, whom he called the 'prince of philosophers'.[1] Specifically, it arises from his discussion of the Spinozian triad, which includes: substance, or God, the oneness of being; attributes, or forms; and modes, or individuals. These terms, which provide the architecture of reality, are immanently related insofar as they can be thought neither separately nor hierarchically. On the contrary, they are mutually constitutive, and so one cannot speak of substance, attributes, or modes except by speaking of the relations between substance and attributes, substance and modes, and attributes and modes. Let us look at these three relations, each in turn, in order to parse out the architecture of Deleuze's immanence.

Central to the *substance-attribute relation* is the wedding of substantial unity with the distinction of attributes. The two attributes of thought and extension are said simultaneously of the one substance, which means that difference (distinction between attributes) and unity (one substance) are not mutually exclusive but in fact symbiotic. This innovation lies at the heart of immanence – recall that Heidegger made a similar move by thinking together difference and sameness – and distinguishes it from the more dominant philosophical tradition, according to which unity has priority over difference. In fact, it is precisely by insisting that unity precede difference that transcendence is introduced; to precede is to transcend, and so the precedence of unity over difference amounts to the transcendence of the (unified) one over the (differentiated) many.

An exemplary instance of this sort of transcendence is the analogical account of being (of which a fuller and more complex account is found in the following chapter). In analogy, truth, goodness, and beauty (forms, or attributes) are convertible in a simple, divine being (substance), such that this simple being possesses them without distinction. Individuals also possess truth, goodness, and beauty, but they possess these only to a certain degree, and only in a dispersed, non-convertible manner. In other words, what makes individuals separate from God is that God possesses these forms in an essential, unified manner, whereas individuals possess them in a partial, differentiated manner; God transcends individuals because unity transcends difference. Deleuze, on the other hand, makes formal distinction (the distinction between attributes) essential to substance (or God), which means that difference becomes intrinsic to God, or substance, itself. The contrast is thus that Deleuze does not distribute difference within a framework where the unified one transcends the diverse many, he instead makes difference intrinsic to, constitutive of, the immanent relation of substance and attributes.

Already in the substance-attribute relation we have glimpsed the *substance-mode relation*: once the difference of attributes becomes essential to substance, the separation between a unitary God, or substance, and differentiated individuals, or modes, disappears. What kept substance and modes separate was the separation between unity and difference, so when unity and difference become immanent, substance and modes are also able to become immanent. Deleuze articulates this immanence of substance and modes by speaking of a 'substantive multiplicity'.

Substance is surely one, but because it is differentiated it is just as surely many. The term multiple, as a predicate of substance, is a response to this difficulty, but it opens the question of the relation between substance-as-one and substance-as-multiple. Does substance exist on two planes, a plane of unity and a plane of the multiple? If we say yes, then we have introduced transcendence. Yet if we say no, then we are left wondering whether unity is an illusion obscuring the reality of difference – or, more likely, whether difference is an illusion obscuring the reality of unity. It is in order to get out of the circulation between the one and the many, a circulation maintained by the concept of the multiple, that Deleuze speaks instead of a *multiplicity*. Against the temptation to translate a difference between individuals into a distinction between a given (and merely apparent, or less real) multiple and a subtending (and true, or ultimately real) ontological unity, Deleuze insists on the immanence of God and individuals, or of substance and modes. This immanent relation is what multiplicity helps articulate. Specifically, the articulation is of a *substantive* multiplicity, meaning that substance is simultaneously unified and differentiated, one and diverse, with neither side taking precedence over the other. How is this possible? It is possible because, as was already displayed in the substance-attribute relation, there is a symbiosis – a mutually constitutive relation – between unity and difference. Whereas the multiple is opposed to the one, multiplicity is simultaneously the one as it is constituted by the many and the many as they are constituted by the one.

Multiplicity thus articulates the immanence of one and many, and in doing so it makes the difference of the many (modal difference) inseparable from the unity of substance. We can thus say that the unity of substance is immanent with difference in two different manners: first we saw the immanence of substantial unity and attributive difference, and now we see the immanence of substantial unity and modal difference. In each case, difference is essential to the constitution of the unity named by substance; difference constitutes the divine essence. Still, in order to complete the triad, and in order to show the relation between the difference of mode and the difference of attribute, we must now turn to the *attribute-mode relation.*

Deleuze states that the attribute, or form, has intrinsic modes, and in doing so he opposes the notion that form is invariable in itself. According to this last notion, different modalities of a form must be explained by the composition of form with some extrinsic mode, creating a scenario in which an invariable form moulds diverse matters. The introduction of something external to the form is required precisely because the form is understood in terms of identity. If the form is invariable, then the only way to account for variation in this form is to combine the form with something external to it, such as material individuals. Once again, we see an instance of transcendence. In this case, it is not that substance transcends forms, nor that substance transcends individuals, it is rather that forms transcend individuals. Here, in the case of the form-individual (or attribute-mode) relation, just as in the cases of the other relations, transcendence is introduced because unity is imagined as preceding the differentiated. And just as he did in the previous cases, so in this case Deleuze will oppose transcendence by calling for an internal or intrinsic differentiation of the supposedly transcendent unity. This means, with regard to the attribute-mode relation, that modal difference will be understood as intrinsic to formal unity.

Specifically, Deleuze contends that 'nature never proceeds by molding'.[2] Form is not something that moulds something else, where this something else is initially external to it or potentially recalcitrant to it. The reason for individual (or modal) difference is not found outside the form. On the contrary, there are different modes of the same form (or attribute) because there is a difference of formal degree in – or *as* – the form. Helpful here is Deleuze's main example (borrowed from Scotus) of a white wall that remains white throughout yet still brings forth various intensities of whiteness. How, in this instance, do we distinguish between shades of white? Not by way of an invariant form of whiteness that is somehow imposed on varying matters (which are external to the form), but rather through a distinction of degrees of whiteness – that is, through a difference intrinsic to the form (or attribute) itself. Deleuze terms the varying, differential degrees of a form 'intrinsic modes'. An intrinsic mode is thus a degree of intensity of the attribute. In the instance of the white wall, we can say that a certain mode of whiteness is differentiated by the degree to which it 'whites', while the different degrees of whiteness constitute the form of white. As Deleuze remarks, 'Degrees of intensity are intrinsic determinations, intrinsic modes, of a whiteness that remains univocally the same under whichever modality it is considered.'[3] Consequently, there is no need to account for differences within the same form by placing them in differentiated external matters; the difference of intrinsic modes accounts of the differentiation of the attribute, and in doing so it constitutes the attribute.[4]

We can now see – having noted his account of the three relations of the Spinozian triad – how reality, for Deleuze, is nothing other than immanence: the immanence of substance, attributes, and modes, or of God, forms, and individuals. As with Heidegger's account of the sameness of thought and being, no one of these terms can be taken as prior to the others. Deleuze's account further resembles Heidegger's insofar as such immanence pivots around, and is unthinkable except as, difference – the difference between substance, attributes, and modes, as well as the difference that constitutes the three relations that emerge between these terms. Where Deleuze goes beyond Heidegger, though, is in his ability to make immanence include individuals. This is especially evident with regard to the notion of substantive multiplicity, according to which individuals, or modes, constitute – in their essential differentiality – the one and only substance. Indeed, Deleuze portrays his use of Spinoza for his own theory of immanence as an attempt driven by 'the hope of making substance turn on finite modes'.[5] In other words, it is not as if substance grounds a movement that, having been generated, is then taken up by or in modes.[6] On the contrary, the diversification of modes is the diversification of substance itself. Substance is one, but its unity does not exist apart from the diversity or distribution of the modes; modal difference is the one and only substance. As Deleuze insists: 'Substance must itself be said *of* the modes and only *of* the modes.'[7]

What consequences does this emphasis on the individuation of immanence have for the question of transformation? How might this account of substantive multiplicity – which makes reality turn on the diversity of modes, on their *modification* – inform a response to the challenge presented by transcendence? How, in other words, might the differential modification of substance enable us to imagine immanence as that which produces the novel? In order to answer these questions, we must now shift our attention from the architecture of immanence to the power of immanence.

Re-expression and the Unconditioned Power of Immanence

God produces because God is; God's existence is production. According to Deleuze, 'God produces an infinity of things by virtue of the same power by which he exists.'[8] These things, taken in themselves, are modes. Things-in-themselves, however, are not actually independent substances, they are rather substantive modifications. Substantive multiplicity is therefore reasserted, since the modal product, through its modificatory power, is not exterior to the substance it produces. The modal product is a modification of the substance that it expresses, such that the substance does not exist apart from – indeed, it turns on – the modification. It is important to observe, as well, that the power of modification is the very same power that enables us to say that substance is unconditioned: the power exercised by modification is precisely the unconditioned power of substance. This leaves us with an unconditioned power that is simultaneously substantive and modificatory – a power of substantive modification.

When I speak of 'the unconditioned', I do not understand it negatively, as *lacking* a proper conditioning or determinacy. The unconditioned, in this latter sense, would be indefinite rather than infinite. But God's existence and production is unconditioned in virtue of its *power*, in virtue of its capacity to cause effects that are conditioned by nothing other than the power of the cause itself. This causal power is infinite, and the infinity of things produced (the substantive modifications) must be located in its infinite power. But if those things that belong to the infinity of things produced by God are substantial modifications, then how can these modifications be determinate yet still inhere in an unconditioned power? After all, the infinity of things, of substantive modifications, are clearly effects of the cause. How, then, can an effect make a claim to the unconditioned power of what causes it? Deleuze's answer is that God is *cause of all things "in the same sense" as [God is] cause of himself*.[9] Modes are distinguished from God insofar as they are effects, insofar as they are not cause of themselves – yet this does not place them outside of or beneath the causal power. A modal essence is a degree of power, but this power is not other than the power of God, for modal power and divine power are in immanence.

We can go some way toward articulating this immanence by comparing it to emanation, which is a paradigm of causation close to but noticeably dissimilar from immanence. *Emanation* refers to a giving that establishes the eminence of giver to recipient; the effect, while born out of the cause, is separated from it in the bearing forth. The emanation that relates effect to cause thus creates a hierarchy of cause over effect, for the effect does not fully remain in the cause. In such a case, an effect belongs to the cause only through the mediation of *exitus* and *reditus*. Now, such emanation is certainly not dualist, for the reason of the effect's production is found in and returns us to the cause. Nonetheless, the production of the effect cannot be said in the same sense as the cause's self-production (or self-existence). The effect remains in the cause in some sense, but not in the same sense that the cause remains in itself. *Immanation*, on the other hand, is marked by the immanence of cause and effect. While the effect is certainly something distinguishable from the cause, it remains in the cause 'no less than the cause remains in itself'.[10] Accordingly, the production of the effect can indeed be said in the same sense as the cause's own production (or existence). It is in this manner, then, that modal power (effect) and divine power (cause) are in immanence.

The immanence of cause and effect introduces affection into the heart of immanence. In emanation, the effect cannot affect the cause, for the effect does not remain in the cause. Concomitantly, the production of effects cannot involve the production of affects by the effects; what is produced cannot affect what does the producing. The cause, in emanation, possesses the capacity to generate effects, but the price of this power is the refusal to be affected by the effects that are generated. It is quite different with immanence, where God 'produces an infinity of things which affect him in an infinity of ways'.[11] God's productive power is not compromised by affection – on the contrary, it is amplified, and this is because power involves

46

not just the capacity to generate effects, but also the capacity to receive (to be affected by) what is produced by the effects. Indeed, while we have already seen that the power of existence is the same as the power of production, and that the power of modification is the same as the power of God, we should now add that the power to be affected is the very same power. The unconditioned power of the infinite can thus be understood as: cause → effect → affection of cause. Just as the production of an infinity of things by God effects a production of substance itself – for substance does not exist except as its modifications – so the affections brought about by an infinity of things are the production of substance itself. The effection and affection of substance, a double constitution, is a consequence of the immanence of cause and effect, where the unconditioned power of God is both causal and affective.

The immanent relation between determinate production (modes-as-effects) and the unconditioned power of production (substance-as-cause) is proclaimed most forcefully in Deleuze's assertion of an expressive *doubling* of immanence. Modal effects immediately express the cause, such that modification is immediately a modification of substance itself. Immanence is thus unlike eminence, in which the effects express the cause at a level that is secondary to the cause. For immanence, the effects express the cause without separation – and, to say it once again, it is because this expression is without separation that the effects can be understood as looping back to affect the cause they express. All of this is to say that modal expression inheres in, but is simultaneously determinative of, the unconditioned power of production; modes are the expression of the power to which they give determinacy. This means that there is a 'double immanence of expression in what expresses itself, and of what is expressed in its expression'.[12] The double immanence of expression and expressed does admit a difference between determination and what is determined, but it simultaneously places determination (the effect, or modal expression) and what is determined (the cause, or substance) in immanence, such that neither can be given priority. Thus there is no identity between cause and effect, but they do immanently relate, so neither is there any real separation between them. Consequently, the expressive effects of God are not situated beneath the unconditioned power of God (that which is expressed), for the cause is determined by these expressive effects.

The doubling of immanence – that is, the immanence of expression and what is expressed, of modes and substance, of determination and the unconditioned – can also be parsed in terms of explication and implication. Effects are explications of the cause; they expressively unfold, or give determinacy to, the unconditioned. At the same time, this explication is never separated from the cause, it remains in the cause just as much as the cause remains in itself. Effects, then, are not just explications of the cause, they also remain implicated in – folded back into – the cause. What we are left with is a process of unfolding and enfolding, a process in which, throughout the diverse unfolds and enfolds, the unconditioned power is never diminished or exhausted. The power of expression, or God, is not absent from any of its expressions, or effects; it remains the 'what is expressed' of every expression. This means that while each expression is determinate, it is never severed from the unconditioned.

An important consequence of expression's double immanence is that every expression contains, within itself, the reason for its re-expression.[13] This is because expression's explication is always convertible with its implication. Let us imagine, for instance, a given expression (E1). As we have seen above, E1 is the explication of the unconditioned cause, and as this explication it gives determinacy to the cause. Yet the power of expression, or the unconditioned cause, does not transcend the given expression. This, after all, is the point of the doubleness of immanence: the expression is immanent to what is expressed, while what is expressed is immanent to the expression. Returning to our instance, then, we see that E1 does not just explicate the unconditioned, it also remains implicated in the unconditioned. This means that even as E1 gives determinacy to the unconditioned, such determinacy never compromises or impedes the power of the unconditioned.

If E1 does not just explicate but also implicates the unconditioned – which is to say that it is not just effected by but also loops back and affects the unconditioned – then there cannot be only an initial expression. There must be a subsequent expression (E2). If E1, the effect, is an immanent double of the cause, then it doubles back on the cause. When it does this, there must be some alteration – that is, when E1 doubles back on the cause, the cause responds by producing a new expression, or E2. It is in this sense that E1, because of its implication in the cause, requires E2. In other words, it is because E1 remains enfolded in the cause that there must be, 'after' its own dynamic of unfolding and enfolding, E2. Of course, E2 has the same status as E1: everything that is said of E1's relation to the unconditioned is equally said of E2's relation to the unconditioned. The point, then, is not that E2 is somehow a necessary improvement on E1, it is merely that an E2 must emerge. And this process continues, such that E2 requires E3, E3 requires E4, and so on. In fact, this process is what I mean when I speak of 're-expression'.

To be re-expressed, then, is not to erase the explication, but to fold the explication back into the power enacting it, and in doing so to bring about the production of a new expression. This logic of re-expression is immensely important, for it allows us to explain how immanence enables the creation of the novel. The challenge of transcendence begins to be answered through the logic of re-expression. This is because re-expression articulates the necessity, within immanence, for the emergence of new states of affairs – that is, for new expressions of reality. We can recall that the challenge, specifically, is to explain how we are able to break with the given coordinates of reality if we do not accept the existence of something that transcends these coordinates. If there is nothing that transcends reality as it is presently given, then on what grounds are we able to imagine something that would escape from the regnant coordinates of reality? How can there be a break with the given if there is nothing that transcends the given?

What re-expression provides, then, is a way of articulating an immanent demand for something that would not be limited to what is given. It articulates how the given exceeds itself, how the present expression – because it remains immanent to the unconditioned power that it expresses – must give rise to another expression: E1, because it is the immanent double of the unconditioned, must give rise to another double of the unconditioned, or E2. Importantly, the production of another expression is *necessary*. Modal expression is produced by the same necessity with which God, or substance, exists, for modal expression is productive of God's existence; since this modal expression must be re-expressed, the modal re-expression is likewise necessary. Yet even as the emergence of another expression is necessary, the nature of this other expression is contingent. Expression must be re-expressed, but whether the re-expression resembles or departs from the initial expression remains up for grabs. Re-expression is thus necessarily contingent. Éric Alliez gets at this very point when he remarks that Deleuze's Spinoza-inspired immanence always proceeds according to the equation: 'expressionism = constructivism'.[14] We can add that expression is immediately construction because expression must necessarily be re-expressed. Construction and expression thus proceed by the same necessity. As soon as we have E1 we necessarily have E2. While E1 is necessary, and while the emergence of E2 is necessary, the specific character of E2 is contingent. It must be constructed.

We can see, then, that the logic of re-expression ably articulates the necessity of emergence, and that it does so without leaving the architecture of immanence. We can see, as well, that none of this immediately speaks to the question of whether the emergently constructed expression will be radically different from the given expression, or even whether it will be better. Re-expression necessitates another expression, but what enables the new expression to be truly novel, to be a *creation* of the new, of something that breaks with the present expression, rather than something that merely rearranges the given?

Giving Intensity to the Mode of Existence

A response to the above questions requires us to look more closely at the role difference plays in Deleuze's immanence. As we already noted in Heidegger, the capacity to produce a difference from, or break with, the present state of affairs depends on the way difference functions in this present. In Deleuze's terms, we can say that there is re-expression, or the emergence of a new expression from a given expression, as a result of the way that difference remains intrinsic to the given expression. This means we must look at re-expression now, not just in terms of an unconditioned power of expression, but also in terms of the difference intrinsic to expression. What we need to see, specifically, is that the unconditioned power of expression is exerted *as* difference. The unconditioned power of expression is fundamentally differential, it is nothing other than its intrinsic difference. In this section, then, I will look at the intrinsically differential character of expression.

Deleuze, in his interpretation of the mode, makes a distinction between intrinsic and extrinsic modes. Accordingly, we may distinguish between situations in which the position of the mode is intrinsic to the attribute and those in which the position of the mode is extrinsic to the attribute. This may seem a rather abstruse point, but it is relevant precisely because it allows us to articulate the doubleness of immanence. If, as we have noted in the previous section, immanence is at once unconditioned and expressed, or implicated and explicated, then this doubleness needs to be articulated at the level of the individual (or mode). What, then, is the distinction between the intrinsic and extrinsic positions of the mode, and how does this distinction relate to implication and explication at the level of the individual?

The intensive position of the mode names its implication in the attribute. Modes, let us recall, are degrees of intensity that intrinsically determine the attribute, and this is what is meant by a mode's intensive position. Yet even as modes intensively determine the attribute, they also explicate the attribute – that is, they extensively develop their intensive determination. This is what is meant by the mode's extensive position. What is important is to understand that the intensive and extensive are two sides of the same modal determination. The intensity of the mode is its implication in the attribute, while the extensity of the mode is its explication of the attribute. Furthermore, we can observe that the intrinsic mode is what generates the extrinsic mode: the extrinsic mode is the result, or the development, of the intrinsic mode; the extrinsic mode is the explication of the intrinsic mode's implication. There is an extensive, explicative infinity of modal determination precisely because the mode is already implicated in – intrinsic to and constitutive of – the attribute. As Deleuze remarks, 'It is not from the number of its parts that the quantity is infinite, but rather because it is infinite that it divides into a multitude of parts exceeding any number.'[15]

Deleuze's insistence that individuals be understood in terms of the doubleness of the intrinsic and the extrinsic allows us to further develop a sense of why immanence is irreducible to the given. In the terminology we are currently developing, the given expression of immanence would be equated with the set of extrinsic modes. The fact that the unconditioned power of immanence is not exhausted by the given is indicated by the implication of these extrinsic modes within the attribute. It is because the mode is never *just* extrinsically positioned, but always *also* intrinsically positioned, that re-expression must take place. The extensive position of the mode is never final, yet neither is the intensive position of the mode simply transcendent – after all, the extensive and the intensive refer to the same mode, and differ only in speaking of the mode's different positions. But how do the extrinsic and the intrinsic relate? If they refer to the same mode in distinct respects, what accounts for these alternative ways of approaching the same thing?

For Spinoza, this relation between intensive and extensive modes involves a one-to-one correspondence (I will call this 'correlation').[16] Where such correlation is in place, it is difficult to imagine a very dynamic process – indeed, it is not clear how a process of explication and implication, a process of re-expression, would be produced by such correlation. For if the intensive and extensive correlate, if they resemble one another, then there would exist no tension between them, no disequilibrium. And if there is no disequilibrium, then there is nothing to catalyse movement. It is thus important that Deleuze develops immanence's account of the individual beyond this correlational framework. Specifically, he evades correlation by articulating intensive modal expression in terms of a field of singularities, which collectively form an intense infinity. Deleuze makes this advance by developing the Spinozian conception of intensive and extensive modes into the conception of the virtual and the actual.

What Deleuze retains from Spinoza is the notion that an attribute is constituted by difference or is intrinsically differential. We have already seen how individual difference was imagined in terms of a difference intrinsic to the attribute: differences between individuals, or modes, are already there in the attribute itself; modal difference is nothing less than a difference of degrees within the same attribute. It is such modal difference, in fact, that is denoted by intrinsic modes. But the question again comes up: if extrinsic modes are the correlational explication of this intrinsic modal difference, then why presume that there would even *be* a dynamic process between the intrinsic and extrinsic? A dynamic process requires disequilibrium between intrinsic and extrinsic, and correlation cannot supply this. But the seed of what needs to be supplied is already here, and this is the notion that the attribute is intrinsically differential.

The difference within the attribute – that is, the difference between intrinsic modes – becomes the motivating force that drives explication. Intrinsic difference is able to act as a motivating force precisely because difference is, in itself, intensive. To see this, it is first necessary to remove intrinsic difference from any relation to extrinsic difference. We must think of intrinsic difference on its own, without the image presented by extrinsic difference. As long as the extrinsic is in view, the intrinsic will be conceived as (correlationally) relating to the extrinsic, and so what gets ignored is the way intrinsic difference functions in itself. How, then, does difference function intrinsically, apart from any model of correlation with extrinsic difference? How does difference liberate itself from, or exert its force against, correlation? Deleuze emphasises its sheer intensity. Once intrinsic difference no longer correlates to another set of (extrinsic) differences, the intrinsic differences are left to relate to themselves. Differences no longer match up with another set of differences, they relate to themselves – and since these are differences relating to differences, we get a rather intense chaos, one filled with differences giving rise to more differences. Difference, left to itself, becomes sheerly intensive, for intensity is what there 'is' between terms that fundamentally differ from one another. Difference itself is intensity, while intensity has a purely differential character; difference is between intensities, but intensity is precisely difference itself. As Deleuze says, 'the expression "difference of intensity" is a tautology. Intensity is the form of difference.'[17]

Deleuze will call this differential intensity the virtual. Similarly, the modal degrees of difference will be called singularities, such that we can define the virtual as a differential, intensive field of singularities. This introduction of the virtual – as differential intensity – has consequences for how we think of extrinsic difference (which will be called the actual). Specifically, it is the pure difference of the virtual that enables us to speak of explication in a non-correlative way. The actual, which is explicated, does not resemble the intensive differential of the virtual. On the contrary, the explication of the actual serves as the resolution of the virtual's pure difference. Modification, then, is not a correspondence between the intrinsic and the extrinsic, but rather a *process* in which difference of intensity, or intensity of difference, is extensively resolved. The given expression of immanence (the actual) is implied in an intensive difference (the virtual), which is the condition not only of that given expression, but also of the necessity of other expressions.[18] In this sense, the virtual is that by which an actual expression is re-expressed.

Virtually New

The virtual is thus the condition of any actual determination. Yet, because the virtual is determined by singularities, when it conditions the actual it does not do so as some kind of undifferentiated reservoir of oneness that transcends the actuality of the world.[19] It is important, when attending to Deleuze's concept of the virtual, to highlight the differentially determinate character of the virtual, as well as the intersection between, or interchange of, the virtual and the actual.[20] Extensive modes (if we wish to keep this language) are actualisations or individuations of singularities – more precisely, they are actualisations of *differential relations* of singularities. These virtual singularities are preindividual – in the sense that they condition actual individuation – but they are not an undifferentiated 'one', for they are determinate as well as relational (even as their relations are purely differential, and therefore name a 'nonrelation'). Deleuze's theory of individuation is indebted at this point to the work of Gilbert Simondon, and no one has developed this link better than Alberto Toscano, who describes Simondon's theory of preindividual relationality as follows:

> Whilst it is yet to be individuated, preindividual being can already be regarded as affected by relationality. This preindividual relationality, which takes place between heterogeneous dimensions, forces or energetic tendencies, is nevertheless also a sort of non-relation: heterogeneity as the anoriginary qualification of being. Being is thus said to be *more-than-one* to the extent that all of its potentials cannot be actualised at once.[21]

What is at issue, then, is the conception of and relation between a virtual or singular manner of determination – itself relational – and an actual order of determination.

The virtual is neither identical (correlational) with nor transcendent to the actual; the relation between the virtual and the actual is neither analogical nor equivocal. Singularities determine the virtual so as to provide a preindividual field that does not resemble what it conditions, yet such non-resemblance does not introduce two levels or planes. This process of individuation must be understood as an *immanent* relation between the virtual and the actual, a relation that emerges through the actualisation of the virtual (E1) and the potential re-expression of the virtual by its newly emergent actualisation (E2). To imagine the virtual-actual relation in terms of correlation or transcendence is to block the dynamic process of individuation.

Against this misconception of the virtual and actual as two-planed, Deleuze insists that the excess of actual determination is due to the virtual's singular determination. A transcendental field of singularities poses a field of differences, a differential field that is objective and determinate. In this way, Deleuze observes, 'the notion of the virtual stops being vague and indeterminate. In itself, it needs to have the highest degree of precision.'[22] To be objective and determinate, however, is not to be closed. This means that the relation of virtual and actual may be conceived as one of problem and solution: the virtual field of singularities is the problem, which conditions the solutions provided by the actual. Deleuze's great advance here is to bring together objective determinacy, on the one hand, and openness or contingency, on the other. The objective determinacy of singularities, or the virtual field of singularities, necessarily gives rise to the question of problematic relation – that is, the question of what contingent relations will be produced in the field of pure, intensive difference. In this sense the virtual is necessary *and* contingent, or objectively determinate *and* problematically open. Singularities make difference objective, but the differential manner in which they do so makes objectivity problematic. Objectivity, as the intensive difference of singularities, gives reality to a problem that exceeds the already given solutions.[23] Accordingly, the task is to problematise given solutions and, in virtue of this problematic horizon, to produce new solutions.

To address the play of the virtual and the actual is thus to invoke a practice of *problematising* – that is, of subjecting the individuated, or the already given, to a virtual, problematic field that may be solved otherwise, or that may enable other solutions. This dynamic of problem and solution – the process of re-expression – must be set within a coexistence of the virtual and the actual. Re-expression, when taken up as a passage of becoming, is capable of producing new, more powerful solutions, but the exercise of this capacity depends on the production of problems. It depends, in other words, on making the problematic, differential field of singularities into a problem for thought. Thought must become adequate to the virtual, but this adequation is not correspondence, it is rather inhabitation and subjectivation of a problematic objectivity. 'Ideas are the differentials of thought', and differentials express the 'objective consistency' of the problematic.[24] Thus we can maintain both that 'problems are Ideas themselves' and that the 'indeterminate horizon of a transcendental problem' is the object of an idea.[25] Passage to the virtual, or the task of problematisation, brings us to the 'objective consistency' of the ideas in which we are involved. This is the first element of adequation, but we cannot stop here. To be adequate to this problematic idea is to re-express the intensity inherent in its differential, to repeat difference nonidentically or productively. Adequation to virtual difference is thus possible only by way of creation.

We are now broaching, after a rather dense stretch of abstraction, the connection between difference and the creation of the new. Immanence, we have seen, is able to imagine the production of expressions of reality that exceed the given expression of reality, and this is precisely because of the intrinsically differential nature of any expression. Immanence exceeds the given due to the virtual nature of what is given. This, in any case, is the logic of re-expression in terms of difference. Having thus articulated this logic in terms of difference, we can now articulate it in terms of an unconditioned power, such that difference and power can be brought together.

The unconditioned power at work in re-expression and the difference at work in re-expression are not separated. On the contrary, the unconditioned power *is* difference. The power of immanence does not transcend its differential architecture, it expresses itself as difference and does not exist apart from differential expression. 'The virtual is never independent of the singularities which cut it up and divide it out on the plane of immanence.'[26] Virtual singularities condition immanence, insofar as they give it determination, while immanence gives the virtual an unconditioned power. Deleuze puts the exchange of difference and power as follows: 'Events or singularities give the plane all their virtuality, just as the plane of immanence gives virtual events their full reality.'[27] The virtual keeps immanence from collapsing into what is actually given: it demands a thought of immanence in terms of unconditioned power, and in doing so it likewise joins this unconditioned power to the differential field of singularities. Thus, while we can look at re-expression in terms of unconditioned power, we can just as well look at it in terms of difference. There is a power of re-expression, but this power is not emanated to individuals, rather it is immanent to individuals as difference. Specifically, the virtual, as differential intensity, is the motivating force behind actualisation. It is the *differential power* of re-expression.

What re-expression – no longer just as a vaguely invoked power, but more exactly as a determinate, differential power – demonstrates is that such a radical break with the given is possible. It shows the possibility of imagining new possibilities. Still, we must ask, how would this work? What is the criterion that must be met in order to make sure that the differential power of re-expression is directed toward the creation of the new rather than toward the maintenance of the given?

We already have something of an answer, namely the demand to problematise, to become adequate to the differential intensity that is implied in any given expression. If creation of the new is possible, then we must become affected by the problematic, by the intensity of difference in itself. This is an ethics of immanence: to become affected by difference, to become adequate to the problematic, and from this point to construct the new. But note the goal of such an ethics. It is enacted in the name of new possibilities of existence. In this sense, an ethics of immanence is ultimately political, for it concerns the making of reality. This means the political question of a radical break with the given is also, for immanence, a question of ethics, which is here understood in terms of becoming affected by the problematic and constructing the new. Relevant, then, is a further articulation of the nature of this ethico-political aspect of immanence. We will eventually turn in this direction, but we must first look at the question of time.

As a way of framing this question of time, we might recall Derrida's objection to Heidegger: the affirmation of difference cannot happen apart from the affirmation of time; difference must be thought, but it cannot be thought ahead of time, it can only be thought *as* time, a time that cannot be anticipated. We have seen, in our account of Deleuze's immanence, the imagination of new possibilities of existence that stem from the differential power of re-expression. We have not seen, however, the role that time plays in this re-expression. This lacuna is a serious one, for re-expression is a process, it is explicitly connected to the temporal. There is no re-expression without time. So how does Deleuze's thought commingle the affirmation of differential power with the affirmation of time? Only when this is understood will we be able to advance to the question of ethico-political creation.

Is Time a Crystal?

The connection between time and the process of re-expression can be approached by looking more closely at the relation between the virtual and the actual. We have noted how the virtual, with its singularly determined intensive power (difference in itself), gives rise to a new process of actualisation. However, this should not be imagined as a two-step process, for neither one precedes the other: 'The plane of immanence includes both the virtual and its actualization simultaneously, without there being any assignable limit between the two.'[28] Yet if this is the case, then what is the sense of distinguishing between virtual and actual? And what is the nature of this distinction – how can there even be a distinction – if it is not possible to assign any limit between what is being distinguished? To get at these questions, we must divide the actual into two sides: actualisation and the actual*ed*.

Actualisation's exhaustion or endpoint is visible as 'the actual', and in this sense, 'the actual is the . . . product, the object of actualization, which has nothing but the virtual as its subject'.[29] But even though the actual is the *object* of actualisation, even though the actual is what actualisation produces, the actual should not be separated from the process that produces it. The actual is the product of actualisation, but it is a product that simultaneously loops back to the virtual, which initiated the process of actualisation. In this sense, the process of actualisation would give rise to an effect (the actual) that does not separate itself from the cause of this process (the virtual). This, at least, is what it means to speak of the actual properly, in its immanence with the virtual. To misunderstand the actual, on the other hand, is to see the actual as having been separated from the process of actualisation. In this case, what is seen is not the actual in relation to the virtual and the process of actualisation; what is seen instead is the actualised. 'The actual falls from the plane like a fruit, whilst the actualization relates it back to the plane as if to that which turns the object back into a subject.'[30] To see the actual simply as actualised is thus mistaken, for it is to miss and deny the immanence of actualisation and the virtual. When we perceive the actual object to have 'fall[en] outside' the plane we see only part of the process; we miss the way that the actual object simultaneously loops back to affect the virtual.[31]

Since actualisation can relate the actual object back to the virtual, even to the point that the (actual) object becomes a (virtual) subject, a straightforward primacy of the virtual over the actual is refused. This process of looping back (from the actual to the virtual) doubles the process of actualisation (from the virtual to the actual), such that we can speak of a 'perpetual exchange' between the virtual and the actual. The plane of immanence, Deleuze says, contains not only actualisation, as 'the relation of the virtual with other virtual terms' – singularities of the transcendental field, or difference in itself – but also the actual, as 'the term with which the virtual is exchanged'.[32] This avoids a predicament in which, when given an actual object, one can only proceed back to the virtual by overcoming the actual, before falling back into the actual and repeating the cycle. We do not need to overcome the actual in order to engage the virtual. The actual can directly articulate its own specific exchange with the virtual.

Along these lines, Deleuze will insist on talking about an image and '*its own*' virtual.[33] In this perpetual exchange of a product and its own virtual, the virtual and the actual intensify their proximity to a degree where they become increasingly indiscernible: 'the virtual draws closer to the actual, both become less and less distinct. You get to an inner circuit which links only the actual object and its virtual image: an actual particle has its virtual double, which barely diverges from it at all.'[34] This 'inner circuit' is a *crystallisation* of the virtual and the actual.

> [The] perpetual exchange between the virtual and the actual is what defines a crystal; and it is on the plane of immanence that crystals appear. The actual and the virtual coexist, and enter into a tight circuit which we are continually retracing from one to the other . . . Pure virtuality no longer has to actualize itself, since it is a strict correlative of the actual with which it forms the tightest circuit. It is not so much that one cannot assign the terms 'actual' and 'virtual' to distinct objects, but rather that the two are indistinguishable.[35]

The crystal thus indicates the point at which the immanence of virtual and actual reaches a kind of purity, the point at which the process of actualisation (where virtual causes actual) and the process of looping back (where actual affects virtual) become indiscernible.

This allows us to see the radical immanence of virtual and actual, as well as the inescapability of re-expression. Yet in doing so it raises the question of time, for it is the relative distinction of virtual and actual, of the processes of actualisation and looping back, that helps us imagine the temporality of re-expression. The distinction between virtual and actual stands in for a distinction between two processes that, while interrelated, seem to feed off of and advance one another, like a two-player game of leap-frog. But crystallisation renders this distinction null, for it refers to a situation in which virtual and actual are indiscernible. Does this mean that the aim of immanence – if indeed crystallisation is this aim – is to annul or even, paradoxically, transcend time? If this were the case, then immanence, despite its affirmation of difference, would fail to affirm time. This is not the case, but in order to understand why, we must look explicitly at how time does emerge in the virtual-actual relation.

Dividing Time

Amidst the inseparability of the virtual and the actual, there is a splitting determined by time – that is, by 'the differentiation of its passage into two great jets: the passing of the present, and the preservation of the past'.[36] Here the temporality of the virtual is indicated by 'the preservation of the past', while the temporality of the actual is indicated by 'the passing of the present'. Though it is tempting to understand the present as 'a variable given measured in continuous time, a supposedly mono-directional movement, in which the present passes up until the exhaustion of that time',[37] this would be to tell time solely in an actual manner. It is to fail to see that there is no (actual) passage from one present to another without a simultaneous jet of time that does not comply with this mono-directional movement, a (virtual) jet that turns toward the preservation of the past. This jet 'appears in a smaller space of time than that which marks the minimum movement in a single direction'.[38] The virtual thus preserves the past, such that this smaller-than-smallest space of time involves a length spanning, or running through, every present, even the longest imaginable period of time. 'The period of time which is smaller than the smallest period of continuous time imaginable in one direction is also the longest time, longer than the longest unit of continuous time imaginable in all directions.'[39] On the one hand, then, this virtual jet of time is so small that it cannot be measured, that it names a real yet disappearing time between one moment and another; on the other, it can be seen as longer than all of these moments added up, for it is that which runs through all of them and thus surrounds them.

How does the crystal connect to this asymmetry between actual and virtual jets of time? It is not that the crystal would somehow annul these jets of time, it is more precisely that the crystal makes them communicate without separation. In fact, the crystal *cannot* annul time, for time is asymmetrical – so even when the actual and virtual jets of time are crystallised, they remain in tension with one another. What crystallisation does, then, is bring us into 'between-times' or 'between-moments'.[40] In other words, it focuses attention not on exhausted, actualised moments, but rather on those interstices between moments, where time is, on one hand, leaving behind one moment for the next, and, on the other, preserving the past. What happens in crystallisation, then, is not the annulment of time, it is instead the affirmation of both asymmetrical jets of time. The crystal thus allows us to leave a temporality of successive presents and to enter into another temporality. As Deleuze puts it, 'we see time in the crystal'.[41] The crystal can become adequate to the asymmetry of virtual and actual because it advances us into time itself, the time that splits into asymmetrical jets.

Crystallisation therefore belongs to the task of seeing time itself. Thus far we have addressed this task conceptually, and while this will continue to be the case, we must now start teasing out the ethical stakes of this task. In other words, we need to start connecting the understanding of time to the possibilities of existence. It is for this reason that we may speak of conceptions of time as practices,

practices that are relations to time and that, in being so, are ways of imagining temporal existence or of inhabiting time. Specifically, we now turn to two practices of conceiving time, those named by Deleuze as Aion and Chronos.[42] The conceptual difference between them entails a difference at the level of temporal possibility, and this is most notably the case when what is at stake is the imagination of the future.

Although it should be noted, as we begin to trace this difference, that Aion enables possibilities that are foreclosed by Chronos, it would be wrong to say that Aion is infinite while Chronos is not. This is because Chronos can go on endlessly, 'it could be circular in the sense that it encompasses every present, begins anew, and measures off a new cosmic period after the preceding one, which may be identical to the preceding one'.[43] Chronos, in other words, may be infinite insofar as it articulates an infinite *succession* of present moments. Indeed, its lure is precisely this capacity to maintain past determinations, or to reproduce them, into the future. It does this through a regulation of the present, a *delimitation* of time to the present. Therefore, while Chronos can be infinite, it cannot be unlimited. But what does it mean to delimit time to the present? How is this possible, since – as we have observed – the present must pass?

For Chronos, 'only the present exists in time. Past, present, and future are not three dimensions of time; only the present fills time, whereas past and future are two dimensions relative to the present in time.'[44] Obviously, then, we are not dealing with a simple present moment that absorbs every past and future. This would contradict the possibility of a Chronic *reproduction*. There is an ineffaceable disturbance of the present by past and future, and the absorptive capacity of a simple present moment would not be strong enough to swallow this disturbance. For Chronos, what matters is not to absorb time into a specific present moment, it is, more precisely, to infinitely narrate the passage from one delimited present to another. It is to think of time only in terms of the present, understood as an undisturbed continuity of presents. Disturbances introduced by the past and future are not denied by Chronos; Chronos does not defend a given present against disturbance. More precisely, Chronos responds to and takes up these disturbances, which are circulated amongst and absorbed by many presents. Included in this 'many' are not just successive presents, but also vaster presents, which encompass disturbance. According to Deleuze's account of Chronos, 'whatever is future or past in relation to a certain present belongs to a more vast present which has a greater extension or duration. There is always a more vast present which absorbs the past and the future.'[45]

The successive presents thus relate to one another through these greater encompassments. While there is necessarily 'a relativity of the presents themselves, in relation to each other', Chronos organises this relativity according to a formidably expansive circulation, a mutable but ceaseless process that, despite its constant addition and fluctuation, can reproduce nothing other than a great, delimited totality – a totality that is delimited not by being finite but rather by infinitely absorbing disturbances.[46] What emerges is an ever-growing inclusion of every present moment within every other present moment, so as to generate an all-encompassing continuity of presence. 'Chronos is an encasement, a coiling up of relative presents, with God as the extreme circle or the external envelope.'[47] There is movement in Chronos, but it always moves 'in order to absorb or restore in the play of cosmic periods the relative presents which it surrounds'.[48] This double-character of Chronos, its capacity to accept a disturbance of one present (by the past and future) and then to restore it (through another present), should not be overlooked. Chronos is not directly opposed to the disturbances of past and future. It acknowledges them, but it can only give them voice according to the form of the present (or the form encompassing various presents).

This is why, despite its willingness to acknowledge their disturbance, Chronos cannot genuinely set forth the potentialities of past and future. These potentialities call into question the delimitation of the present, whereas the essence of Chronos is the commitment to such delimitation. These potentialities disturb the present, but Chronos responds by supplying another present to absorb the disturbance and re-establish the priority of the present. This newly supplied present is, then, in its own turn disturbed, which necessitates the supplication of yet another present, and so on . . . infinitely, never-ending, but always in the name of delimitation. We have constant movement, but it is always regulated by the coiling and encompassment of relative presents in an eternal present. Thus Chronos does 'express the revenge taken by future and past on the present', but it always does so 'in terms of the present, because these are the only terms it comprehends and the only terms that affect it'.[49]

The Aion, however, provides another theory of the present, another practice of temporality. For the Aion,

Only the past and future inhere or subsist in time. Instead of a present which absorbs the past and future, a future and past divide the present at every instant and subdivide it ad infinitum into past and future, in both directions at once. Or rather, it is the instant without thickness and without extension, which subdivides each present into past and future, rather than vast and thick presents which comprehend both future and past in relation to one another.[50]

The present is no longer a vast, circular encompassment, but a crack of the instant. There is a 'sidestepping' of the present, but the present that is sidestepped is the Chronic one.[51] Aion puts forth a different present, one that belongs to future and past potentialities themselves (and therefore is not simply present). Future and past are not subjected to the present, the present is subjected to a becoming-future and becoming-past at the same time. 'It is no longer the future and past which subvert the existing present; it is the instant which perverts the present into inhering future and past.'[52] Against Chronos's circle, which contains past and future disturbances in its coils, Aion 'stretches out in a straight line, limitless in either direction', for it binds the present *to* its disturbances – disturbances that make it 'always already passed and eternally yet to come'.[53]

The Aionic present is smaller than Chronos's vastness because it offers only a cut, a sliver or crack – constituting a between – in an otherwise homologous past and future. What is important, though, is that this is a genuine fissure, that time itself is extracted from a homologous development. It is in this sense that Aion is larger than Chronos: within its fissure there opens 'an unlimited past-future', unthought by the entire cycle of history (the accumulation or totality of presents). Aion is not merely a relativising of the present, it is the 'eternal truth of time'.[54] It introduces the break of past-future precisely because it introduces this eternal truth, a pure and empty form of time prior to the organisation of time by an ever-encompassing Chronos. The break or crack conditioned by the pure and empty form of time is one where past becomes future and future becomes past. With the Aion, there is no re-establishment of the present, for there is instead an opening-up of the present to becoming.

Accordingly, the Aionic present is not a moment in or of time, it is the introduction of time as such; time does not come to some determinate mode of presence, it winnows out every determined presence with its emptiness. An immense ocean then opens up, beyond the continuously imagined limits of the unbroken chain linking past, present, and future. But this beyond emerges as nothing else than this time that is pure and empty. The beyond is opposed to the limit, but the beyond is nothing other than the immanence of time. Time bears an oceanic immensity, it is unlimited in nature, but this unlimitedness is in common with the finite. 'Whereas Chronos was limited and infinite, Aion is unlimited, the way that future and past are unlimited, and finite like the instant.'[55] Becoming's power does not compete with, is not in a zero-sum relation with, a finite and contingent grasping. The ocean has its island, the empty and immense time has its emergence in an instant.

What I wish to indicate with this phrasing is the way in which an unlimited time – where the unconditioned power of immanence emerges – is always juxtaposed with the contingent striving of determinate, individual beings. We must take seriously the understanding of Aion and Chronos as two *practices* of temporality. The unlimited is not an object but a passage, the intensive practice of which may be undertaken or neglected by individuals. Neglect is often furthered by the fact that such a passage requires resistance to the given, or invocation of the crack – a crack that means the fissuring of the individuated being.

It is precisely this sort of ascesis that Deleuze finds in Kant's critique of Descartes. According to Deleuze, the central and most radical impetus in Kant is his emphasis on time, which had been ignored by the Cartesian self. 'Temporally speaking – in other words, from the point of view of the theory of time – nothing is more instructive than the difference between the Kantian and the Cartesian Cogito.'[56] The Cartesian 'I think' is meant to function as the determination of existence, but it does not fully succeed: what the 'I think' determines, namely 'I am', denotes an existence that ultimately remains underdetermined. Why is this the case? The difficulty lies with the incompleteness of the relation between the determination ('I think') and the determined ('I am'). Descartes fails to consider the condition of possibility for existential reception of the determination. According to Deleuze's reading of Kant, we find – in addition to the determination and the determined – 'a third logical value: the determinable, or rather the form in which the undetermined is determinable (by the determination)'.[57] There can be no determination of an existence as thinking, of an 'I am' by 'I think', without the form of determinability, and for Kant, 'the form under which undetermined existence is determinable by the "I think" is that of time'.[58]

In other words, Descartes' project of determining existence, 'I am', in virtue of the determination 'I think', remains incomplete insofar as it does not address time. It is time, after all, that allows for the determination of 'I think' to be received by existence. Once this Kantian critique of Descartes has been taken up, the payoff, for Deleuze, is that the subject must be constituted not just in terms of thought and existence, but also in terms of time – so much so, in fact, that time becomes prior to thought and existence (both of which depend on time). Both thought and existence are suspended by the milieu of time, a milieu on which their relation depends, and in relation to which their relation is undetermined. Time suspends both because time remains unthought. The subject, the supposed relation between thinking and existence, thus emerges as 'fractured from one end to the other . . . by the pure and empty form of time'.[59] Before the subject, there is time – or, as Deleuze often proclaims, 'the only subjectivity is time . . . it is we who are internal to time'.[60] The subject does not act upon time, and it does not even act within time; time cracks the subject, and the subject is able to act only insofar as it is cracked.

The subject enters into becoming through this temporality because the subject is related to time itself, and time is unlimited. 'Time . . . divide[s] itself in two as affector and affected', and the subject emerges as this division of time – indeed, 'the affection of self by self' becomes the 'definition of time'.[61] The subject thus inhabits the crack of, or is produced by, time's division. It is affected by time (time as affector), but this affection by time opens up the subject, it makes the subject *become*. The subject, thus opened, is able to act, and its action loops back to affect time itself. In other words, the cracked, or opened-up, subject can act on the basis of time's unlimited nature and thus affect time (time as affected). The subject exchanges the subjectivity of the identity-based 'I' for the subjectivity of time, the cracked 'I', but in doing so it affects the very articulation of time. Once again we find ourselves face-to-face with the power of re-expression, now as a *temporal* expression and construction of the unconditioned power. This logic of time is extremely similar to the logic of the Spinozian God, the immanent cause: just as the power of the cause to produce effects is inseparable from its power to be affected by the effects, so time's affection of the subject is inseparable from its being affected by the subject it cracks.

The Autonomy of the Product

Yet it is not enough, having extracted a re-expressive process of temporal subjectivation, simply to valorise this process. We must attend to the product created by the process, to the fact that this process of temporal subjectivation creates a product. I have already spoken of a process of crystallisation, though I must now qualify it: the crystal is preliminary to the product, but it is not the product itself; the crystal must be cracked. The crystal is 'not time, but we see time in the crystal. We see in the crystal the perpetual foundation of time, non-chronological time'.[62] It is because the crystal gives us vision of time itself that it can weave together the virtual and the actual in a non-mutually-exclusive manner. This insertion of virtual and actual into time itself is why the crystal 'constantly exchanges the two distinct images which constitute it, the actual image of the present which passes and the virtual image of the past which is preserved'.[63] The crystal is of immeasurable value because it enables an oscillation between the distinctly virtual and the distinctly actual jets of time, an oscillation so intense that the two become indiscernible. No potential is precluded, for the crystal 'absorb[s] the real which . . . passes as much into the virtual as into the actual'.[64] The crystal produces a profound circuit, but its profundity is bound up in its *penultimate* status in the process it realises. After the crystal, there is still something to be produced; something 'will come out of the crystal, a new Real will come out beyond the actual and virtual'.[65]

It is in service of this 'new Real' that the crystal, having been formed, must be cracked. The crystal gives us vision of time, it puts the virtual and the actual in circuit, but it does not yet produce something new from time; it is the necessary preparation for creation, but it is not yet the act of creation. Beyond crystallisation, thought must be committed to something that 'takes shape inside the crystal which will succeed in leaving through the crack and spreading freely'.[66] Crystallisation is thus a condition of creation, but we must leave, or crack, the crystal in order to produce 'a new reality which was not pre-existent'.[67] Presents that pass (the actual jet of time) are related to the preservation of the past (the virtual jet of time) through the crystal, but they must emerge from it once again in a tendency that 'launches itself toward a future, creates this future as a bursting forth of life'.[68] In this sense, production of the future requires, but then exceeds, crystallisation.

It is clear that, for Deleuze, the question of time always gives rise to the question of thought's capacity to temporally access and extract a power to create something that breaks with the given. The manner in which this creation produces a new reality – or a real future – is most explicitly presented in his account of the three syntheses of time, which articulate an Aionic relation of past, present, and future. 'The past and the future do not designate instants distinct from a supposed present instant, but rather the dimensions of the present itself in so far as it is a contraction of instants.'[69] What matters here is the interplay between past and future within the present; there is no discrete present, for the present is nothing other than an interplay between its conditions (which may become crystallised) and what these conditions produce (the future that is created). Let us now turn to this interplay, noting first the role of the conditions – habit and memory – and then proceeding to look at how the unconditioned power is re-expressed for the creation of a future that breaks with the given.

Habit, which Deleuze sees as a kind of contemplation, is said of the first, passive synthesis of time. An individual exists only through contemplating, it is made up of that which it contemplates. This synthesis is passive in virtue of the fact that the contemplative agent does not pre-exist its contemplations, but is instead made up by what it habitually contemplates. 'We do not contemplate ourselves, but we exist only in contemplating – that is to say, in contracting that from which we come.'[70] Habit's temporal synthesis, the contraction of what is contemplated, thus condenses a multitude of elements, and this condensation shapes the present. The present is shaped by habit; the habitually contemplated is the most contracted. Habit, as 'a *contraction* of instants with respect to a present', synthesises time and thus determines the present, but it cannot account for the fact that this present passes.[71] In other words, habit accounts for the contraction into a present, the condensation of a given moment, but it cannot account for the fact that this given moment does not stay. The given moment gives way to another moment, which is also a contraction, and so habit once again comes to the fore. However, the question remains: Why did the first moment pass away? Habit is the basis for the contraction of every present moment, but it cannot be the basis for the passing away of each one of these moments.

It is here that Deleuze's insistence on a contemporaneity of past and present is set forth. The past cannot be derived from the passage of contracted presents, because this would leave unexplained the fact of the present's passing.

> In effect, we are unable to believe that the past is constituted after it has been present, or because a new present appears. If a new present were required for the past to be constituted as past, then the former present would never pass and the new one would never arrive.[72]

In other words, the past does not come after the passing of the present. If the past had to wait for the present to pass, if the past came about only after the present passed away, we would have no reason for the fact that the present does pass away. There must be something that motivates the present to pass away (a jet going in the other direction). This motivation is the past: the past does not come after the present passes away; the past is already there as soon as the present is there. Only if the past is already there can the present be motivated to pass away. This is why the present and the past are contemporaneous: 'No present would ever pass were it not past "at the same time" as it is present; no past would ever be constituted unless it were first constituted "at the same time" as it was present.'[73]

Contemporaneity of the past and the present thus explains the passing of the present. But this then raises another question: how should we explain the contemporaneity of past and present? One must introduce a *pure* past. The past, in order to be contemporaneous with each present that passes, must exist in a pure state – it must exist in such a way that it is not relative to, or dependent upon, the passing of the present. 'The past does not cause one present to pass without calling forth another, but itself neither passes nor comes forth.'[74] The past, in other words, is not merely a past present, it is not even a collection of past presents. On the contrary, the past must somehow be there as soon as any present is there, it must not be waiting for the present to pass, and it must not be derived from the passing of the present. Yet this can only be the case if the past has its own manner of existence, if the past is autonomous from the present – and this is why the past must be understood as a 'pure past'. The past, as pure past, is thus an *a priori* condition of time.

It is also what grounds the second, active synthesis of memory. Therefore we have two passive syntheses working together, but according to significantly different rhythms:

> Whereas the passive synthesis of habit constitutes the living present in time and makes the past and the future two asymmetrical elements of the present, the passive synthesis of memory constitutes the pure past in time, and makes the former and the present present . . . two asymmetrical elements of this past as such.[75]

The first and second syntheses correspond respectively to the actual and the virtual, but there remains a third synthesis, which corresponds to production of the new, or creation. On one hand, the third synthesis exceeds the first two syntheses. It is that by which the

actual and the virtual are re-expressed. As such, it names the unconditioned power that enables a break with the given. On the other
hand, the third synthesis does not transcend the first two syntheses.
It is immanent with them, and so we advance to the third synthesis
only by repeating the first two syntheses. The third synthesis is the
production of the new, but this production must emerge from the
crystallisation of the first two syntheses (even though it ultimately
cracks this crystal).

Habit, as repetition of the present again and again in different
modalities, is metamorphosis, the change from one moment to
another; memory, because it concerns the pure element of the past
in every present, conditions these metamorphic movements and
repeats them through reproduction and reflection. These two conditions must be together affirmed and crystallised. Nonetheless, if we
had only these two repetitions, they would, despite their intrinsic
dynamism, circle back on one another. Crystallisation would be
splendid entrapment. Immanence, despite its dynamism, would then
amount to a re-shuffling of the given, to something that cannot truly
break with the given and create the new. But this is not the case, for
crystallisation is penultimate, not ultimate. What is ultimate is the
third synthesis, which addresses the excess harnessed by the crystal
in order to create something new from it.

> We produce something new only on condition that we repeat – once in
> the mode which constitutes the past, and once more in the present of
> metamorphosis. Moreover, what is produced, the absolutely new itself, is
> in turn nothing but repetition: the third repetition, this time by excess.[76]

This third repetition, that of the eternal return, draws on the first
two repetitions, but it does not make them return. What returns
is nothing but the excess – or, more precisely, excess as what is
produced by the third repetition. Eternal return 'causes neither the
[memorial] *condition* nor the [metamorphic] *agent* to return: on the
contrary, it repudiates these and expels them with all its centrifugal
force'.[77] Memory and habit are thus displaced by what they prepare.
They are determinate conditions, but through this passage of repetition they are joined to the power of the unconditioned. The virtual
and actual conditions (or jets) of time are undone in favour of the
pure and empty form of time. This form, in the practice of the third
repetition's eternal return, enacts 'the revelation of the formless' and
'causes only the yet-to-come to return'.[78] The eternal return is the
constitution of the new out of the interplay between determinate

processes of conditioning (the virtual and the actual, or memory and habit) and the power of the unconditioned (the pure empty form of time). What is created through the third synthesis *breaks with*, or is irreducible to, the pre-existent, for the third synthesis 'constitutes the autonomy of the product, the independence of the work' – it brings about 'the new, complete novelty'.[79] Importantly, it does so not by reference to the transcendent, but by re-expression of determinate (virtual and actual) conditions in virtue of the unconditioned. Re-expression, through the pure empty form of time, immanently constructs the new.

The Ethics of Re-expression and the Naming of God

This conjunction of re-expression and temporality is central. Re-expression may be understood as Deleuze's response to both the potentiality and the difficulty that we saw posed, in Chapter 1, by Heidegger's attempt to bring together the themes of immanence and difference. Deleuze's differential immanence thinks the sameness of these two themes in such a way that differentiality becomes the intensity that produces both expression and the immanent demand for re-expression. Furthermore, we can see that it is because immanence is a matter of re-expression that it cannot be equated with acceptance of the given. The necessity of re-expression precludes anything approaching such acceptance. On the contrary, re-expression makes it possible for immanence to imagine new possibilities of existence. Still, because these possibilities concern a re-expression of what is already expressed, they have nothing to do with the imagination of a novelty that wants nothing to do with, or that would functionally transcend, what is given. Re-expression is simultaneously a matter of refusing to transcend what is given and refusing to accept it. If re-expression refuses both of these options, then it can do so only because of the sort of temporality that it involves.

This is to recall our observation, also in Chapter 1, that Heidegger's connection of immanence with difference ran into an insuperable ambiguity when it came to the nature of this connection's temporal constitution. We then noted how Derrida's account of différance sought to elaborate and address this difficulty. Deleuze's differential immanence can thus be understood as sharing Derrida's concern insofar as the thought of re-expression requires the thought of temporality, especially as this last is understood in relation to an Aionic inhabitation of time. What temporal re-expression makes possible, as we have just seen, is creation of the new, where what is productively re-expressed has an autonomy that can distinguish it from the past and the present, even as it takes its material from them.

It is in this regard that Deleuze surpasses Derrida, whose différance turned itself against every return of transcendence, but in doing so remained extrinsic to the difference it protected. It left unthought the possibility of an intrinsic relation to difference, a relation in virtue of which difference's excess would become productive of the new. Deleuze, by way of the Aionic temporality of re-expression, has provided us with such an intrinsic relation to difference. For Deleuze, the affirmation of difference just is the affirmation of time; these affirmations are direct, or intrinsic, and so much so that the affirmation of difference and time affects, or cracks, the affirmer. In other words, to affirm difference and time is to re-express all that is given, to leave nothing out, not even the subject of expression, but to do so by way of the crack – the crack of intensive differentiality, the crack of the Aion. The re-expression that comes after this cracking is yet to be seen, for it comes from the affirmation of time itself.

These remarks give us a glimpse of the ethics of immanence. Ethics is central to immanence, for the capacity of re-expression to produce the new depends on whether individuals seek to encounter difference, to enter the crack of immanence. Only if this is done is there the chance of making the difference that runs throughout reality into a weapon against what has presently settled in. The creation of the new, in immanence, does not happen without an ethics of the crack. When we recall that politics concerns the imagination of new possibilities, then we can see how such ethics is inseparable from this political task. To give attention to this ethical dimension of the political is therefore to give attention to the fact that the political demand for change is inseparable from the ethical demand to respond to suffering, to dissatisfaction with the present, to the pain of what is given. Such a response is also a matter of re-expression.

The imagination of new possibilities of existence is thus bound up with the imagination of suffering. To take seriously the possibility of these new possibilities is also to take seriously the task of being critical about the inherited habits of our imagination when we encounter both dissatisfaction and the demand for change. As we observed by way of introduction, there will be no break with the coordinates of the given, with the coordinates in which we imagine possibility, unless we directly encounter the enabling condition of these given coordinates. This enabling condition, following Nietzsche's proclamation, is the name of God. Whether the name of God is necessarily transcendent – that is, whether it necessarily forecloses immanence – is a question that we have yet to answer. Regardless of how we answer it, the process of attempting to do so, of interrogating the naming of God (which is the task of the following two chapters), is necessary in order to understand how temporal re-expression can be brought to bear on inherited habits of imagination. Such an interrogation also allows us to articulate more precisely the manner in which temporal re-expression plays out ethically. In other words, its rivalry with the transcendent tendency involved in the naming of God, and with this tendency's claim that immanence cannot ultimately break with the given, allows us to develop more fully the distinctive way in which temporal re-expression responds to the experience of dissatisfaction.

Notes

1. Gilles Deleuze and Félix Guattari, *What is Philosophy?*, trans. Hugh Tomlinson and Graham Burchell (New York: Columbia University Press, 1994), p. 48. He is elsewhere referred to as the 'Christ of philosophers' (ibid., p. 60). I am, by relying on Deleuze's account of Spinoza for an introduction to immanence, eliding somewhat the distinction between Deleuze's 'historical studies' and his more obviously 'constructive' work. Of course, Deleuze himself engenders such an elision, given his well-known preference for 'revisionist' representations of figures within the history of philosophy. But my decision to draw on Deleuze's interpretation of Spinoza is driven by something more substantial than Deleuze's own interested manner of interpretation – namely, the essential importance of Spinoza (and even more, of *Deleuze's* interpretation of Spinoza) to the thought of immanence. When it comes to grasping immanence, then, Deleuze's interpretation of Spinoza has immense value, despite the fact that Deleuze's 'own' philosophy might not ultimately maintain certain properly Spinozist features (such as the triadic architecture of substance, attributes, and modes) that Deleuze nonetheless foregrounds.
2. Gilles Deleuze, 'Cours Vincennes: Spinoza: February 17, 1981', available at <http://www.webdeleuze.com/php/texte.php?cle=38&groupe=Spinoza&langue=2> (last accessed 18 February 2013).
3. Gilles Deleuze, *Expressionism in Philosophy: Spinoza*, trans. Martin Joughin (New York: Zone, 1990), p. 196.
4. This, in fact, would bring us back to the multiple.
5. Ibid., p. 11.
6. As Deleuze puts it: 'God does not produce [substantive] modification outside the modes' (ibid., p. 111).

7. Gilles Deleuze, *Difference and Repetition*, trans. Paul Patton (New York: Columbia University Press, 1994), p. 40.
8. Deleuze, *Expressionism*, p. 94.
9. Ibid., p. 164.
10. Ibid., p. 172.
11. Ibid., p. 102.
12. Ibid., p. 180.
13. I have discussed this notion of re-expression, as it relates to the notion of 'spirituality', in Daniel Colucciello Barber, 'Immanence and the Re-expression of the World', *SubStance* 39.1 (2010), pp. 36–46.
14. Éric Alliez, *Signature of the World: What is Deleuze and Guattari's Philosophy?*, trans. Eliot Ross Albert (London: Continuum, 2005).
15. Deleuze, *Expressionism*, p. 203.
16. The task of identifying and opposing correlationism is now understood as an essential characteristic of the movement known as 'Speculative Realism'. This text is not the place to enter into a debate with the movement, or more precisely with its general indifference to (and even disregard for) Deleuze's thought. However, my insistence on Deleuze's evasion of and opposition to a correlational tendency should be taken as an indication that his thought is not subject to the critique set forth by Speculative Realism. In fact, I imagine that Deleuze's work presents a possibility of thought too often ignored by this movement.
17. Deleuze, *Difference and Repetition*, p. 222.
18. This does not mean Deleuze is advocating some kind of otherworldliness, for his point is not that the actual is unreal or relatively unimportant. On the contrary, he is trying to uncover the immanent conditions of possibility for the given. He claims, for instance, that 'difference . . . is the sufficient reason of all phenomena, the condition of that which happens' (ibid., p. 228). The given expression, then, is not to be suppressed or excised. It is simply to be understood in its genesis, which is intensive; explicated bodies are not to be replaced by what they implicate, rather they are to find and involve themselves in the intensity in which their bodies are already involved.
19. Such a misguided assumption seems to subtend Peter Hallward's critical claim that invocation of the virtual is nothing other than a vaguely mystical tendency that, at best, calls for a movement 'out of this world', out of actual bodies. Hallward wishes to highlight 'the degree to which [Deleuze's] work, far from engaging in a description or transformation of the world, instead seeks to escape it'. Hallward claims that 'although Deleuze equates being with the activity of creation, he orients this activity toward a contemplative and immaterial abstraction'. See Hallward, *Out of this World: Deleuze and the Philosophy of Creation* (New York: Verso, 2006), p. 7.
20. The actual is not an emanation of the virtual – indeed, the relation of

the two should be taken in the direction of what Anthony Paul Smith calls an 'ecological relationship between the actual and the virtual'. See Smith, 'Review of Hallward, *Out of this World*', *Angelaki* 12 (2007), p. 154.

21. Alberto Toscano, *The Theatre of Production: Philosophy and Individuation between Kant and Deleuze* (New York: Palgrave Macmillan, 2006), p. 138.
22. Gilles Deleuze, *Bergsonism*, trans. Hugh Tomlinson and Barbara Habberjam (New York: Zone, 1991), p. 94.
23. For a mathematical account of the fundamentally problematic character of difference in Deleuze's thought, see Simon Duffy, *The Logic of Expression: Quantity, Quality, and Intensity in Spinoza, Hegel, and Deleuze* (Surrey: Ashgate, 2006).
24. Deleuze, *Difference and Repetition*, pp. 178, 181.
25. Ibid., pp. 162, 188.
26. Gilles Deleuze, *Dialogues II*, trans. Hugh Tomlinson, Barbara Habberjam, and Eliot Ross Albert (New York: Columbia University Press, 2002), p. 149.
27. Gilles Deleuze, *Pure Immanence: Essays on A Life*, trans. Anne Boyman (New York: Zone, 2005), p. 31.
28. Deleuze, *Dialogues II*, p. 149.
29. Ibid.
30. Ibid., p. 150.
31. Deleuze, *Pure Immanence*, p. 27.
32. Deleuze, *Dialogues II*, p. 152.
33. Ibid.
34. Ibid., p. 150.
35. Ibid., pp. 150–1.
36. Ibid., p. 151.
37. Ibid.
38. Ibid.
39. Ibid.
40. Deleuze, *Pure Immanence*, p. 29.
41. Gilles Deleuze, *Cinema 2: The Time-Image*, trans. Hugh Tomlinson and Robert Galeta (Minneapolis: University of Minnesota Press, 1989), p. 81.
42. I interpret Chronos and the Aion as theories of time, of course, but also as ways of inhabiting time. What distinguishes the Aion is its ability to theorise a presentation of pure time, of time as such. A temporal practice of the Aion, then, is orientated around the pure and empty form of time – that is, around the unconditioned nature of time. Time, I should make clear, is not intrinsically or automatically creative, but it is certainly the case that pure time, due to its unconditioned nature, enables creation. Temporal practice of the Aion thus names the endeavour to

make the unconditioned nature of time into the ally – or enabler – of creation. Where time is understood in terms of Chronos rather than of the Aion, a corresponding temporal practice of Chronos emerges. In short, the temporality of Chronos – theoretically and practically – does not accede to the pure and empty form of time.

43. Gilles Deleuze, *The Logic of Sense*, trans. Mark Lester with Charles Stivale (New York: Columbia University Press, 1990), p. 163.
44. Ibid., p. 162.
45. Ibid.
46. Ibid. It is worth noting that I have here associated 'circulation' with Chronos, rather than with the temporality that belongs to the creative capacity of immanence. Circulation, as I approach it, is not a good. It is rather a way of maintaining the present, and specifically of doing so by way of the metaphorics of fluidity. Immanence, whatever it is, ought to be understood not as the affirmation of but rather as the break with circulation.
47. Ibid.
48. Ibid., p. 163.
49. Ibid., p. 164.
50. Ibid.
51. Ibid., p. 165.
52. Ibid.
53. Ibid.
54. Ibid.
55. Ibid.
56. Deleuze, *Difference and Repetition*, p. 85.
57. Ibid., p. 86.
58. Ibid.
59. Ibid.
60. Deleuze, *Cinema 2*, p. 82.
61. Ibid., p. 83.
62. Ibid., p. 81.
63. Ibid.
64. Ibid., p. 85.
65. Ibid., p. 86.
66. Ibid.
67. Ibid.
68. Ibid., p. 88.
69. Deleuze, *Difference and Repetition*, p. 71.
70. Ibid., p. 74.
71. Ibid., p. 81.
72. Ibid.
73. Ibid.
74. Ibid., p. 82.

75. Ibid., p. 81.
76. Ibid., p. 90.
77. Ibid.
78. Ibid., p. 91.
79. Ibid., p. 90.

3

Stuck in the Middle:
Milbank, Hart, the Time of Chronos

There are many variants of theology, especially when one defines it (as I do) literally and broadly as the naming of God. Yet the interrogation of the naming of God that I am now commencing addresses the specific theological discourse of Christianity. Why do I make this selection, which could seem to perpetuate the hegemony of Christianity? Are there not other ways into theology apart from Christian discourse? There are – but to focus on Christian theology, rather than on some other form of theology, is not necessarily to participate in the hegemony of Christian discourse. The fact that I am focusing on Christian theology is not because I wish somehow to legitimate it at the expense of alternative theologies, or of alternatives to theology. The reason I focus on Christian theology has to do with the historical force that Christianity exerts on our present moment. As I discussed at greater length by way of introduction, it is precisely because of the hegemony of Christianity in relation to the act of naming God that I am focusing on Christian theology. If we wish to understand the inherited condition that imposes itself on our imagination of new possibilities of existence, then we must understand the specific contours of the inherited condition. In this sense, my attention to Christian theology is driven by a concern not to further, but rather to directly encounter, understand, and contest, its hegemonic position regarding the naming of God.

It is in virtue of the same line of reasoning that I have chosen to address, within Christian theological discourse, the work of Milbank and Hart. They are theological thinkers whose work is attuned to contemporary philosophical debates; they are, at the same time, explicitly committed to a version of theology that is in accord with Christian orthodoxy. In other words, they are exemplary because even as they attempt to articulate the mode of theology that has been most dominant, they do so by responding to the very philosophical problematics and figures that we have already mentioned. Milbank and Hart thus stand at the conjuncture between a contemporary account of differential immanence and a more classical account of theology.

They have a distaste for immanence, but because they are explicit about their opposition, and because they are forthright about the theological discourse they advance against immanence, they are of immense diagnostic value. Indeed, what is fascinating about their thought is the way it is simultaneously concerned with the aims that immanence seeks – to conceive difference, as well as possibilities of existence exceeding the given – and radically opposed to immanence. Their antagonism, in other words, is symptomatic of the political and ethical stakes of the conceptual distinction between immanence and transcendence. They are of interest because they make manifest certain habits of imagination that might otherwise remain latent in more explicitly secularising discourse, where the question of theology is either quarantined or disregarded.[1] While there are reasons to support secular discourse's opposition to the sort of theological trajectory pursued by Milbank and Hart, we cannot overlook the fact that such secular opposition is not expressed at an essential level. This also means that we cannot overlook the possibility that the secular – because it quarantines theology more than it opposes the essence of theology – still inherits many of the habits of imagination produced by theology.

The theology that Milbank and Hart advance is the analogy of being. According to this approach, being is said ultimately and fully of God, but it is also – analogically – said of individuals; individuals do not exist in the same sense as God (this would be univocity), but neither is their existence utterly separated from the existence of God (this would be equivocity). The relation between God and individuals is one of both distance and presence, distinction and union. The God named by analogy is transcendent, but it is a transcendence that is not otherworldly in any simple sense. The transcendence of Milbank and Hart is of a kind that speaks to, from, and within the world – hence it is not just distant but also near. This analogical approach was most notably expressed by Thomas Aquinas, but what makes Milbank and Hart relevant is that they advance a kind of 'updated' version of analogy – one that takes into account the philosophical innovations that shape contemporary philosophical discourse.

Milbank and Hart thus inhabit a position that seeks to defend and advance theological analogy, but in such a way that theological analogy responds – even amidst its antagonism – to the aims articulated by certain philosophical concepts. Their implied strategy, then, is to show that philosophy, if it is to truly fulfil its own stated aims, must turn to the analogy of being. This means that, for them, the analogy of being is both a theological critique of philosophy and a theological fulfilment of what philosophy already seeks. In fact, analogy is especially relevant to the argument of this book because it seeks to imagine, and makes the claim that it can best imagine, the possibility of transformation.[2] It is thus in the work of Milbank and Hart that we find the most thoroughgoing case for transcendence as that which is necessary for any attempt to imagine new possibilities of existence. If, as we have seen in the previous chapter, differential immanence ends up with the ethico-political task of creating the new, then the challenge of analogy is that this ethico-political task cannot be fulfilled unless we invoke the transcendent.

'The Dog is in the Garden': God's Being and the Meaning of 'Is'

We began our philosophical account of immanence with Heidegger, and our account of the immanence-theology relation likewise returns to him. Theology has a complicated relation with this thinker of immanence. There are theological thinkers who have found various reasons for appreciating his work: he critiques overly abstract thinking; he poses the question of being itself, which raises the question of God; he develops themes and concepts that appear quite similar to themes and concepts developed, throughout history, by theologically orientated philosophers. At the same time, there is no escaping the fundamental antagonism that emerges between theology and Heidegger's immanence.[3] Nor is there any escaping the fact that Heidegger's thought is ultimately indigestible for theology. Though it can serve as a momentary ally of theology, and though it can make certain theological motifs seem relevant, it cannot genuinely collaborate with theology.

This fundamental antagonism is especially evident when Heidegger includes 'God is' as one among a set of 'ises': 'We say, "God is." "The earth is." "The lecture is in the auditorium." ... "The dog is in the garden."'[4] The point of Heidegger's statement is to insist that the being of God has no special character, such that the 'is' attributed to God is no different from the 'is' attributed to a blade of grass or a speck of dust. Any affirmation of a particular entity requires a prior ontological horizon, the being of beings; one can think the 'is' of a particular entity only if being – considered independently of the existence *of* the particular entity – is already there. This is the upshot of Heidegger's ontological difference, which insists on thinking being as such, and on doing so by thinking the *difference* between being and beings. What matters for Heidegger, then, is not a specific being but the question of being as such, which concerns the difference between being and beings. Statements regarding specific beings are concomitantly subordinated to statements regarding ontological difference. While this may be a rather uncontroversial move with regard to statements such as 'The dog is in the garden', it is more controversial with regard to the statement 'God is.' After all, for theology, God is no being among beings – God is the act of all beings, the source of being, and therefore not on the same plane as all other beings. Accordingly, when Heidegger includes God as one among a multitude of entities, all of which are set against the common, prior horizon of being, he refuses the basic starting point of theology.

For Milbank, even a qualified appreciation of Heidegger's thought is too much. If being is truly analogical, then it simply cannot be adequately thought, not even in a partial manner, apart from analogy. Against Heidegger, Milbank argues in favour of the equation of the 'is' of God and the 'is' of being.[5] What matters is not the being that is at stake when we say, 'God is', but rather the way in which God and being are convertible. God is being, and being is God – if this is the case, as it is for Milbank, then how could the question of being ever emerge except as a question of God? To be sure, when Milbank identifies God and being he is not seeking to place God in a limited category, he is instead expanding being beyond its limits. According to this manner of thinking, God expands being beyond its supposed immanent limits, but in doing so God simply allows being to fulfil itself.

The distinction and union of being (the natural) and God (the supernatural) forms an analogical interval. The analogical interval is stretched between the contours of the natural and the gift of the supernatural, but in being stretched it holds together what stretches it, such that the natural and supernatural are able to intertwine. Natural and supernatural are distinct terms, but they cannot be thought separately. Being, because it is always already an analogy between the natural and the supernatural, because it is given by and drawn to divine transcendence, is always already grace, or gift, when it is mundanely encountered. This means the question of how to exceed the given is already answered within the given, for the given is given *by* the transcendent. The given bears the beyond within itself, and this beyond holds forth possibilities exceeding what is given.

Hart concurs with Milbank's thesis that Heidegger's immanent account of being closes in on itself, and that the desire to think difference can be fulfilled only by turning to theological analogy. He states, for instance, that once

> it is disentangled from Heidegger's *Seinsgeschichte*, Christian philosophy proves to possess resources for understanding and overcoming the 'nihilistic terminus' of modernity . . . and it can, moreover, provide an account of the ontological difference far more cogent than any Heidegger ever enunciated.[6]

More precisely, he claims that while ontological difference justly distinguishes being from beings, it is undermined by the fact that the so-distinguished being cannot finally ground these beings. The conceptualisation of the being of beings never finds its proper independence, it remains defined solely in terms of its opposition to beings – as, for example, non-being, or nothing.

As much as Heidegger may see the sameness of thought and being, their immanent relationality, as an advance, for Hart this amounts to a denial of the properly transcendent aims of thought. Sameness cuts us off from the possibilities of the infinite. According to Hart, Heidegger's supposed advance is 'merely a stepping away from the infinite into the finite . . . a descent into a passive self-sealing immanentism'.[7] This is to say, furthermore, that Heideggerean thought blocks thought's desire for the transcendent. While the question of being ought to call forth the transcendent, Heidegger, according to Hart, denies 'any stirring of reason's necessarily ecstatic movement toward a horizon continuous with and yet transcending the scope of experience'.[8] Heidegger binds himself to a Sisyphean immanence, for the horizon opened up by awareness that there is an excess to given beings is prevented from opening fully.

Hart, however, overlooks the presence of such excess in Heidegger. There is, for Heidegger, no transcendent form of excess, but there is excess as a result of difference. Difference is the excess of the given because it is what has remained unthought. It is therefore not enough for Hart just to say that Heidegger blocks thought's striving for excess. The question begged by Hart's argument is: Why does reason's longing for excess require analogical transcendence rather than Heidegger's immanent ontological difference? Indeed, we might imagine Heidegger, for his own part, responding to Hart's challenge by observing that it is precisely reliance on the transcendent as a means of resolving ontological difference that prevents thought from genuinely encountering difference. Instead of encountering what is unthought, we invoke something that simply transcends the very matter – difference – that must be thought.

But what, Hart asks, *is* difference? Even if we admit that difference is unthought, must not difference still have some kind of ground? To think the difference of being, must we not, at some point, think that which makes difference possible? Difference, then, may name possibilities that we have not yet thought, but these possibilities themselves must be grounded in something that transcends difference. Instead of addressing this challenge, Hart notes, Heidegger resorts to the language of nothingness. This indicates that being, when it is thought in terms of difference, and without transcendence, leads us into an all-pervasive nihilation that is at odds with the very desire for different possibilities of *existence*. In fact, for Hart, Heidegger's terminology amounts to a stark admission of anti-analogical thought. It names quite explicitly what there is, apart from analogical participation of individuals in the divine, ontological gift: nothing. There is nothing there to answer the question of what makes possibility possible. According to Hart, 'Heidegger has merely elevated possibility over actuality. What he certainly has not done is address the essential mystery: How is it that either possibility or actuality *is*? Whence comes the "is" in "it is possible"?'[9] It is not, in the end, coherent to make possibility anterior to actuality, 'for possibility – however one conceives of it – must first *be*'.[10]

We now have an initial sense of the incommensurability between analogy and immanence. From the vantage of analogy, immanence appears as vacuous flailing, as a collapse of the eminent, or the transcendent, into the finite prison of the given; from the vantage of immanence, analogy appears to sever us from that which must be thought. Analogy locates excess in a beyond that is within the given and sees immanence as a foreclosure and annihilation of possibilities; immanence locates excess in unthought difference and sees transcendence as an evasion of that which generates possibilities. We can anticipate, furthermore, how the question of time will be central to this conflict. In analogy, time is understood as a process of participation in the transcendent source of being. Milbank, for instance, recommends that the difference between being and beings be cast in terms of a temporal process of analogising. According to Milbank, if one is to avoid a nihilistic exhaustion of difference, then 'one has to posit a plenitudinous supra-temporal infinite which has "already realized" in an eminent fashion every desirable effect'.[11] For immanence, on the other hand, a 'desirable effect' is not already established by the transcendent, awaiting our temporal participation. On the contrary, a 'desirable effect' must be temporally created, through an encounter with unthought difference.

Violent Origins

We must now progress beyond this initial account of the rivalry between analogy and immanence. Such a task is aided by shifting immanence from a Heideggerean to a Deleuzian form, for while Heidegger is quite relevant insofar as he functions as a point of entry, any consideration of the rivalry will be lacking if we do not proceed to Deleuze's articulation of differential immanence. Milbank provides a useful way of adjudicating this conflict when he makes a taxonomic bifurcation between 'ontologies of peace' and 'ontologies of violence'.[12] Ontologies of violence – and Milbank places Deleuze's ontology under this heading – are such because they presuppose an 'original violence'.[13] They provide a contemporary version of the pagan (pre-Christian) cosmos, where chaos is perpetually and necessarily at war with meaning. One can affirm the excessive chaos, or one can affirm meaning, but one can never affirm both. Any meaning will be inadequate and tragic, for it must be set against a chaotic backdrop (much like Hart saw Heidegger's being as set against a backdrop of nothingness). Chaos, in fact, will undermine not just meaning, but also the purposive production of collective goods, such as peace. As Milbank, drawing on Giambattista Vico, puts it, 'for the pagans, "meaning," or the sign-relation, is always construed as "inhibition of chaos". *Logos* is a counter-violence that "stays" an always more primordial violence.'[14] Thus, when ontologies of violence name being as originally chaotic, they are forced into a consequent war between meaning, or collective goods, and being. It is this sort of dialectic that prevents them from providing the conditions for genuine peace.

Milbank contends that Christian theology does provide such conditions. It 'recognizes no original violence', and this is because it 'construes the infinite not as chaos, but as a harmonic peace'.[15] While ontologies of violence set up a dialectic between the infinite and the finite, or between chaos and meaning, theology – understood as analogy – enables a finite participation in the infinite. The finite/infinite limit does not involve a dialectic between infinite violence and finite counter-violence, for every finite limitation can exceed itself in virtue of its participation in the infinite, and this infinite is harmonious. Accordingly, Milbank prefers a definition of finite essence 'which no longer figures [it] as the definitely identifiable principle of finite limitation but marks an active, open – and not predetermined – possibility sometimes transcending given actuality'.[16] Violence, then, is not necessary but rather a contingent, 'secondary willed intrusion upon' the divinely gifted harmony.[17]

This possibility of violence's non-necessity is linked to the question of difference, for in its contemporary variation the ('pagan') ontology of violence tends to present the chaotic infinite as the dynamical power and play of difference. While there is still, in Milbank's eyes, a dialectic at work, it is no longer one that settles for a tragic balance between meaning and chaos (as was the case for the pagan imagination). Now the chaotic side, though still dialectically opposed to meaning or order, is valorised; the significant contemporary intervention is to liberate difference from the inadequate totality of stable meaning. The 'untruth' of this last is presented by contemporary thinkers with a certain fervour, and lots are cast with the 'truth' of difference's excess to totality. Milbank echoes Hart when he claims that this can amount to nothing other than 'nihilistic difference', a difference that annihilates the very possibilities it promotes.[18] The truth of difference immediately becomes the truth of original violence. But, Milbank asks, is it not possible to assent to the reality of difference without placing it in an interminable dialectic with order and meaning? Analogy's distinctive contribution here is the nomination of an infinite that is differential (and therefore not totalising) as well as capable of order and meaning (because it is a *harmonious* infinite). Peace, for analogy, is 'beyond the circumscribing power of any totalizing reason', it 'no longer depends upon the reduction to the self-identical', which excludes difference. On the contrary, analogical peace is 'the *sociality* of harmonious difference', meaning that it is intrinsically relational and open.[19]

While Milbank's description of Deleuze's ontology as violent depends on an extremely tendentious reading (one I will contest further on), his taxonomy is beneficial because it makes explicit two central elements of debate. First, he notes that the discourse of difference requires a 'metadiscourse' – that is, a discourse that argues for a particular discourse of difference – and that the specific character of this metadiscourse is, for the most part, undecidable.[20] The ontology of violence is, in the end, nothing more than one 'particular encoding of reality', and the ontology of peace is another, 'the coding of transcendental difference as peace'.[21] It is a matter of one encoding against another, one 'unfounded' myth against another.[22] Precisely for this reason, rival accounts of difference cannot be measured according to the degree to which they objectively correspond to a datum of difference – they are undecidable.

The second element Milbank makes explicit is the basic link between the ontological and the political. Such a link is perhaps obvious, but by foregrounding it – in the ontological bifurcation between 'violence' and 'peace' – he makes it a point of entry into evaluation of rival metadiscourses. The imagination of political possibilities emerges through metadiscourse. This is because a metadiscourse, when it presents an argument for a specific discourse, will do so by imagining the possibilities of existence enabled by that specific discourse. In other words, the appeal of a specific discourse is articulated as a metadiscourse, and this articulation will involve showing the political superiority of the specific discourse, or the way that the specific discourse is better able than others to fulfil a general political need. Therefore a key criterion for evaluating rival metadiscourses – in our case, between the alternative ways in which difference is conceived by ontologies of peace and ontologies of violence – will be the degree to which these metadiscourses are able to imagine new possibilities of existence.

Milbank, throughout his work, leans heavily on this ontological-political link as a criterion of metadiscursive evaluation. For instance, he addresses the Marxist project by claiming that it lacks an ontology adequate to its political aims, and that only analogy can supply this ontology. One cannot

> simply dispense with ontology in order to concentrate upon practice: Marxism, and indeed every socialism, requires an account of human nature and of the role of human beings within the cosmos; otherwise it is not clear why there is something now lacking that needs to be emancipated, nor why one should suppose that we live in a reality within which such emancipation is possible.[23]

The thrust of this point – and what links it to his taxonomic bifurcation between ontologies of peace and violence – is that political desire and enactment will be stifled as long as they are not connected to the conception of a 'hospitable cosmos'. Liberatory hope 'is possible only if the cosmos is secretly such as to be hospitable to human harmony and to humanity living in harmony with the cosmos'.[24] In other words, political liberation, when it does not understand itself in terms of analogy, grants itself a tragic fate in advance because its ontology is violent. The possibilities of existence that it imagines cannot be sustainably enacted; the possibilities that would break with the given cannot be enacted within the realm of the given, they can only be posed as a sublimely tragic rejection. Such enactment will take place only insofar as an analogical paradigm is presumed, for analogy makes the transcendent intertwine with the given; the imagined possibilities transcendently break with the given but, because the transcendent and the given are analogically related, these imagined possibilities can be hospitably received anew by the given.

The Interstice and the Accord

But is this actually the case with Deleuze's immanence? Is it true that, for Deleuze, the liberation of excess, as difference, cannot sustain itself in this world? Here I must foreground the claim, implicit in Deleuze's immanence, that the interstice (difference in itself, or the virtual field of differences) is prior to the accord (the given actualisation of virtual difference). The accord, if we imagine it as a resolved or actualised relation between elements, is conditioned by the interstice, which in this case amounts to the 'between' of these elements (the problematic difference that the accord resolves). Although the interstice is the condition of the accord, they are, as noted in the previous chapter, immanent to one another; the interstice is actualised as the accord, which is able to loop back and act upon the (virtual) interstice. This means the accord cannot be discarded (then we would, in fact, have the dialectical scheme presented by Milbank's accusation, namely the destruction of meaning and order in the name of difference). It means, furthermore, that an accord cannot be thought apart from its interstice. The power of any accord, which consists of the relations between its elements, is greater or lesser in virtue of the intensive difference (of the elements) that it enables to consist. The accord's power, in other words, stems from its immanence with the problematic, differential character of the interstice; the more an accord enters into this interstice, the more powerful it will become. It is therefore a matter not of destroying accords in favour of difference, but rather of re-expressing accords, such that they are adequate to the intensity of difference in itself, and such that they consequently increase their power.

For immanence, then, the power of an accord is measured in an entirely different manner than it is in analogy. Power is found not in the transcendent but in difference. Differential excess to an accord indicates the inadequacy of an accord; it indicates an unconditioned power that exceeds – but that may also be re-expressed by – an accord, or a constellation of accords (an accord of accords). From Milbank's analogical perspective, this predicament amounts to war: given accords provide the object of difference's violence. But what Milbank fails to grasp is that the differential pressure of the interstice, which is exerted on the given accord, is immanent with the accord. This is to say that difference is not imposed upon a given accord, it is rather that in which the given accord is intrinsically involved, or implicated. For Deleuze, an accord's interstitial difference is its immanent power of re-expression. Consequently, while differential excess marks an accord's inadequacy, it likewise marks a return to the interstice, and thus to the production of other possible accords; the resolved accord loops back to the problem it resolved in order to create new solutions. Difference, for Deleuze, is not the inverse of accords – as Milbank presumes – but rather the immanent condition of their production.

There is a genuine parting of ways here, for in analogy accords are measured by their resemblance to the transcendent accord of accords, rather than by their interstitial, unresolved difference. With analogy, the excess of a particular accord, what is incommensurable to or in it, is conceived in terms of a hyper-accord. In this sense, analogical discourse must conclude in 'an analogy of analogies'.[25] The excess of any horizontal analogical interval finds its condition in a vertical analogical interval. This is but another way of phrasing Milbank's insistence on a supra-temporal infinite: the excess of any temporal and finite analogical interval is already realised within, and issues forth from, a transcendent, supra-temporal infinite in which finite intervals temporally participate. Because the vertical interval is analogically related to every horizontal interval, each horizontal interval can exceed its limits while simultaneously remaining within the same source. Vertical analogy means that there is an excess to any given horizontal accord, and that a new horizontal accord may be generated as a result of the vertical. Yet because every horizontal accord – every one that is exceeded and every one that is subsequently produced – maintains a vertical analogy with the transcendent, the movement from the exceeded horizontal accord to the subsequent horizontal accord is not violent. The subsequent horizontal accord breaks with the previous one, but the new possibilities it brings about were already there in the previous horizontal accord's vertical analogy with God.

It is due to this fact that, for analogy, the distinction between the vertical and the horizontal is never absolute. There is, of course, a distinct verticality, since the supra-temporal infinite really is eminent to finite accords, but at the same time these finite accords cannot be discretely separated from the infinite. This is one of the key aspects of Milbank's 'suspended middle', wherein the finite/infinite difference – the difference between, on one hand, given, finite horizontal accords, and, on the other, the vertical, infinite accord that exists between God and every finite accord – can be addressed only by way of its middle. He says we must move 'from cosmic immanence to supernatural transcendence', from the given to the divine, but we do not do this according to an inverse proportionality between cosmos and transcendence.[26] The aim of this movement is not to negate the given in favour of the transcendent, it is to see the horizontal accords of the former as analogically related, via a vertical accord, to the latter. What is required is an account of the supernatural *in* the natural, an affirmation of the 'orientation of the *cosmos as such* to the supernatural'.[27] Once again, we see the claim that politics, as the imagination of new possibilities of existence, and philosophy, as conceptualisation of the world, can only accomplish their aims by turning to analogy. As Milbank puts it, 'speculation beyond finite bounds is necessarily constitutive of our apprehension even of the finite'.[28]

Analogy, because it brings us to the 'middle' of the finite and the infinite, enables us to affirm that the natural, in order to be thought, must be related to the supernatural, and that this relation must be articulated without leaving behind the natural, indeed that this relation allows us to truly grasp the natural. The middle is 'suspended' between finite and infinite, but not in a privative manner. It must be supplementally articulated: the excess of any horizontal analogy requires supplementation by the vertical, but this vertical analogy, in order to be adequately participated, requires a horizontal supplement. The same basic paradigm is at work in Hart's more pulchritudinous account of analogy. The divine beauty of the infinite, he claims, is expressed to some degree by every (horizontal) analogical interval, while also being the interval of intervals. Beauty 'inhabits' and 'belongs to' every interval of distance.[29] Furthermore, it 'possesses' distance, and this is because 'it gives distance'.[30] In other words, every horizontal accord, as well as every distance between horizontal accords, inhabits a distance that is always already included in, or possessed by, the transcendent God's beauty: 'Beauty crosses every boundary, traverses every series, and so manifests the God who transcends every decision.'[31]

For both Hart and Milbank, then, there is no outside to analogy – in fact, any notion of an outside-the-finite is already included in the finite's analogy with the infinite. The infinite possesses the outside. In Hart's case, this is articulated in terms of a *correspondence* between finite creation's difference and God's infinite difference – one that links the two while maintaining the eminence of the latter to the former. Just as God perichoretically differs (the difference between the three persons of the Christian trinity), so creation differs in a perpetually serial manner (the difference between horizontal accords as they constantly exceed and displace one another). This seriality of finite creation is not separate from God's infinite difference, rather it is the result of an excessive overflowing of difference out of God. Creation's difference, Hart says, should be seen as an 'infinity of difference from God, its free, departing, serial excess of otherness'.[32] The finite expression of this seriality is thus a departure from God that is never separate from God, for it analogically participates in God's infinite difference. God 'is not the high who stands over against this low, but is the infinite act of distance that gives high and low a place'.[33] In this sense, Hart's account of distance functions in a manner similar to Milbank's account of the middle.

While analogy permits a sharing of being between the finite and the infinite, and thus makes horizontal and vertical inseparable, it nonetheless maintains a real, inextinguishable distinction between the two. Hart states this quite perspicuously: 'The insuperable ontological difference between creation and God – between the dynamism of finitude and an infinite that is eternally dynamic – is simultaneously . . . a partaking by the finite of that which it does not own, but within which it moves.'[34] Yet there is no implication of the finite in the infinite: 'for while the finite belongs to the infinite, the converse cannot be so, except through an *epektasis* toward more of the good'.[35] The line between Hart's formulation and Deleuze's articulation of the double immanence of substance and modes, of cause and effect, is thus impermeable. Milbank's account of the relation between infinite and finite also refuses Deleuze's double immanence. Creation, Milbank remarks, is not a once-for-all event, but rather 'the serial occurrence of differential reality in time' – yet this seriality must be 'related to God by a plus sign'.[36] The 'plus sign' here indicates that serial difference participates in – or adds itself into – a transcendent source, that is, God. When we recall Milbank's assertion that God names a supra-temporal infinite in which every desirable effect is already realised, it becomes apparent that serial difference amounts to the temporal effectuation of eminently or transcendently *pre-established* possibilities. All possibilities, then, are already existent, it is just that their existence is posed at a level that transcends the existence that is already given. This means that even as new possibilities emerge temporally, these new possibilities are not so much created *within* time as they are effectuated – from the transcendent to the given – *through* time.

What analogy provides, then, is an account of difference that is never finally vulnerable to the passage of time. No matter what 'happens' in time, no matter what time brings, it will be given by the transcendent, it will be analogically related to God. This means, furthermore, that no matter how bad a given expression of being may appear, the possibility for a break with this given is guaranteed – in fact, it is, analogically, already *there*, already present in what is given. It is not just that we can create new possibilities of existence (as is the case for immanence), it is that new possibilities of existence are waiting to be effectuated. In fact, it seems that in Milbank and Hart's metadiscourse, in their argument for the superiority of their discourse on difference, what is paramount is this sort of guarantee. Analogical relation to the transcendent is necessary, with regard to the question of difference, because it guarantees the 'peaceful' outcome of difference. When Hart, for example, casts finite, serial expression as part of an infinite, ontological music, he notes that the latter 'eminently *contains* all transitions and intervals together', such that no serial digression can reach a point of abandon.[37] Since every divergence or digression, every dissonant moment – in short, every difference – shares in the eminent, harmony cannot be lost. Everything shares in God, and thus possibility is guaranteed.

For Deleuze, on the other hand, the only things shared, according to Hart, are 'ruptures between differences'.[38] The intent of Hart's statement, of course, is to drive a wedge between sharing in difference and sharing in an eminent accord of accords. But, to say it once again, accords and interstitial difference are not mutually exclusive in Deleuze, for to share in the interstice is to share in the unconditioned power of immanence, which conditions the production of new accords. From the perspective of immanence, the key distinction is not between peaceful and violent ontologies, nor is it between harmonious and dissonant accords; it is between accords that seek to creatively re-express the interstice and those that do not.

Of course, what Deleuze cannot provide is a *guarantee* that future accords will be 'better' or 'more peaceful' than present accords – and this ultimately seems to be what makes his thought, according to Hart and Milbank, 'nihilistic' or 'violent'. But why must the ultimate criterion, when evaluating rival metadiscourses, involve the provision of a guarantee? What is at stake here is a question about the very nature of the ethical: Is ethics a matter of incarnating transcendent possibilities? Or is ethics, on the contrary, a matter of experimentally producing non-pre-existent possibilities that endeavour to liberate, but that also – because this endeavour departs from what is already established – risk destruction?

Ethics of the Crack

In order to further develop this question of ethics, we will now look at how, for Deleuze, the interstice is connected to an ethics of the crack. The interstice is the crack running through immanence. In the double immanence of substance and modes, or of what is expressed and its expression, the crack of difference is the line that runs through the middle of these reciprocal inclusions. For immanence, then, the middle is not suspended, it is not that of a positive supplementation between the natural and the supernatural, it is instead difference. It is, in other words, the crack, which allows the given to be broken down and presents the chance for something else. As such, the crack not only belongs to expression, it also marks the necessity of re-expression. The crack of an individual's differential expression provides the path – the line of flight – into a re-expression of substance, or a substantive modification. Each expression itself is conditioned by the interstice, and this interstice also provides the condition for another expression. Therefore an evaluation of the possibilities of immanent expression is never final – we do not yet know what re-expression can do.

When we are faced with the limits of the given and the concomitant political failures of a people, the task is to find a point prior to this blockage, and thus to give birth to the struggle for new possibilities of existence, for the creation of a new, cracked, and bastardised people. Yet for Deleuze, unlike for analogy, to be prior to the given possibilities is not to possess transcendent possibilities; it is nothing more and nothing less than to turn the unconditioned into a chance, to bring the contingently given into immanence with the unlimited. The task is not to trade the bad for the good but to renew thought, struggle, and their contingent but unconditioned possibilities. The only 'end' of philosophy is its constant and repeated auto-constitution, the 'reason' of thought is 'its own birth'.[39] Similarly, the aim of a people, in the wake of its failure, is not to fulfil the telos or destiny it has lost, it is on the contrary to produce a new path for itself, a bastardised rather than pure path. The aim, in other words, is to cease being a people in order to follow a path of bastardisation. This path is found in the crack, the undecidability of which is indicated by the fact that it breaks down given consistencies while opening up the unconditioned.

The dangers of proceeding through the crack should not be ignored – in this sense, analogy is not wrong to claim that the risk of violence remains. While the crack breaks open a power exceeding the given, there is no guarantee that the 'outcome' that emerges from following it will be measured as beneficial. Furthermore, passing into the crack does mean foreswearing certain consistencies that, in spite of their limits, do provide stability. Yet if the crack is not without risk, if it is never fully defended against the black hole, it is nonetheless preferable to the given – secure but limited – possibilities of health. The reason for this is that the crack 'give[s] us the chance to go farther than we would have believed possible'.[40] When existence becomes unimaginable apart from its limits, the securities of good health can themselves become chronic; the loss of 'good health' becomes the risk worth running in order to imagine existence apart from these limits. In such a predicament, the insecurities of sickness, suffering, and exposure to death need not be viewed as *lacking* health. They can, on the contrary, name what is involved in a path that seeks something beyond the limits of given existence. It is in this sense that an immanent ethics does not try to overcome, but rather begins from, the fact of suffering.

The crack introduces into limited thought (and its corresponding notion of health) the unconditioned power of immanence. The crack 'runs through and alienates thought in order to be also the possibility of thought', it is 'obstacle to thought, but also [its] abode and power'.[41] The political concomitant is that a people, given the obstacle of its suffering, must endeavour not to exchange the suffering it faces for the given health that is this suffering's inverse, the health of the people, but instead to refuse the entire scope of given possibilities and to invent its own new ones. It is from a vertiginous complication of suffering and power that both thought and a people assert: 'better death than the health which we are given'.[42] Of course, it is not as if one immediately trades health for death – for even if death becomes the risk, what is immediately opposed to the health of the limit is not death but the pure and empty form of time. Just as time introduces the crack into Chronos, or into chronic health, so the endeavour to live from the crack must give this time to itself, as much time as possible, an extensive inhabitation of the Aion, in order to invent a different, more powerful health, a health that would be coextensive with life beyond limit. Indeed, 'we must take risks and endure the longest possible time, we must not lose sight of grand health'.[43]

The fact that the crack has nothing to do with any transcendent unity is affirmed most forthrightly by Deleuze in his discussion of cinema. There he insists, against any attempt to produce a Whole through an association of elements (in this case, images), on the fundamentally opposed practice of thinking the fissure conditioning, and unthought by, any association. This is but another way of affirming that the interstice (the problematic fissure between elements) is prior to the accord (the resolved association of elements). Cinema, for instance, does connect with the 'innermost reality of the brain, but this innermost reality is not the Whole, but on the contrary a fissure, a crack . . . un-linking' images.[44] Instead of association or accord, then, thought connects itself to 'interstice' and 'differentiation'.[45]

There can be no gathering of the many into the One, no association of elements into an accord, or into an accord of accords, since the means of harmonising the many – that is, association – has been put aside; neither can there be a simple affirmation of the many against the One, for the elements forming any set of the 'many' are the conditioned of which the interstice is the condition. 'The fissure has become primary.'[46] Against both One (accord) and many (elements simply lacking accord), what is enjoined is a becoming-different of thought through cracking. 'There are no longer any perfect and "resolved" harmonies, but only dissonant tunings or irrational cuts . . . only "unlinked" tones forming the series.'[47]

Dissonance is thus freed from its two prevalent functions, where it is either the ruin of harmony (what analogy calls violence) or, through its eventual resolution, the elaboration and amplification of harmony (what analogy sees as participation in the transcendent). In each of these cases, dissonance is viewed through the lens of harmony, or accord. An ethics of the crack, however, views dissonance on its own terms. Just as the virtual's differential intensity was thought without correlation to the actual, so dissonance must be thought without correlation to harmony. Dissonance – or ethically speaking, the experience of suffering – becomes anterior rather than posterior to the association of which harmony is said. Concomitantly, any harmony worth seeking must be conditioned by the crack that dissonance presents. Harmony – ontological as well as political – ceases to be the starting point or the telos and instead becomes a matter of contingent temporalisation and construction. What matters is not whether accords are bound to be good or bad, but how we might find, in the dissonance of the interstice, the capacity to construct new accords, to enter into new becomings.

An ethics of the crack has to do with becomings; we become only insofar as we are able to crack the given. Becoming, then, should not be confused with the increase of communication, for communication remains caught up in the logic of association. Communication may expand the reach of an accord, it may increase the number of accords, but it does not encounter the interstice by which genuinely different accords would be produced. Communication, Deleuze says, has 'nothing to do' with becomings, which is to say that it has nothing to do 'with minorities speaking out'.[48] But what is this connection between becomings and minorities? It is that both have to do with the interstice, or the problematic. The minoritarian begins from the problem of being a minority in relation to the given; to differ from the majority – the given norm of existence – is to encounter existence as a problem. It follows that the minority can exist only through becoming, only through creating possibilities of existence that depart from and exceed the given. The minoritarian thus exists through an ethics of the crack.

The contrary of the minoritarian, that which turns away from the crack instead of pursuing it, that which refuses the problem in the name of already-given solutions, is called majoritarian. It is worth noting that no individual is essentially or fully majoritarian, for every individual is conditioned by difference. Deleuze notes that 'the majoritarian is nobody. Everybody's caught, one way or another, in a minor-becoming that would lead them into unknown paths if they opted to follow it through.'[49] The fact that the majoritarian is nobody is an ontological fact: immanence itself is cracked, and so there is no individual that escapes the crack. Nonetheless, a distinction between the majoritarian and the minoritarian can be made in virtue of time, or more specifically, in virtue of the ethics an individual follows in response to this ontological cracking. A majoritarian individual is one that does not follow a minor-becoming: the majoritarian individual, rather than pursuing the crack, and the struggle involved in the crack, resorts to pre-existing accords; he attempts to organise re-expression so that it harmonises with the 'good' accords, the dominant accords that are given.

Immanence thus turns on ethics, on the decision to either become-minor or become-major, to affirm the crack that runs through all individuals or to refuse it in the name of the given accords. Suffering is a fact, it is what there is, or what is given. Yet suffering, and all the violence that it undergoes and can engender, need not be the last word on what is possible. Suffering, when it is affirmed through an ethics of the crack, may open onto new possibilities. Suffering can give way to becoming.

The 'Suspended Middle'

This discussion of an ethics of the crack sheds light on the recurrent criticism, advanced by Hart and Milbank, that immanence, because it thinks difference in itself and cannot analogise difference, inscribes violence within being. According to Milbank, immanence 'tends to eternalize and positivize evil and to make agon an ultimate and not contingent reality'.[50] Because it offers 'a cosmos without ultimate meaning or order, the consequently manifest violence of the arbitrary will itself be sacralized'.[51] But does not this criticism implicitly conflate the violence of a given expression with the differential (or interstitial) character of being? Deleuze would not claim that the violence involved in one ontologically expressive moment (the actual) conditions the full range of ontological possibilities (the virtual). On the contrary, it is difference that conditions expressive moments, whether they are more or less violent, more or less peaceful. So Milbank's demand that we 'should not *ontologize*' violence 'but instead insist on its contingency', does not seem to distance him from Deleuze as much as he presumes.[52]

For Hart, immanence's tendency 'to deduce from the features of the existence of the world the principles of the world' means that 'it must see all the characteristic conditions of the world as manifestations of its ground'.[53] Such a statement presumes that only the transcendent can provide a ground that does not correlate with the limiting principles of the world. But again, Hart's conception of immanence directly reverses the order of determination articulated by Deleuze. In Hart's interpretation, a determinate ontological expression manifests the very nature of being, whereas for Deleuze, an actualised expression is conditioned *by*, and not the condition *of*, the difference intrinsic to being. Determinate states of the world are 'manifestations of [the world's] ground' only if the determinate states exhaust the ground – and Deleuze's virtual, preindividual field of difference is certainly not exhausted by actualisations. Consequently, Hart's assertion that immanence 'must embrace, not merely as elements but as principles of being, all the tragic and negative aspects of existence', is off-target.[54] These aspects can be described just as contingently in Deleuze as they can be in analogy. In neither case is it necessary to turn these 'aspects' into 'principles of being': just as Hart renders them contingent before the divine act, so Deleuze renders them contingent before the unconditioned, differential power of re-expression.

There is, because of re-expression, a reality of the future. The future belongs to the power of re-expression and is presented in the crack. When Hart asserts that 'for beings, in their becoming, being is absolute futurity', he is not far from Deleuze.[55] While Hart's future is eminently contained, and thus guaranteed peace in a way that it is not for Deleuze, Deleuze's future is truly produced, and thus is unconditioned in a way that it is not for Hart. Yet Hart tends to overlook the role of the future in Deleuze's thought, and this is because he overlooks the role of the product in Deleuze's thought. The connection between Hart's two evasions is not arbitrary, since, for Deleuze, the future *is* produced, it belongs to the autonomy of the product. There can be no ontological whole in differential immanence, no totality, because no communication or mutual supplementation of accords can erase their interstice. So when Deleuze enjoins an affirmation of immanence, this affirmation is of a product rather than of a whole, of what is created from the crystal rather than of the crystal itself.

But this is precisely what Hart fails to grasp when he asserts that 'Deleuzian affirmation is always an affirmation of the whole as force'.[56] If Deleuze's ontology essentially amounts to a chaotic becoming, Hart argues, then all immanence can offer is a way of contemplating this chaos, of affirming the lack of peace.

> For Deleuze, such is the world, in its ceaseless transience and eternal eventuality: the will to power is the force of ontic becoming, while the eternal return describes the only possible ontology. If, though, this is the game of the world, and thought must now inhabit this interminable immanence of chaos, sealed within the necessary event, it might quite plausibly fall prey to sadness and simply withdraw into itself, impotent and disengaged; in the face of so terrifying and inescapable a power of becoming and perishing, only the highest power of the will can preserve itself intact: affirma-

tion. This henceforth, holds Deleuze, must be the supreme philosophical ethos.[57]

Hart is right to say that, for Deleuze, 'eternal return describes the only possible ontology', but wrong about what this means. If we listen to Hart, the eternal return means that whatever is given must simply be. The possibilities of existence are coextensive with whatever is given. But, as I have argued, eternal return belongs to the third synthesis, the production of the new. Such production expels its conditions – that is, the virtual and actual, which have been crystallised – as if by 'centrifugal force'. Eternal return's affirmation, then, is of the product, it is of the creation of the future, which expels the very thing (the crystallised whole) that Hart claims is affirmed.

Milbank also fails to recognise the role of creation, or of the product. According to Milbank, Deleuze's thought is 'subservient to the excluded middle'.[58] The point of this criticism seems to be that Deleuze requires an absolute separation between the dynamic of difference and the stability of order. One can praise the former, but one can only live, or sustain oneself, in the latter, and this is because the middle of these two – the analogy between difference and order – is excluded. We are forced to choose or to oscillate between difference and order. 'Deleuzian univocity . . . spells out the always somewhat futile and not finally winnable war of sheer difference (without real constitutive relation) with temporarily stable hierarchies that always emerge as the only possible expression (and yet simultaneous inhibition) of difference.'[59] Difference, then, can never be realised because of the excluded middle between itself and order. But Milbank's interpretation of Deleuze misses the mark, for the 'middle' in Deleuze is the product of the third synthesis, which involves and goes beyond both virtual difference and actual order. For Deleuze, it is precisely by weaving together, or crystallising, virtual and actual that one is able to create the new, to generate a product that draws on both. The middle is not excluded, as Milbank believes, it is in fact produced.

Milbank's middle is also produced, though in an alternative manner. He repeatedly insists that the made is not beneath the transcendent, but rather coincident with it – or, more precisely, coincident with the three classical transcendentals whose degrees of being provide analogical paths between created beings and uncreated being. Created beings participate to some degree in the true, good, and beautiful, which exist absolutely and convertibly in the being of God. When we add the *factum* to these three, we can also analogise an eminent – or, as Milbank sometimes qualifies it, a 'supereminent' – being's *creatio ex nihilo* and human making.[60] In this respect, Milbank again recommends Vico, 'who proclaimed ... that the transcendentals *verum* and *bonum* also convert with a new transcendental, the *factum*, meaning the historically and even eternally "constructed"'.[61] The made is thus properly ontological, properly divine, at least through an analogical middle.

Yet there is something of a paradox here – and this is what separates the analogical product from the Deleuzian product. The paradox is that the made must be new, for it is produced in time, and yet it must also already exist, for its production involves participation in an ontological (super)eminence that contains all of the made, all possibilities of making. Are we then, on Milbank's account, making what is already made by God? But then it would be difficult to see such making as a genuine creation. Or perhaps our temporal act of making is simultaneously God's act of making – but then how could Milbank speak of God as *supra-temporal* infinite which has "already realized" in an eminent fashion every desirable effect'?[62] The already realised and the being made cannot be simultaneous. It seems, at this point, that the 'suspended middle' is indeed suspended, but not in the sense that Milbank intends. It is suspended between two roles: it mediates the difference between finite and infinite being (the ontological middle, or the vertical analogy), but it also mediates the difference between what is given and the product that is made (the political middle, or the horizontal analogy). Why are these two roles in suspension? How, in other words, are they confused?

In its ontological role, the middle ensures that we are peacefully 'placed', that we are always contained within a peaceful infinite. No excess to the finite can displace us from an infinite peace, for when excess pushes us outside of the given accord, this outside is still granted by God. To leave the finite accord that is given is not to enter a sheer outside, it is to inhabit the middle of the finite and the infinite. The ontological middle thus articulates the analogy between finite and infinite, such that any exceeding of a finite given will be continuous with the finite that is exceeded. In its political role, on the other hand, the middle denotes that what is made from our place – or what is produced from and in excess of the given – is analogically related to what was given in the first place. The political middle thus articulates the analogy between the accord that was given and the accord that comes to be produced. Now, one would expect that these two accords would need to be significantly different from one another. After all, if they are not significantly different, then in what sense can the newly made accord be described as new? If the product (the new accord) is demanded by what exceeds the given accord, then the product would be 'successful' only insofar as it responds to this excess and thus differs from the given accord. So what makes these accords different?

This question becomes especially pressing when we recall that they are analogically related. They are both 'middle'. Therefore the post-productive middle (the middle that arises after the product) must significantly differ from the pre-productive middle (the middle that was there prior to the product). Yet Milbank has no conceptual means of distinguishing these two moments of the middle. Yes, they are temporally different, insofar as one succeeds the other, but in what sense can this succession be seen as a genuine change? In what sense can we say that the product has broken with the given and brought about a new state of affairs? The new accord, or the product, is analogically related to the given accord, and both the new and the given accord are analogically related to the infinite. There is, then, nothing within these relations that would indicate the basis for the production of something new, something different. Whatever novelty the political middle seeks to articulate is swallowed up in the ontological middle. We are assured of never being separated from the infinite, but this also ensures that we have no way of conceiving a radical break from what is given. The possibilities of existence imagined by analogy are thus guaranteed participation in the infinite, but then it becomes impossible to imagine in what sense these possibilities would be able to differ from what it is given. Such guaranteed participation is a trap. The place produced by the political middle is unable to differentiate itself from the place where we already are. We are suspended in place, in the present. We are suspended in the middle.

But perhaps this description of the politics of analogy is due to my dependence on spatial imagery. Might not an account of the politics of analogy be altered if we emphasised the role of time? Yet we cannot even do this, for Milbank excises time from God's supereminent being – indeed, the supereminent *is* supereminent precisely because it is supra-temporal. Thus the only means that remain for description of the transformations made by middle-products are spatial, since the source of both that which already is and that which will be made is beyond time. There is, of course, a temporality involved in making, but it is present as that which distinguishes making from its eminent source. In other words, to be temporal is to be involved in making, but God, the source of the power of making, is distinguished as God *precisely by being beyond time*, by being supra-temporal. The power that would bring about the transformation of existence is beyond time, and so a difference in time cannot be meaningful for a difference in the possibilities of existence. Accordingly, the difference between the place preceding and the place produced by the middle's making cannot be accounted for through time. In fact, the difference brought about by temporal dynamism is constantly explained by relating it to what the dynamism already possesses, and the circularity thus introduced can be resolved only through vague qualifications. When discussing the human soul's identity with God, for instance, Milbank must explain it as both a temporal aim and a presupposed reality: 'Spiritual beings in their deepest identity are lured to unity with God – even in some sense already possess this unity.'[63]

Back to the Present

Let us now revisit the criterion Milbank presents for deciding the rivalry between analogy and immanence: How do they imagine the relation between the ontological and the political? For Milbank, an ontology of peace is the condition of political peace, so much so that political peace would be possible only insofar as ontological peace is first imagined. Ontology and politics thus circle back upon one another. The ontological grounds the political, but the political produces the reality, or at least the manifestation, of ontological peace. Manifest violence is resolved through assertion of a prior ontological peace, but ontological peace can be manifested only through a political production. This circularity of the ontological and the political is confirmed, furthermore, by the fact that the production of peace, while manifested through the political and creaturely act of making, is said to be ontologically and eternally already there. We are once again swallowed up in the confusion of the political middle and the ontological middle.

With immanence, however, one can speak of an ontology of difference and a politics of peace. There is necessarily difference, but it is an entirely contingent matter whether this differential ontology produces manifest violence. An ontology of difference, therefore, does not amount to an ontology of violence. It is politics that decides the peaceability or violence of the various manifestations – or, in Deleuze's terms, expressions – of intrinsically differential being. The intrinsic difference of being does not exclude peace, it is rather the interstitial condition by which it may or may not be effectuated. The power of re-expression, necessitated by difference, requires politics, it demands the imagination and construction of possibilities of existence, but the possibilities selected – the accords that are produced – remain contingent.

The consequences of the divergence between the ontological-political relations advanced by analogy and immanence are starkest with respect to the question of struggle. Kenneth Surin makes this point central to his treatment of analogy. He notes that analogy 'necessarily introduces a hierarchy among beings, this hierarchy being specified in terms of a being's proximity in principle to the Godhead (angels being nearer the Godhead than humans, and so forth)'.[64] The political peace and flourishing promoted by Christianity's analogy depends on a prior consensus that such an ordering of creation by essence is properly harmonic. As Surin observes, 'Christianity's "peaceableness" is thus guaranteed only when there is logically prior commitment to the ontological requisites of a preestablished harmony (in fact acceptance of this divinely ordained harmony becomes an ontological condition for being a Christian).'[65] Analogy may articulate an order that is peaceable to some, but there will no doubt be those who experience this order in terms of suffering.[66] There will be minorities – all individuals are cracked, and so all, on some basic level, will be disaffected with the peace that order offers.

In what sense, then, can analogy speak to the desire for a break with what is given, to the experience of suffering? The only way analogy's order could remain peaceable, in light of such desire and experience, is to demand their stifling. In fact, the very possibility of addressing and re-expressing the presently disaffected desire is precluded by analogy's order of peace. It is in this sense that the ethics of analogy are majoritarian. For immanence's minoritarian ethics of the crack, on the other hand, dissatisfaction with, or intolerance of, given accords is a kind of infant resistance, an interstitial affection, and it can set one on a path toward the production of new accords. Yet it is precisely this affection of dissatisfaction with given accords that analogy seems to excise. We can consider, for instance, Milbank's remark that analogy, when properly developed, 'implies . . . analogical continuity between the "sameness" of given hierarchy and the constant temporal intrusion of difference'.[67] What is striking, when this claim is set against an ethico-political background, is how much the emphasis is placed on protecting the 'given hierarchy'. The concern is not to speak to, and from, the experience of suffering; it is to ensure that the 'temporal intrusion of difference', or contingent possibility, not be allowed to undermine the hierarchy that is already in place. We must, it seems, stay in the middle . . . some difference, some excess, sure, but not so much that it would disturb the order that is now regnant. This 'temporal intrusion of difference' seems less to call forth a break with the given than to indicate an excess in need of accommodation, a *disturbance* to be addressed but ultimately pacified. In fact, analogy's attitude toward temporal difference is, in this respect, precisely what Deleuze attacked under the name of Chronos.

In the temporality of Chronos, we can recall, past and future are dimensions of a constant present: 'only the present fills time, whereas past and future are two dimensions relative to the present in time'.[68] Against this, Deleuze poses the time of the Aion, which recommends an 'instant without thickness and without extension, [which] subdivides each present into past and future, rather than vast and thick presents which comprehend both future and past in relation to one another'.[69] Milbank's middle, we can now see, belongs to the temporality of Chronos – for what is the middle if not the construction of a 'vast and thick present', one that is able to absorb every potential disturbance of difference? Milbank does, of course, speak of old and new accords of being, of the past of the given and the future of the made. Yet, as we have seen, both old and new determinations are indistinguishably middle. The middle-product may be past or future, but the place it makes is, without exception, the eternal place of the ontological middle. It is this ontological middle that determines the present. Middle-products enable variations of the present, constant bifurcations of the present into the past and future, but they also recuperate these bifurcations into the present. Each middle-product's variation is related back to the present. The assertion, 'all of being is analogically contained in God', can therefore be rewritten: 'all of being is analogically contained in the present'.

It is in view of this concern to accommodate disturbance by way of an all encompassing present that we should take up Milbank's attempt to articulate analogy in terms of a 'romantic orthodoxy'. He opposes this to classical orthodoxy, which he criticises for too strong an emphasis on 'objective reason'.[70] The manner of this opposition is telling, for it indicates the difficulty to which he sees himself responding, namely a relation between the divine and the world in which the latter is seen as threatening the former, such that refusal of the latter is necessary for affirmation of the former. And it is true that analogy, as Milbank articulates it, does quite well in responding to this difficulty – for analogy does not immediately appear to aim at a negation of materiality. All of the world, or everything that is natural, is already imagined as participating in the being of God, so there is nothing in the world that could presently cut one off from the divine. As Milbank remarks,

> the entirety of the natural world constitutes a book signed by its author in whose being it participates by virtue of that author's creative action. We can read the symbols of this world because our intellect is illumined (and so able to think at all) through its participation in the very mind of this same author.[71]

There is something quite alluring about this vision, as its romanticism seems to simultaneously offer a maximal inhabitation of the world and a plenitudinous understanding of the divine. Specifically, the allure emerges at the level of the imagination, for it makes plausible, and affirms the desire to believe, the notion that every image that has been produced, or that could be produced, points toward the divine. The name of God, with all the connotations that it carries, is applied to every possible image from the past or the future. But it is precisely this allure that must be resisted, for to follow Milbank in this regard is to transform every disturbance of the past and future, every image of disturbance or disturbance of imagination, into an affirmation of the present – a present that, because it is said to analogically participate in the divine, is able to accommodate every mode of dissatisfaction with the present. It is in the name of this affect of dissatisfaction, of a temporal intrusion of difference that disturbs the present order of things, that we ought to refuse the very way that Milbank frames the issue. The key opposition is not between an objective reason that negates the world and a romantic imagination that affirms the world; it is between an imagination that absorbs the disturbance of the world through guaranteed participation and an imagination that commences with a refusal to moderate the force of such disturbance.

We can say, in fact, that Milbank does not here affirm the imagination of the world as such, despite what his framing of the issue wants to imply. What he affirms, more precisely, is the imagination of a world without disturbance. He demands that we imagine the world in such a way that disturbance is mollified by or subsumed in an all-encompassing transcendence of the present. This, it seems, is to assume that only such a world is worth imagining, or that the power of the imagination calls us to define the world in this way. Yet, as we have observed, the world cannot be plenitudinous as long as there are cracks. There is more to the world than the richness of images, for there are cracks running through these images. Cracks are disturbing. What is necessary, from this vantage, is not to patch over the cracks with an invocation of the transcendent, but rather to move into them in a more engaged manner, to make disturbance into an occasion for breaking with the present. From this vantage, it does not matter whether one is supplied with an archive of images, for such an archive is without cracks and thus requires the refusal to think from the cracks of dissatisfaction with the present. To inherit this archive, to participate in it, allows one to avoid becoming emptied of images. Yet it is only by running the risk of such emptying, of such senselessness – as I will argue in the final two chapters – that one can break with the present and create something new. In fact, it is only by running this risk that one can affirm the world in its excess. After all, the world is more than we presently imagine, and so the failure of inherited imagination, or the risk of being stripped of images, does not amount to an affirmation of the world. On the contrary, it is in the name of the world that we must demand the rejection of such an ultimately undisturbed imagination. This demand is disturbing only insofar as one does not want to be disturbed.

We are now able to see how the challenge posed by transcendence – that immanence cannot, on its own, provide the basis for a break with the given – undermines itself. Analogy's discourse of transcendence, far from supplying a basis for the production of new possibilities of existence, actually ends up supporting the present. In fact, the challenge posed by transcendence appears ultimately to be a conservative, even reactionary one. Furthermore, its tendency to misread the way differential immanence functions appears to be symptomatic of a reading practice that devalorises change wherever such change cannot be imagined in continuity with the given order of things and thus guaranteed in advance. What becomes clear, now that analogy has been set in contrast with immanence, is that the latter is far more capable of imagining possibilities that would liberate us from the regnant modes of domination.

All of this advances our attempt to diagnose the relation between immanence and theology. What remains to be looked at is whether the failure of analogical transcendence is determinative for all theology. In other words, while it is clear that immanence is not subject to the critique of theological transcendence, it is not yet clear that immanence must therefore steer clear of all theology. In fact, there is some ambiguity here, even after such a detailed discussion of analogy. Specifically – and to recall our introductory discussion of the slippage, within Nietzsche's proclamation, between the name of God and otherworldly hopes – it is ambiguous whether the failure of analogy is driven by its commitment to transcendence or by its commitment to theology. We can say with certainty why it is that transcendence must be opposed, but does this entail that theology as such, the very act of naming God, must be opposed? In other words, might not the problem with analogy be its involvement in transcendence more than its involvement in theology? Might not it be possible to imagine theology otherwise – indeed, to imagine theology in terms of immanence?

The relevance of such questions can be seen when we recall that God is the name by which many will imagine the possibility of possibilities, or possibility in its most radical sense. If the use of such a name requires transcendence, then we must discard the name. But why discard this name before we know that we must? Why not consider the possibility of making use of this name from the perspective of immanence? Let immanence take over the name of God – let it steal the name, let it mimetically subvert the name's inherited power – if it can. This is to say that where the naming of God engenders the transcendent, such naming ought to be refused, for only through such refusal can we liberate the imagination of new possibilities from its foreclosure. It is also to say, however, that what immediately matters is not the naming of God but the imagination of new possibilities. In fact, the suspicion that hangs over the secular is that it is concerned more with evading discourse about God than with imagination of the novel. To consider the possibility of an immanent naming of God is thus to distinguish immanence from secularisation. It is also to find a way out of the 'return of religion' war in which we find ourselves – a war in which theology, or religion, is on one side and the secular is on the other. As I discussed by way of introduction, the opposition between these two sides is actually derivative. Accordingly, to attend to the battles between them is to direct our attention away from the imagination of new possibilities of existence; it is to keep us focused on a war that proceeds within the given coordinates of the present. My thesis, then, is that what matters is not the opposition between theology and the secular but the opposition between transcendence and immanence. To imagine an immanent expression of theology, an immanent naming of God, is to refuse the terms of the war, or to break with the terms of the present.

It is in order to advance this thesis that I next turn to the work of John Howard Yoder, a Christian theologian, but one whose work, I will argue, can be understood in terms of immanence. There are no doubt other theologians, especially from other religious traditions, who could likewise be aligned with immanence. Once again, however, I believe it is important to take seriously the sort of historical pressure that Christianity still exerts on the contemporary imagination. It is for this reason, then, that my proposal for an immanent theology, like my critique of a transcendent theology, focuses on the Christian tradition. My aim is thus to establish that even within Christianity, that historical bastion of transcendence, immanence can find theological allies. It is, furthermore, to show how differential immanence and its capacity for re-expression cuts across the diversionary oppositions between theology, or religion, and the secular.

Notes

1. The fact that the movement ('Radical Orthodoxy') aligned with their thought has gained attention in various academic and popular circles indicates that theological transcendence still has force in the imagination of the present. John Milbank, for instance, has published a debate with the widely read (atheist) philosopher Slavoj Žižek. See Milbank and Žižek, *The Monstrosity of Christ: Paradox or Dialectic?*, ed. Creston Davis (Cambridge, MA: MIT Press, 2009). And David Bentley Hart's response to Richard Dawkins's criticism of the 'God Hypothesis' – *Atheist Delusions: The Christian Revolution and its Fashionable Enemies* (New Haven: Yale University Press, 2009) – has been promoted in the *New York Times*. See Ross Douthat, 'Notes on the New Atheists', 22 April 2010, available at <http://douthat.blogs. nytimes.com/2010/04/22/notes-on-the-new-atheists/> (last accessed 18 February 2013). The point of mentioning all this is not because it somehow validates their thought. It is simply to provide some anecdotal indexes of the significant hearing that the position of analogy is able to get, today, in the public sphere. It should also be noted that the movement of Radical Orthodoxy, despite Milbank's interest in socialist traditions of thought, seems in recent years to have turned in an increasingly conservative political direction. (Milbank, far from being exempt from this turn, is often at its vanguard.) This fact, taken together with the public attention its position is able to get, makes analogy all the more important to diagnose.

2. Let me take this moment to offer a quick qualification of my use of

the term 'transformation'. I intend it in the broad, popular sense of changing from one situation to another. In that sense, re-expression is transformation. But the point of re-expression, we have seen, is not just to find a better form, it is to exist in relation to a difference that is prior to any form – the virtual's difference in itself. So transformation is never final, it is always required to repeat itself, differentially.

A related point can be made regarding the term 'possibility'. I intend it, once again, in the broad, popular sense of the capacity for something that is not actually present. The term 'potentiality' might be just as good. But what we must watch out for is the tendency to imagine possibilities as somehow 'pre-existing' their realisation. Possibilities, as I am developing the term, are not like commodities on the shelf from which one chooses. To speak of possibility, in the sense that I intend, is to speak of something that could be, but is not yet – not even as possibility. In other words, the aim is not to realise possibilities that are already existing, it is rather to create possibilities themselves.

3. For some examples of theological attempts to both appropriate and resist Heidegger, see: Hans Urs von Balthasar, *The Glory of the Lord, Volume V: The Realm of Metaphysics in the Modern Age*, trans. Oliver Davies and Andrew Louth (San Francisco: Ignatius, 1993); Gustav Siewerth, *Das Sein als Gleichnis Gottes* (Kerle, 1958); Erich Przywara, *Analogia Entis*, trans. John R. Betz and David Bentley Hart (Grand Rapids: Eerdmans, forthcoming).

4. Martin Heidegger, *Introduction to Metaphysics*, trans. Gregory Fried and Richard Polt (New Haven: Yale University Press, 2000), p. 93.

5. This argument runs throughout his work, but it is most explicit in John Milbank, *The Word Made Strange: Theology, Language, and Culture* (Malden, MA: Blackwell, 1997), pp. 36–53.

6. David Bentley Hart, 'The Offering of Names: Metaphysics, Nihilism, and Analogy', in *Reason and the Reasons of Faith*, ed. Paul J. Griffiths and Reinhard Hütter (New York: T & T Clark, 2005), p. 261.

7. Ibid., p. 270.

8. Ibid., p. 263.

9. Ibid., pp. 268–9.

10. Ibid., pp. 269–70.

11. John Milbank, *Theology and Social Theory: Beyond Secular Reason* (Malden, MA: Blackwell, 2006), p. 309.

12. For an extended contrast of these two ontologies, see Milbank, *Theology*, pp. 278–325.

13. Ibid., p. 5.

14. Milbank, *Word Made Strange*, p. 108.

15. Milbank, *Theology*, p. 5.

16. Milbank, *Word Made Strange*, p. 15.

17. Milbank, *Theology*, p. 5.

18. Ibid.
19. Ibid.
20. Ibid., p. 260.
21. Ibid., p. 6.
22. Ibid., p. 279.
23. John Milbank, 'Materialism and Transcendence', in Creston Davis, John Milbank, and Slavoj Žižek (eds), *Theology and the Political: The New Debate* (Durham, NC: Duke University Press, 2005), p. 393.
24. Ibid., p. 424.
25. Ibid., p. 414.
26. John Milbank, *The Suspended Middle: Henri de Lubac and the Debate Concerning the Supernatural* (Grand Rapids: Eerdmans, 2005), pp. 53–4.
27. Ibid., p. 53.
28. Ibid., p. 64.
29. David Bentley Hart, *The Beauty of the Infinite: The Aesthetics of Christian Truth* (Grand Rapids: Eerdmans, 2003), p. 18.
30. Ibid.
31. Ibid., p. 21.
32. Ibid., p. 180.
33. Ibid., p. 181.
34. Ibid., p. 193.
35. Ibid., p. 194.
36. Milbank, *Theology*, p. 438.
37. Hart, *Beauty*, p. 209; my emphasis.
38. Ibid., p. 66.
39. Gilles Deleuze, *Cinema 2: The Time-Image*, trans. Hugh Tomlinson and Robert Galeta (Minneapolis: University of Minnesota Press, 1989), p. 165.
40. Gilles Deleuze, *Logic of Sense*, trans. Mark Lester with Charles Stivale (New York: Columbia University Press, 1990), p. 161.
41. Ibid., p. 332.
42. Ibid., p. 160.
43. Ibid., p. 161.
44. Deleuze, *Cinema 2*, p. 167.
45. Ibid., p. 179.
46. Ibid., p. 180.
47. Ibid., p. 182.
48. Gilles Deleuze, *Negotiations*, trans. Martin Joughin (New York: Columbia University Press, 1995), p. 175.
49. Ibid., p. 173.
50. Milbank, 'Materialism and Transcendence', p. 423.
51. Ibid.
52. Ibid.

53. Hart, 'Offering of Names', p. 273.
54. Ibid., p. 273.
55. Ibid., p. 229.
56. Hart, *Beauty*, p. 66.
57. Ibid., p. 62.
58. Milbank, 'Materialism and Transcendence', p. 418.
59. Ibid., p. 419.
60. Ibid., p. 394.
61. Ibid.
62. Milbank, *Theology*, p. 306; my emphasis.
63. Milbank, *Suspended Middle*, p. 50.
64. Kenneth Surin, 'Rewriting the Ontological Script of Liberation', in Davis, Milbank, and Žižek (eds), *Theology and the Political*, p. 258.
65. Ibid.
66. Looked at from this perspective, it seems no surprise that colonisation historically emerged out of an analogical imaginary. If peace can be brought about only through conversion, then not only does one have a motivation for the conversion of others to one's own position, one also has a justification for 'whatever it takes' to bring about this conversion – it is all done in the name of 'peace'. (In this sense, the logic of just war seems peculiarly dependent on an analogical position.) Therefore we must note not only analogy's inability to address or speak from the minoritarian tendency of life, but also its need to conquer those who actively dissent from the established order.
67. Milbank, 'Materialism and Transcendence', p. 419.
68. Deleuze, *Logic of Sense*, p. 162.
69. Ibid., p. 164.
70. John Milbank, 'The New Divide: Romantic Versus Classical Orthodoxy', *Modern Theology* 26.1 (2010), p. 28.
71. Ibid., p. 30.

4

Yoder: From the Particular to the Divine

Yoder's theology begins by giving attention to the particularity of Jesus. His approach thus contrasts with the one adopted by Milbank and Hart, which makes theology a matter of understanding a supereminent being and the consequent relation between the supernatural and the natural. On their reading, the figure of Jesus must be positioned in relation to questions of being; the importance of Jesus in analogical theology is to dramatise, or to serve as the essential instance of, the natural's participation in the supernatural.[1] It is in this sense that Jesus functions as a figure of universality. To say that Yoder's Jesus is particular, in contrast, is to say that Yoder refuses to put him in the service of a more generic ontological claim. Indeed, there is a kind of empiricism that runs throughout Yoder's theology: the goal is one of understanding what this figure is, what this figure does, what this figure makes interesting.

Yoder's approach has the effect of re-positioning excess. For analogy, excess is transcendent, and so Jesus functions to incarnate this eminent reality within the world. Yoder's particularistic approach also sees in Jesus the emergence of excess. Yet rather than begin from a position of transcendence – a position that would ground the excess – Yoder just begins with Jesus. To understand the excess of Jesus, in Yoder's approach, it is not necessary to find the (transcendent) ground of that excess, it is enough to follow the excess as it (immanently) emerges. Accordingly, Yoder's emphasis is not on the difference and continuity between the world and an eminent being. The difference that concerns him is less continuous and more discontinuous, or less ontological and more political: it is the difference between the particular existence of Jesus, with the possibilities it imagines, and the structures of existence that Jesus stood against. There is excess in Jesus, but it begins from and must loop back to this basic antagonism over the possibilities of existence.

Yoder's insistence that theology begins as witness to the particularity of Jesus can be taken as a refusal to countenance any *a priori* presupposition according to which we would comprehend this particular. Jesus's particularity must not be subjected to already decided upon rules governing thought, it instead must force new manners of thinking. The value of Jesus for thought, in other words, comes from the ability of a particular to call into question the given regime of possibility, to unground the presumed ground. We can, in order to get a better sense of the political stakes of Yoder's theological approach, look briefly at some remarks Derrida made about a problem that occupied his later work:

> I do not know if this structure [a phenomenologically delineated *khôra*] is really prior to what comes under the name of revealed religion or even of philosophy, or whether it is through philosophy or the revealed religions, the religions of the book, or any other experience of revelation, that retrospectively we think what I try to think.[2]

What Derrida is observing is the problem of determining the order of priority between a particular revelation and the structure of revelation, or revealability. On one hand, it would seem that the structure must come first, since every particular revelation, insofar as it is named as a revelation, must belong to a condition held in common with every other particular revelation. On the other hand, it seems impossible to think such a condition – the structure of revelation – without beginning from a particular revelation. Derrida admits his own confusion about how to resolve this problem:

> I must confess, I cannot make the choice between these two hypotheses. Translated into Heidegger's discourse, which is addressing the same difficulty, this is the distinction between *Offenbarung* and *Offenbarkeit*, revelation and revealability. Heidegger said ... that there would be no revelation or *Offenbarung* without the prior structure of *Offenbarkeit*, without the possibility of revelation and the possibility of manifestation. That is Heidegger's position. I am not sure. Perhaps it is through *Offenbarung* that *Offenbarkeit* becomes thinkable, historically. That is why I am constantly hesitating.[3]

What is interesting about Derrida's hesitation, with regard to Yoder's theology, is that he does call into question the Heideggerean assumption that the structure *must* come first, that particular revelations are nothing more than incarnations of a universal structure. Derrida notes the viability of the claim that any structure of revelation – that is, any set of rules about the possibilities of revelation – should be seen as secondary to the emergence of a particular revelation. Yet even as Derrida admits the legitimacy of this claim, he hedges his bet in undecidability. Yoder, however, does not hedge.

For Yoder, there cannot be any compromise between the priority of rules about revelation and the priority of a particular revelation. We must side with the latter. This, once again, is his empiricism: to say that a particular revelation is secondary to a structure of revelation is to say that the possibilities that are revealed by a particular must enter into compromise with predetermined rules of possibility. But the very point of giving attention to a particular is to see how reality is not fully understood by the ideas we already possess. This is especially so when it comes to a particular *revelation*, since what is at stake in such a case is not just any particular but rather a particular that claims to reveal something not already given. If a particular revelation is subjected to pre-possessed rules, then what is the point of the particular, and what is the sense of calling it a revelation? If we say that a particular revelation, a particular act of naming God, must be subordinated to an already-determined structure, then we are saying that the emergence – the 'revelation' – of new possibilities must be subordinated to what we have already decided to be possible. This philosophical question of a particular and its condition, or this theological question of a particular revelation and the structure of revealability, never stops becoming a political question. Accordingly, Yoder's particularistic approach to theology is always already political, in fact it imagines the theopolitical in the direction of the new, of the possibility of the particular to break with the given.

Against the Powers

Yoder conceives the given – or the expression of reality with which Jesus breaks – in terms of 'the Powers'. What does he mean by this concept? 'The Powers', he says, are not unlike what we are today wont to call 'structures'.[4] They have their own style of coherence or self-maintenance: 'the concept "structure" functions to point to the patterns or regularities that transcend or precede or condition the individual phenomena we can immediately perceive'.[5] We thus find, in the Powers, the sort of rules that Jesus refuses – that is, the given range of possibilities that he will call into question. These rules, however, are not separate from individuals. The Powers, by providing social, political, and economic structure, also produce individuals that are capable of responding to them, that are complicit with the possibilities they express. Thus the social, political, and economic structure the Powers provide is not something separate from the individuals they produce (or from the field of possibilities conceived and sought by these individuals). The Powers express the world and the individuals of this world at the same time – or, to put it otherwise, they determine the relation between, and the realm of possibility common to, individual and world. Furthermore, the process of individuation they govern is not simply given, but instead must repeatedly make itself. It subsists only in this repetition, only by Chronically incorporating temporal divergence. The concept of the Powers, then, allows Yoder to talk about transindividual modes of social (and political and economic) organisation. By dramatising the life of Jesus in relation to these Powers, he situates theology within a fundamentally political register.

As for the ethical status of the Powers, Yoder makes use of a creation and fall narrative. The Powers 'were part of the good creation of God', for 'society and history, even nature, would be impossible without regularity, system, order'.[6] This acknowledgement indicates that organisation or the process of individuation – that is, actualisation – is not an obstacle *in itself*. The difficulty, in other words, is not that there is actual organisation, it is rather that the actual organisation that is given does not advance the free imagination of possibilities. Yoder understands the world to be in a deep sleep of sin where we have become enslaved to these Powers. The mediators of 'good creation' have become objects of addiction – and addiction is a felicitous term, for though these Powers are modalities of domination, we find ourselves incapable of living without them. The Powers produce an actual world as well as individuals that are addicted to the given form of this world; the Powers sustain themselves by serving and reproducing a function we seem incapable of abandoning. It is this tireless co-dependence of individual and world, mediated by the Powers, that Yoder claims is cracked when Jesus, as a particular human being, 'unmasks the Powers'.

Yoder frames the passion narrative – the narrative in which Jesus freely suffers (and in doing so unmasks) the violence of the Powers – not as a backdrop for the reversal of humanity's guilty juridical status, but instead as the conflict between a sociality dominated by the Powers and a new, emergent one that wants to be free of such blockage. The passion narrative, then, is not ultimately a story about being forgiven for one's transgressions. It is, on the contrary, a story about politics, about the sort of world that we imagine to be possible. What is central is that Jesus, as a human, opened a new *possibility* for humanity – namely, the capacity to live a life not essentially determined by the Powers. Jesus thus marks a point in concrete history where the Powers, which are initially and for the most part taken as something inescapable for humans, become underdetermined. They are no longer the matter to be thought, for something apart from them has become available to and for historical humanity. Putting this in Deleuze's terms, we can say that Jesus *problematises* the Powers – he poses a problem for Rome, for the religious authorities, and for the course of history they demand. When we recall that the problematic field is the condition for any process of actualisation, we can say that Jesus's exteriority to the Powers 'unmasks' them precisely because it reveals them as a contingent actualisation, as something that can be resisted. Before the Powers, there is the problem to which they are but one contingent answer.

Jesus, by problematising the Powers, is able to exceed them, even when he suffers for his refusal of their health. In fact, it is because his problem is prior to the Powers' solution that his sickness is not the final word, but instead the advent of struggle. 'If . . . God is going to save his creatures *in their humanity*, the Powers cannot simply be destroyed or set aside or ignored. Their sovereignty must be broken. This is what Jesus did . . . by living a genuinely free and human existence.'[7] Jesus introduces an affirmative possibility for common life, which is to say that what was previously organised by the logic of the Powers may be liberated from them, but not only that. Life is not just liberated from the Powers, as a momentary subversion; it is also reorganised, or organised anew.[8] There are possibilities of life in common that are not determined by the Powers. Accordingly, it is not necessary to choose between the Powers' health or sickness's inevitable destruction, for a different health has become available.

This, in any case, is what is at stake when Yoder speaks of 'the creation of a distinct community with its own deviant set of values and its coherent way of articulating them'.[9] It is *deviant*, because it cannot be subsumed under given structures, but it is nonetheless *coherent*, because all of life can be reimagined and restructured within the possibility of life invoked by Jesus. At stake here is the outworking of a fundamental opposition between two kinds of communities, two ways of imagining the possibilities of social existence. The passion narrative is thus a political conflict, or a dramatisation of logically incommensurable commitments. Conflict, in this instance, is a consequence of the fact that Jesus does not operate within the field of possibilities determined by the Powers. The lived affirmation of Jesus exceeds the sovereign operation of the Powers, and this is evident as the latter keep coming up to their limit in the former. Jesus, much like the product of Deleuze's third synthesis of time, expels pre-existing, supposedly final determinations, and stands out beyond any totality of being.

How does one conceptualise something exceeding the conditions of one's conceptual paradigm? A paradigm undertakes strange contortions when it comes up against its limit. The passion narrative is, for Yoder, a concrete struggle that embodies this question. The limits are established when Jesus is criminalised and given the supreme punishment of death. The contortions are also undertaken. Powers previously disjoined come together against the excess that unites them negatively. 'In his death the Powers – in this case the most worthy, weighty representatives of Jewish religion and Roman politics – acted in collusion.'[10]

The mobilisation of the Powers is occasioned by something outside them, so their extreme production marks most perfectly their limit. Accordingly, any expansion of the Powers can be asymptotically graphed; they stretch without end, but cannot gather the excess in their sweep; their sweep expands and falls short at the same time, precisely because they cannot credit the excess. If Jesus is the exception to the Powers, then this is only as an ancillary function of his independence: Jesus was a 'threat to [the Powers'] dominion' because 'he existed in their midst so morally independent of their pretensions'.[11] To be independent in this way is to be irreducible to the Powers at a constitutive level. It is to re-express the problematic field independently of the Powers' form of expression. Yoder elucidates this irreducibility according to a hyperbolic logic of being 'more' and 'greater': Jesus 'incorporate[s] a greater righteousness than that of the Pharisees, and a vision of an order of social human relations more universal than the Pax Romana'.[12] The apparent maximum of Rome's universality is unmasked as a limit, but this unmasking takes place in a particular encounter. It is not, in other words, as if Jesus presents a theory of universality to be compared with that of the Powers. His excessive universality must be grasped precisely as a particular refusal of the Powers' universality, and as a particular production of something 'more'. Jesus is more universal in the strict sense of enabling something in excess of the Powers' universality; his logic is more universal because it is more than the universal. This is to say that the political logic of Jesus is more universal not in virtue of some standard of universality, but rather because it insists on the particular excess to universality, as well as on the possibility of such particular excess to re-express a problematic field prior to – more 'universal' than – the Powers' form of resolution. The question of universality, then, must be framed in terms of the 'limit' and the 'more'.

There is no compromise between a 'limit' and a 'more', there is only temporalisation and spatialisation of the limit running up against the more. The impossibility of compromise is most perspicuous in the turning of life and death. Jesus demonstrates his radical independence by taking upon himself death. One might assume that life and death are sufficiently universal or essential to serve as neutral mediators, but Jesus insists that even these terms split apart under the incommensurability between the Powers and his new possibility. 'Not even to save his own life will he let himself be made a slave of these Powers. This authentic humanity included his free acceptance of death at their hands.'[13] To kill, or to determine life and death, is the highest function of the Powers. Jesus, by *freely* assuming this death, reveals the Powers' apparently absolute function to be a relative one. The rules of possibility that the Powers express, and that they protect through the threat of death, are ultimately conditioned by something else.

It is because Jesus does not pull back in the face of this threat that we are able to conceive the claim that the cross – the execution that stands at the heart of the passion narrative – is victory. The event of Jesus's death indicates an historical body that so outlives the structure of the Powers that it can underdetermine this structure from another vantage – that of the production of new possibilities. In fact, the cross is verbal: it is a matter of 'what Christ and his death *did to* the Powers'.[14] The action is so capacious that the Pauline corpus resorts to three different verbs to account for the way Jesus unmasks the Powers. Yoder mentions this by borrowing from Hendrikus Berkhof:

> [Jesus] 'made a public example of them'. It is precisely in the crucifixion that the true nature of the Powers has come to light. Previously they were accepted as the most basic and ultimate realities. [Yet the Powers] are made a public spectacle. Thus Christ has 'triumphed over them' . . . The concrete evidence of this triumph is that at the cross Christ has 'disarmed' the Powers. The weapon from which they heretofore derived their strength is struck out of their hands. This weapon was the power of illusion.[15]

We can isolate, within this particular, historical unmasking of the powers, Yoder's conceptual innovations, beginning with a certain logical operation of overdetermination and underdetermination.

The Powers assert their capacity to govern each and every situation. Such an assertion amounts to a logic of domination, but what is central to this domination is its overdetermination-function, which gives it a significant degree of flexibility. Yoder notes the way in which legal and religious establishments, when confronted by Jesus, will transgress what they have posited as normative if this transgression is necessary in order to extend domination. The Powers, when confronted by Jesus, found themselves in need of recourse to the brute function of overdetermination. It was no longer a matter of extending domination through established legal or ethical norms, for what the particular independence of Jesus demanded was the assertion of the Powers' sheer functionality. And when Jesus freely accepts death, he underdetermines the Powers' overdetermination. The bare overdetermination-function of the Powers runs up against a particular life that it cannot fully determine. If we do not grasp this, then we miss the way in which terms determined by one condition (the Powers) are displaced when conceived according to another (problematically antecedent) condition. Death, for example, is determined by the Powers as the nullification of life, but with Jesus death becomes verbal.

The logic of overdetermination and underdetermination that I am using to make sense of Yoder's theology might be usefully contrasted with the logic Hart extracts from the passion narrative. For Hart, the key is that the 'cross marks the place where the totality, in its most naked manifestation as political terror, attempts to overcome infinity . . . but the cross ultimately fails to put an end to the motion of Christ's life, to the infinity of his gift'.[16] While my reading of Yoder would obviously agree that Jesus demonstrates the limits of the logic that demands his crucifixion, a difficulty nonetheless remains. Hart, by framing the passion narrative simply as a conflict between totality and infinity, fails to capture the temporal and political elements that are at stake.

With regard to time, Hart's account is too synchronic, and consequently renders the actors ('totality' and 'infinity') too static. While the Powers are ultimately committed to a kind of totality, it is also the case that this commitment is temporally enacted. Totality is not only an abstraction, it is also an expression of being that the Powers seek to re-express time and again. In other words, essential to the totality of which Hart speaks is a totalising-*function*: a temporalisation of totality, or a totalising manner of inhabiting time (Chronos). This is an important qualification, for it maintains the political character of the Powers, or their interest in making reality by overdetermining it. When Hart speaks of totality's 'political terror' as a moment *within* the passion narrative, he supports the misguided notion that this is not a political matter from the beginning. What is basic to the passion, in his account, is an ontological conflict (between totality and infinity). But ontological conflict must simultaneously be political conflict, the conflict between the Powers' and Jesus's respective ways of making being, of producing being's future. Emphasising this fact allows us to see why the Powers were compelled to kill Jesus: he refused to be actualised within the world to which they were committed, to be subject to their overdetermination-function. It also allows us to speak of the political temporality ensuing from his refusal, the continued conflict over the production of being. The logic of overdetermination and underdetermination thus stands against the too-synchronic logic of totality and infinity, it allows us instead to conceive the inescapably diachronic – and political – character of the passion narrative.

What happens in this diachronicity, this passage of time that cannot be understood from an eternal point of view? The operation of underdetermination disengages being from death and life as determined by the Powers, it opens a crack between them. An operation is at work whereby a minor term – death – which is determined within the paradigm of the Powers as lesser or as loss, is affirmed from the perspective of Jesus's independence. This is not because the minor term is 'really' major or objectively primary. It is a matter not of reversing, but of underdetermining, the order of determination; the order of determination is underdetermined not through internal critique, but through confrontation with an independent commitment, a particularity that asserts its autonomy with regard to this order. The problem is prior to the Powers' order of determination, but this priority does not assert itself by transcending determination. No, the priority of Jesus's problem to the Powers' solution emerges from within his particular historical existence.

'A Host of Other Free Agents': Exceeding the Frame

The Powers overdetermine the world, and Jesus resists them by problematising them. What must be stressed, however, is that this sort of resistance proceeds as underdetermination. In other words, the resistance of Jesus is not in the name of a positive, transcendent infinity, it is instead immanent. It is immanent because what it affirms is already there: Jesus's resistance is in the name of that which is real, yet denied or dominated by the determination of the Powers. The protest of Jesus is not primarily a negation of the order sustained by the Powers, it is primarily an affirmation of something immanent in reality that this order rejects – such as the demand for justice in this world, here and now. So while Jesus does stand against the Powers, this is as an effect of standing for the fullness of the world's possibility. This standing *for* the world is what undoes – or underdetermines – the apparent solidity of the Powers' given order.

It is along these lines that Yoder argues for the centrality of 'jubilee' to Jesus's work. There is, of course, a long prophetic tradition of jubilee-preaching that involves, among other things, the forgiveness of debt and the destruction of wealth accumulation – which might be understood as an underdetermination of overdetermining wealth. This jubilee-preaching can sometimes be read as a regulative ideal against which actual political processes fall short or as a promised reconciliation to come in some future messianic age. What is important about Yoder's jubilee is the way it insists on the real, present possibility of such liberation through the historical emergence of the human Jesus. Yoder pushes us to come to grips with the way Jesus claims to fulfil the jubilee tradition, or to bring about the messianic kingdom that involves this fulfilment, such that the demand for freedom and equality imposes itself here and now.

The kingdom whose form is 'jubilee' must involve 'a visible sociopolitical, economic restructuring of relations among the people of God'.[17] To fulfil the kingdom is to make this form both a demand and a real possibility. There is, in this way, a politics internal to the jubilee-form of the kingdom, which I will call the 'first sense of the political'. This jubilee politics stems from and goes beyond Jesus's fulfilment. Jubilee is proclaimed by Jesus but it immediately becomes the object that engenders and is sought by a political community. The political community of Jesus lives as 'a movement, extending his personality in both time and space, presenting an alternative to the structures that were there before'.[18] 'Church' (the name given to this political community) is therefore 'interior' to – that is, necessarily and directly constituted by – the particularity and logic of Jesus, and separate from the coordinates of the given expression. Separation and antagonism are thus central to any concept of church. 'To organized opposition [Jesus] responds with the formal founding of a new social reality', a 'political, *structural* fact which constitutes a challenge to the Powers'.[19]

Yet Jesus's proclamation of the here-and-now character of the jubilee, along with his establishment of a jubilee-formed community, only intensifies the reaction of the Powers. His willed separation from the Powers occasions their antagonism. Accordingly, it is not enough merely to speak of the independent politics of jubilee. We must also address the Powers' reaction to Jesus, their attempt to put to death the kingdom he makes a real possibility. But we must do so in a manner that keeps faith with the jubilee-logic's independence from the Powers.

Such a task forms what I will call the 'second sense of the political'. The first sense of the political, then, concerns the organisation of jubilee in its utter independence and constitutive capacity (its inherence in the particular Jesus), while the second sense of the political concerns the relation between this independent, constituent logic and the reaction visited upon it by the Powers. The second sense of the political reminds us that the political community of Jesus finds itself enmeshed in a situation of conflict. It raises a question of arms. There is a battle underway between the Powers and the social reality of Jesus, and this battle is complicated by the sword – not the way the sword is used, but the sheer recourse to it. The prospect of violence, though I have not addressed it as such, has been everywhere present; it is the musculature of what I have talked about in terms of the domination and limitation by the Powers. The question that now emerges (how can we battle violence without recapitulating the form of this violence?) belongs to one I have already stated (how do we overcome the Powers without being determined by them while doing so?).

Mere resistance, according to Yoder's concept of 'nonresistance', amounts to a reversal of direction by preservation of style.[20] It means fighting the sword with the sword, the Powers with counter-Powers – maybe even, in my nomenclature, overdetermination with another, transcendent overdetermination (the mistaken approach of analogy). There is much displeasure, much disenchantment, much desire for something else, yet nothing changes. The reason for this is not that one is too antagonistic, but instead that one is not antagonistic enough, for one who resists creates an analogy with what is resisted. 'What is wrong with the violent revolution according to Jesus is not that it changes too much but that it changes too little; the Zealot is the reflection of the tyrant whom he replaces by means of the tool of the tyrant.'[21] The life of Jesus offers an irrecuperable antagonism, but resistance, as Yoder defines it, loses track of the independence that occasions this antagonism. Resistance reacts to, rather than acts against, its opponent. Yoder's concept of nonresistance, on the other hand, affirms that the more can exceed the limit without having to react against it, and that the more only undermines itself when it tries to express itself within the logic of the limit. This should remind us that nonresistance is not a matter of empirical violence in itself but rather one of determining the position and field of a pervasive and unlocalisable antagonism. Violence is refused, insofar as it creates an analogy with the Powers, but militancy is required.

It is necessary to think together the two senses of the political because of the immanence of the messianic kingdom implied by Yoder's understanding of the jubilee. The jubilee cannot be analogically distributed between a transcendent plane and an immanent plane, where the former indicates its supra-temporal, already-accomplished existence and the latter names its finite degree. Such an observation provides a way of understanding Yoder's opposition to the logic of just war, which assumes, to use Milbank's terminology, a distinction between the supra-temporal and the temporal: the peace of the supra-temporal can be legitimately furthered by means of state-sponsored war because the reality of this peace is not said in the same sense with regard to finite temporality. Analogy permits the violence of the state – which accomplishes a limited, temporal peace – to serve as a finite participation in transcendent peace. Just war is then that which mediates the finite's intrinsic aim at infinite peace (via its analogical participation) with its equally intrinsic limit (its finite degree). But if there is immanence of infinite and finite, then the peace made possible by the former's unconditioned power cannot have a different meaning when it is sought in this world. It is thus just war, rather than Yoder's nonresistance, that is otherworldly.

The 'non-' of nonresistance distinguishes the political logic of Jesus from any analogy with what it stands against. To say that this logic is independent is to say that it is prior. It is because of this priority or independence that nonresistance is never passivity before or capitulation to what it refuses. But the logic of Jesus is not only separated from the Powers (the first sense of the political), it is also in confrontation with them (the second sense of the political). Confrontation is inescapable because the logic of Jesus, while being independent of the Powers, lays claim to the same matter of determinability, the world. The excess of Jesus is excessive precisely because it is a *worldly* more – in other words, it goes beyond overdetermination by virtue of its inseparability from the matter of determinability. Jesus's political logic is all the more independent because it is independent of the Powers and *not* independent of the world. It does not hope for independence from the world, it hopes for a worldly independence.

Yoder emphasises that nonresistance's antagonism toward the Powers involves antagonism toward frameworks of causation. Why is this the case? The short answer is that to accept a framework of causation is to accept the terms of the given expression of being. The first sense of the political loses its power of independence because the second sense of the political is itself lost; the admission of a causal framework turns antagonism into mere resistance. This is because a framework of causation is essentially the reification of the logic of what is already established. It does not reflect the movement of the world, it reflects the movement of a thought that dominates the world – in other words, a framework of causation is transcendent to the world and its immanent possibilities. This is the short answer to the question of why causal frameworks must become the object of antagonism. A more elaborate answer, however, comes by attending to three specific weaknesses.

First, causal frameworks produce a mutually delimiting complicity between possibility and effectiveness. The only effective path is the one we can see as possible; what is impossible, or what we cannot imagine presently, becomes ineffectual. Problems, rather than enabling the construction of alternative expressions, are dissolved in the face of already given expressions. The realm of effectiveness cuts off what is possible: what seems impractical becomes essentially impossible, and the endpoint of our political possibility is chalked up to the realm of the real rather than to the blindness and impotence of our imagination.

Second, causal frameworks produce an autonomously functioning sphere of relevance. Everything is justified in virtue of a relevance granted by the cause, which is transcendent. Any expression is permitted, but only in virtue of its relation to this transcendent cause and its form of relevance. To isolate relevance as such is to think outside the antagonism between the life of Jesus and the Powers, from a point transcendent to this conflict of the limit and the more.

Third, causal frameworks break down not so much in the manner of their management as in their very assumption that history *can* be managed. We might discern, with this statement, an indication of Yoder's philosophical position. He believes it to be evident, apart from theological commitments, that the world is not adequately considered within a pre-established network of causality. There are, in the world and its history, 'a host of other free agents'.[22] One implication of this is that particularity cannot be reduced to universality. Therefore we have a philosophical reason for approaching Jesus through particularity: sufficient reason, when conceived as universality, is insufficient; causal frameworks cannot negotiate sufficiently with elements of chance and contingency, or with the capacity for re-expression; 'universality' cannot be thought of as universal in the first place.

Yoder's particularistic approach to the logic of Jesus is thus consistent with the claim that particularity exceeds any presupposed notion of universality, or that the world labours in ways unimagined by logics of transcendent causality. It is important to note the logical inseparability of Yoder's Jesus with that which emerges contingently, with that which *becomes*. Yoder can, as a result of this inseparability, refuse the overdetermination of causal frameworks without being forced to champion their opposite. In other words, the unmanageability of the 'host of other free agents' can be affirmed at the same time as the political logic of Jesus. The particular Jesus breaks open, or cracks, the world as it is given, providing a passage that exceeds the present. Furthermore, since this logic is inseparable from the matter of determination, the politics of Jesus must also be inseparable from a politics of the world. What is common to these two politics, what enacts their link, is the nondenumerable 'host of other free agents'.

Where causality is absent, revolution is present. That which cannot be managed is always already in revolt against the reign of managerial control, even where it does not tag itself as 'revolution'. It is the world, with its excessive particularity, that cannot be thought universally or causally – thus we can ascertain the worldliness or secularity of revolution. If there is splendour in revolution, it is a mundane splendour. To challenge the domain of causal frameworks is to speak of and from the world. A causal framework knows only what it sees, it is the totality of visibility; revolution emerges from a possibility of the world outside the sightlines of causality. We should be unsurprised, given the particularity and concreteness of his approach, that Yoder finds 'revolution' to be an apt term for talking about the life and logic of Jesus.

If the world revolts against its subjection to overdetermination-functions and predetermined causal networks, and if the independence of Jesus's political logic is all the more independent due to its inseparability from the world, then Jesus's claim to fulfil the jubilee kingdom must be a worldly revolution. And it is precisely in the sense of a worldly revolution – and only, strictly in this sense – that we may speak of secularity in Yoder's thought. In other words, secular, in my reading of Yoder, refers to the world, and even more precisely to the world in its independence from any correlation with the transcendent, or in its revolt against the regnant discourse of the present. It is in this sense, then, that Yoder's secularity can be distinguished from the presuppositions of what is normally recognised as the secular: whereas the normative secular is a discourse about the world as it should be, thus implying a standard conception of the world, Yoder's secular is a discourse about the world in revolt against given discourses of standardisation; whereas the normative secular valorises itself as that which is able to separate the world from the theological, Yoder's secular is indistinguishable from the theological; and whereas the normative secular establishes the world in the present, Yoder's secular turns the world against what is presently established. This last point is evident when Yoder speaks of the secularity of the gospel, or the good news, at the same time that he speaks of the revolutionary nature of such news: 'The root meaning of the term *euangelion* would today best be translated "revolution." Originally it is not a religious or a personal term at all, but a secular one: "good news." '[23]

The world revolts against frameworks of causality, and the political logic of Jesus says the revolt as 'love'. When Jesus lived the cross as verb, 'effectiveness and success were sacrificed for the sake of love', and 'this sacrifice was turned by God into a victory which vindicated to the upmost the apparent impotence of love'.[24] Underdetermination and nonresistance place us within the antagonism that Jesus poses to overdetermination and domination; 'love' offers a criterion according to which we should construct a social life internal both to the novel difference of Jesus and to the world. Nonresistance is convertible with love because the matter that separates itself by nonresistance lives the condition that separates it according to love. Yoder asserts that 'the love of the Gospel ethic' is 'nonresistance, unconditional obedience to the nature of love', and that one attribute shared by these terms – nonresistance and love – is their 'making no promise of effectiveness'.[25] Both live according to an excess that refuses effective causality. 'It is of the nature of the love of God not to let itself be limited by models or options or opportunities which are offered to it by a situation. It does *more* because the very event of exceeding the available models is itself a measure of its character.'[26]

In this sense, the love of God names the immanence of being's more – its excess – and that which is limited by 'available models'. Unlike causal frameworks, where the cause is transcendent to its expressions, the causal love of God is immanent to excessive expression. The measure of its character, its 'more', is not imposed on expression, but rather is immanent to 'the very event' of an expression's act of 'exceeding'. To love the world is to re-express it in excess of the regnant model of expression. In fact, the immanence of Jesus's divine particularity and the particularity of the world, or of Jesus's original revolution and the revolution of the world, is reinforced by Yoder's claim that 'people who bear crosses are working with the grain of the universe'.[27] The key phrase is 'working with'. This phrase indicates the insufficiency of saying that the grain is to be imposed on the universe. On the contrary, the political logic of Jesus and the grain of the universe are in immanence: the original revolution directed by the particular Jesus and the revolution of worldly particularity *work with* each other. For this reason, the revolutionary 'more' is the immanence of the love of God and the love of the world.

Secular Creativity

One consequence of the independence of Jesus's logic is that its political community, the 'church', is to be thought of as a 'social minority' – an imperative blatantly refused by the history of Christianity, so much so that we might imagine Christianity *as* the history of this refusal. It is interesting here to note a comment that Deleuze makes in connection with his minoritarian ethics. What defines a majority, he says, is not quantity but quality, not number but standard: 'Majority implies a constant . . . serving as a standard measure by which to evaluate it. . . . Majority assumes a state of power and domination, not the other way around. It assumes the standard measure, not the other way around.'[28] A majority, then, has nothing to do with the greatest number but with the nature of a given power. It is produced by its appearance as standard *and* variable, it is both norm and that with which variability is required to accord. Concomitantly, a minority has nothing to do with being quantitatively smaller, it is rather about becoming involved in a quality of existence that varies from the given standard.

Yoder sees the concept of minority in a remarkably similar manner. The church is a minority not because of its number, but because of its commitment. And that which it stands against, the 'establishment' (or majority), is defined by its social dominance and illusory claim to universality. '"Establishment" does not mean the [numerical] majority; it means the [numerical] minority who are in dominant social roles and claim the authority to speak for everyone.'[29] The minority status of the church thus derives from its antagonism to this numerically minor, but politically majoritarian, establishment. 'To recognize that the church is a minority is not a statistical but a theological observation.'[30] In other words, the church is a minority because its political logic commits it to a minoritarian way of being. It is minoritarian because of its commitment to what is unthought by the majoritarian determinations of causal frameworks and the Powers. Yoder demands, in a rigorous and consistent manner, that the church – because it is a social minority – seek a politics apart from the state. His tendency to conceive the church as a 'movement' rather than as an institutional 'denomination' is not unrelated to this.[31] The question of institutionalisation must be secondary, for otherwise the church-as-movement risks fitting itself into a social role provided by the state. To take a minority position is not to ask for respect within a whole governed by the state, but rather to assert one's autonomy from, and antagonism toward, a state-determined whole. As Yoder says, 'the church is more truly political . . . than is the state'.[32] It is 'more truly political' because it poses the question of the making of being *in the world* and thus apart from the majoritarian causality of the state.

The grand virtue of this political logic, then, is that it breaks, without remainder, the possibility of any analogy between the state and the movement of the political, and that it does so precisely through intensified commitment to movements from below. Yoder, by tying together a social minority and secularity, implies that the movement of the world is found at its edges and in its initially indiscernible phenomena. The church and the world can relate without this relation having to be mediated by the state:

> In modern usage the application of the term *political* to the state rather than to the church . . . leads to a distortion . . . for in biblical thought the church is properly a political entity, a *polis*. In both biblical languages the word *church* (*qahal*, *ekklesia*) refers originally to a deliberative assembly of the body politic.[33]

The politics of the church is inseparable from an operation of assembling. An assembly is not just a gathering of people, it is an assumption, in common, of the tasks, operations, and modes of production that explicate and implicate our particular worldliness. The practices or processes named by assembling express and construct the world, along with the manner of our existence in it. They are processual modes of individuating both humans and world. To see the way we are formed by these processes, the way these processes enable an inhabitation of the world, is to see that assembling is a production of political possibility.

Jesus's logic, in calling forth unthought possibilities that are in excess of given limits, is immediately secular (because this possibility is *of the world*) and political (because these possibilities must be assembled or constructed). We must pose, in this sense, the political and the secular against the cultic.[34] The cult cannot shake itself from the grip of mediation. It revolves around an object or mode of exchange that is transcendent to the political process of expression and construction. The cultic functions to divert attention from the immanent processes of the world by focusing attention on a mechanism of cause and effect claiming to explain the events and possibilities of the world. In this sense, the cultic alienates agents of the world from their expressive or re-expressive capacities, for these productive capacities are captured by the cultic object or mechanism.

Even if the cult is not identical to the state as such, it functions as its handmaiden – and thus plays an essential role in the Powers' overdetermination – due to its ability to divert the desire for new possibilities of existence. And the church has historically played this cultic role due to its 'Constantinian' willingness to fuse itself with the state. In such an instance, 'The church is no longer the obedient suffering line of the true prophets; she has a vested interest in the present order of things and uses the cultic means at her disposal to legitimize that order.'[35] In fact, one can easily see analogy as playing such a legitimating role. Thus Yoder's insistence that the logic of the particular Jesus is secular rather than cultic is no small matter, for it is here that the capacity to stand against the given, as well as against theology's collaboration with the given, succeeds or fails.

One might object that the logic of Jesus has a certain cultic character, in that it is given *through* Jesus. Does not Jesus serve as yet another cult? This point is not entirely untrue, but it misses the nature of Jesus's 'mediation'. Jesus mediates not by setting himself apart from the world, but through extreme inseparability with it, whereas the cultic mediates by taking remove from it. For Yoder, Jesus introduces a clearly-defined life-style distinct from the crowd [yet] this life-style is different, not because of arbitrary rules separating the believer's behavior from that of 'normal people,' but because of the exceptionally normal quality of humanness to which the community is committed. *The distinctness is not a cultic or ritual separation, but rather a nonconformed quality of ('secular') involvement in the life of the world.*[36]

The particular Jesus separates itself, but it does not separate itself from the world, it separates itself from the cult of the given – which has already separated itself from the world. In this sense, Jesus's separation is in the name of the world, it is a separation from separation. The 'more' of being is not above the world, it is within the world, beneath the above imposed by the cult. There is thus an irreversible movement toward the co-inherence of the possibility named by the particularity of Jesus and the possibilities of the world.

The process of living this co-inherence must be creative. Creation here has nothing to do with an origin of the world and everything to do with a politics of the world. The minimum that co-inheres (in the world and the logic of Jesus) must be *creatively* expressed and constructed precisely because this minimum is a possibility (of re-expression) rather than something given. Yet the secular character of this minimum means expression and construction are contingent, worldly matters. Accordingly, the political community of Jesus is properly concerned with 'the creative construction of loving, non-violent ways to undermine unjust institutions and to build healthy ones'.[37] To create, once again, it is necessary to underdetermine the Powers: 'social creativity is a minority function'.[38] The deed of state violence manages and enforces overdetermination's limit, and so such violence cannot overcome or pass beyond itself. One who takes power – who takes the state, or takes responsibility for the functioning of the Powers – is bound by what one assumes.

A social minority, however, can risk failure. It can, for instance, undertake 'pilot projects' that address a new problem experimentally. The most minute gain from such experimentation far exceeds the preserve of the state and its overdetermination, for the pilot project adheres to a point of emergence that the state can attempt to manage, but never know. In other words, the state's Chronic temporality can aim to manage the excess of past and future to the present, but it cannot think *from* this excess, it cannot proceed from the crack of the present. This is why the 'creativity of the "pilot project" ... is more significant for a social change than is the coercive power which generalizes a new idea'.[39] Overdetermination arrives late on the scene of emergence, so late that it no longer sees the emergence of the emergent.[40]

Equality With God is Not Something to be Emanated

I am aware that, even as I argue for an account of Yoder's theology in accord with immanence, an important objection might still linger – namely, that Yoder's theology, because it involves the claim that Jesus is the Son of God, must ultimately contravene immanence. After all, if the particular Jesus is said to be divine, doesn't such a particular become transcendent? This objection can be addressed by examining the sense Yoder gives to the Christian claim that Jesus is of the same substance as God.

Yoder constantly qualifies the Nicene proposition of *homoousios*. He adopts, in *Preface to Theology*, a somewhat historico-genetic approach to Christian theology, the purpose of which is to contextualise theology as something done in history and out of a commitment to historical events (cross, resurrection). Consequently, when thinking about the assertion that Jesus is God, it becomes important not to think from the general proposition that Jesus is co-essential with God, but rather to commence with the events that press the need for this proposition. Yoder makes two points, along these lines, that we should foreground.

First, he emphasises the ethical and historical, or lived, character of Jesus's identity with God. He argues that 'when, in the New Testament, we find the affirmation of the unity of Jesus with the Father, this is not discussed in terms of substance, but of will and deed. It is visible in Jesus's perfect *obedience* to the *will* of the Father.'[41] What makes Jesus divine is the quality of his life. Yoder remarks elsewhere that the biblical report of God's statement at Jesus's baptism, 'Thou art my Son', is 'not the definition or accreditation of a metaphysically defined status of sonship; it is the summons to a task. Jesus is commissioned to be, in history, in Palestine, the messianic son and servant, the bearer of the goodwill and the promise of God.'[42] Jesus is the Son of God by virtue of a thoroughly historical possibility. Sonship involves a particular capacity as well as a temporality according to which this capacity is lived.

Second, Yoder makes a case for the apologetic origin of assertions regarding Jesus's pre-existence. His point is that the proposition that Jesus exists with God, prior to world, was a result of the historical conflict between the community of Jesus, with its own political logic, and other political logics, which had an alternative logic or cosmology that would have rendered the political logic of Jesus as an impossibility. These alternative cosmologies spoke of a logos that mediates the creation of the world, and so the church, in order to avoid identifying Jesus with such a creative principle and to assert his political priority over such a principle, claimed that Jesus was with God before creation. In other words, the claim that Jesus pre-exists the world is not a genuinely ontological claim but instead an act of subversive mimesis: that which the other says is ultimate, 'the logos', is copied and taken up by Jesus. Yoder wants the cosmological or ontological implications of this 'before' to be secondary to the way 'before' expresses the precedence of the political life of Jesus's community over rival political projects.[43]

The narration of Jesus as divine logos is thus in service of new possibilities of relation amongst the elements that belong to these alternative cosmologies. Take, for instance, the confrontation with cosmologies in which the eternal, timeless One is eminent, while all other beings emanate (through the logos) from this One. There is, in this instance, an inverse proportionality between One and many, or cause and effect, as the higher and the lower, the emanating and the emanated (I am speaking, in other words, of the emanative ontologies against which Deleuze posed his immanative ontology). What is important is not simply that the logos, as Jesus, is no longer the medium and principle of emanation, that Jesus is instead anterior to any mediation of God and the world, of eternal unity and temporal divergence. It is just as important to grasp that what is anterior is thoroughly historical – in the sense of an immanence of the particularity of being and the cause of being. To claim that Jesus is God is thus to affirm a coincidence of God and the world, of the eternal and the temporal, in a way not imagined by cosmologies of emanation and hierarchy. The hierarchy managed by the emanative logos is short-circuited because what is historical is also 'pre-existent' – that is, prior to the historical-as-emanated. Yoder makes this point quite nicely:

> instead of tailoring Jesus to fit the slots prepared for him, John breaks the cosmology's rules. At the bottom of the ladder, the Logos is said to have become flesh, to have lived among us as in a tent, symbol of mortality, and to have suffered rejection by us creatures. At the top of the ladder, the Logos is claimed to be coeval with God, not merely the first of many emanations. *But then there is no more ladder*: the cosmology has been smashed, or melted down for recasting.[44]

The claim that Jesus is God may give rise to a doctrine of co-essenti-
ality, but such a doctrine functions just to insist that *there is* history.
To say that Jesus is divine, then, is not to analogically coordinate the
world's history with something transcending this history, it is to deny
their very separation, it is to make the world's history immanent with
the openness named by divine possibility. The doctrine of co-essence
means that the world is immanently *more*, where this more is prior
to the distinction between the world and the divine (and hence to the
analogy that depends on this distinction).

This more, in the political logic of Jesus, is historical, or a historical process by which a supposedly eternal possibility *is* eternal
only to the degree that it *becomes* historically. The point of saying
'Jesus is Logos' is neither to join what is separated, nor to register
analogically what was previously in hierarchy; it is to indicate the
inescapably worldly and particular movement of divine existence.
'No longer does the concept of the Logos solve a problem of religion,
reconciling the eternal with the temporal.'[45] This is what an analogical ontology still does, for making analogous two separated terms
amounts to 'reconciling' them. Yoder's Jesus, instead of *reconciling* a
pre-given religious or metaphysical problem, actively *problematises*
the political making of being. He does not provide an analogical
peace for an overdetermined ontological hierarchy, he instead 'melts
down for recasting' the distinctions brought about by this hierarchy.
In other words, he underdetermines this hierarchy, expels its very
terms, through the force of his problem. According to Yoder, the
logos of Jesus 'carries a proclamation of . . . incarnation, drawing
all who believe into the power of becoming God's children'.[46] This
'incarnation' indicates an irreversible inseparability of what is normally divided between God and creation.

Time for Re-writing

We can now see how Yoder's theology, even as it takes up the
discourse of logos, insists on the priority of historical possibility;
possibilities in excess of the given are theologically imagined, but this
excess indicated by the name of God is never supra-temporal. It is no
surprise, then, that we find Yoder insisting on the theological centrality of time and history. Biblical language, he says,

> is significantly different from the Platonic worldview in which time is a
> disadvantage. There, the eternal is genuine. Our wearing out and getting

old represents the passage of time. Essential reality is the nontemporal, therefore the most essential hope is a nontemporal hope, so it is rather crude to talk about Christian hope or the passing of time.[47]

In the Christian paradigm, however, 'history [is] more basic than timeless language'.[48] It understands the eternal, the working of God, to be temporal through and through, from emergence to conclusion. 'If real events are the center of history – certainly the cross was a real event, certainly the resurrection is testified to as in some sense a real event – then the fulfilment and culmination of God's purposes must also be really historic. The God of the Bible is not timeless.'[49] In other words, if the practice of divine power and possibility is really available through Jesus's fulfilment of the jubilee kingdom, then historical existence is the condition of a creativity that is at once divine and temporal.

Along these lines, Yoder says that 'the eternal is not atemporal. It is not less like time, but more like time. It is like time to a higher degree. The kingdom is not immaterial, but it is more like reality than reality is.'[50] I have throughout emphasised the way that the logic of Jesus introduces a 'more' in virtue of which the given Powers run up against their limit. The life of this more does not require renunciation of the temporal world dominated by these Powers, but rather infinite intensification of it. This more's hyperbolic power is expressed by its divine status, but the construction of this more involves an inescapably temporal and historical process. There is no need to take remove from the contingency and disaccord of history; one can affirm this disaccord, this intrinsically differential character of being, not from the vantage of pure eternity or of analogical peace (as the mediating accord of this disaccord), but from the more through which such history is loved and composed. Disaccord becomes affection of the more. For this reason, the value of disaccord is not measurable in terms of ultimate accord. Disaccord is valuable in itself, for it makes us encounter, *temporally*, what exceeds the given order of things.

Opacity is a consequence of temporality. History is lived in a certain blindness, and this is not to be lamented. The more of history, which co-inheres with the unconditioned more of divine potency, is the edge internal to temporality. One who talks about the infinitude of this temporality in terms of two different times or ages has fallen short of its demand. The same could be said of one who places the temporal beneath the supra-temporal. According to Yoder:

What we are now doing is what leads to where we are going. Since the 'this-worldly' and the 'otherworldly' [are] not perceived in radical dichotomy, to be 'marching through Emmanuel's ground' today is to be on the way to Zion. Terms like 'hereafter' are in that kind of context affirmations, not negations. *They do not say that that to which we look forward is in a radically different kind of world from the world in which we now live, but rather that it lies farther in the same direction in which we are being led.* The unforeseeable future is farther along in the same direction as the foreseeable future for which we are responsible.[51]

The old aeon and the new aeon are not two different times, but two ways of inhabiting time: the old aeon belongs to the limit, the new aeon to the more. As temporal practices, the old aeon and the new aeon correspond respectively to Deleuze's Chronos and Aion. Just as Chronos cannot affirm production of the new, so the old aeon cannot countenance the proclamation of the new aeon; just as the Aion cracks the Chronic present, so the new aeon breaks in on and underdetermines the vision of the old aeon. Furthermore, for both Deleuze's Aion and Yoder's new aeon, what matters is the nature of time itself, rather than some reference to a chronological period.

The old aeon becomes old, or fulfils the oldness that testifies to its always-already-dying, by collapsing in on itself rather than by being replaced. And the world determined by the old aeon is not so much destroyed and supplanted as it is displaced and refashioned, released from subjection and opened to experimentation. Jesus's fulfilment of the kingdom is not the establishment of a wholly other time, or of a different kind of world, but rather the new possibility of living the time of this world, the only world there is, in a different manner; the political logic of Jesus makes possible the radically new by calling forth a temporal process of the world.

This account of time also enables one to provide something like a Yoderian 'metanarrative'. Such a term can assume many connotations, but my interest lies in its specific function of narrating history according to the uncontrollability of time. What is intriguing about Yoder's metanarrative is its ability to move beyond a strict opposition between time as infinite and history as closure of temporal possibility. The two epochal hinges of history are indicated, for Yoder, by 'Constantine' and 'Jeremiah' or by the 'Constantinian' and 'Jeremian' tendencies. These epochal events or tendencies provide the key orientation for *telling* history. The telling or narration of history is not historicism. As Yoder notes,

Each of these defining events, like the New Testament itself, must be exposited in a larger-than-life way . . . as 'legend', as something having to be recounted, bigger in its meanings than what the historians' questions about documents and causation can contain.[52]

'Constantine' names the tendency of history that must be refused. It names, as well, a metanarrative unto itself, one in which Jesus's political logic is compromised through its attempt to take over, or at least to mediate itself through, the state. We can therefore understand Yoder as attempting to provide a metanarrative antagonistic to the Constantinian metanarrative.

At the same time, it would be insufficient simply to 'out-metanarrate' Constantine; antagonistic metanarration would be meaningless without an antagonistic *concept* of metanarrative. In other words, it is not enough just to have a different metanarrative, it is also necessary to have a different kind of metanarrative, a metanarrative that is different in its very essence. Stanley Hauerwas, in a dialogue co-written with Chris Huebner, suggests that 'the way to oppose the Constantinian reading seems to require something like a metanarrative'.[53] Huebner responds that Yoder does this insofar as he 'offers a *continuous rewriting* of history'.[54] Yoder's metanarrative, then, is essentially different from Constantine's because Yoder understands metanarration as an open process. Thus Huebner remarks that Yoder 'appears to focus more on the constant process of narration and re-narration itself rather than on the actual narrative produced'.[55] This seems to be the precise path a Yoderian metanarrative should take. I would add that Yoder's re-writing is not a quantitative but an essential imperative; re-writing is demanded not just *a posteriori* but also *a priori*. We do not re-write because there happens to be quantitatively more history, we do so because of the more of time itself – in this sense, Yoder's 're-writing' is intrinsically necessary, just as is Deleuze's re-expression. There is quantitatively more history only because of the unconditioned more of time.

Yet it is not enough just to oppose unconditioned time against quantitative history. We must fold time's excess back onto the historical in order to speak differently of history, to speak of the more of history or of a historical more. Constantinian history is closed off not simply because it is a history, but because of the way its history excludes time's excess. Within Constantine's overdetermination, there are only two positions: the dominator and the dominated. One must either side with the Powers or be dominated by the Powers. Consequently, the church, or the political community of Jesus, abandons whatever historical possibilities it might open when it adopts the Constantinian strategy. In this case, the only aim it can serve is that of making history come out right. This is a history from above, narrated by the establishment. The 'right' history is one that preserves the Powers' overdetermination and domination. Even if the church, in such a case, calls attention to the domina*ted*, it still accepts the overdetermined logic of dominator and dominated. The most one can then hope for is a softening of domination, or some pious expression of mercy toward the dominated. As Yoder says, 'the meaning of history is not what the state will achieve in the way of a progressively more tolerable ordering process'.[56] Indeed, the notion that the dominated or the poor are passive recipients, rather than powerful actors, is due to a failure to underdetermine the binary of dominator and dominated.

Before we can settle into the roles of dominator and dominated, time must first emerge – and the re-writing function of a Yoderian metanarrative makes the production and narration of history inseparable from time. This is made explicit by Yoder's constant assertions that the politics of Jesus has nothing to do with making history turn out 'right'; the politics of Jesus stands or falls on its capacity to be affected by what does not fit into the 'right' history. It is also implicitly asserted by Yoder's concept of 'patience', with its insistence on the centrality of reception. Hauerwas notes how Yoder peculiarly emphasises the necessity that the gospel be received – in fact, the gospel is not fully gospel outside of its reception. As Hauerwas continues, 'The good news the gospel is becomes good news through its reception by us.'[57] The possibilities of the new aeon do not exist apart from temporal becoming. The gospel must be received because the process of reception is an affective process, an affection of time. It is through this affective-receptive process that the divine or the eternal affirms its essential temporality, and that, correspondingly, time becomes 'more like time . . . time to a higher degree'. Temporal becoming is the end, or the means that is never resolved in an end, the means of the emergence of new historical paths.

This production of new historical paths is indicated in a Yoderian metanarrative by the 'Jeremian' tendency. Jeremian logic, the historical locus of which is Israel's exile in Babylon, is one by which God (as the prophetic voice of Jeremiah) has

> instructed the people in Babylon to stay there, to renounce notions of an early return to Judaea, to settle in, to buy land and plant gardens and vineyards, to marry off their children and enjoy their grandchildren, and (especially) to, 'Seek the welfare of the city where I have sent you into

exile, and pray to the LORD on its behalf, for in its welfare you will find your welfare.'[58]

The point is that minority status is not something to be overcome. The notion of returning to a place where one is at home, where one can be a majority, is rejected. It is best to stay where one finds oneself, even as a minority. But how should one conduct oneself as a minority? Should one try to take over, to impose one's minority way of life on the majority? Should one instead forget the minority way of life and conform to, or at least compromise with, the majority?

Yoder's account of the Jeremian logic is subtle. On one hand, there should be no takeover attempt. Yet, on the other, there is no contrary demand to hole up and preserve some imagined purity of minority identity. To do so would be to turn minority identity into a kind of mini-majority. It would be to conceive minority identity in terms of the majority's model. Thus, while one is to remain a minority and to affirm one's variation from the standard, one must simultaneously become affected by this new encounter. 'Jeremiah does not tell his refugee brothers and sisters to try to teach the Babylonians Hebrew. The concern to learn goes in the other direction.'[59] This ability to be affected is an increase of power, for it expands one's capacity for re-expression or re-writing. Yoder continues by noting that, 'Jews will not only learn the local languages; they will in a few generations (and for a millennium and a half) be serving the entire ancient near eastern world as expert translators, scribes, diplomats, sages, merchants, astronomers.'[60]

The upshot of this Jeremian logic is that minoritarian existence is to be affirmed, but that doing so requires hybridity. Jeremian logic calls for the minority to encounter and inhabit the world of the majority, and in doing so to bring about new, differential, hybridised possibilities. On this point Yoder is in agreement with Deleuze, who says that the issue, when it comes to a minoritarian ethics, 'is not the distinction between major and minor language; it is one of a becoming'.[61] The minority is to use the major language in a new way, but it can do so precisely because its entrance into the major language makes the major language encounter the language of the minority. As Deleuze enjoins: 'Use the minor language to *send the major language racing*.'[62] Minority existence is minority not because it has its own identity but because it re-writes itself through encountering other modes of existence. A particular political community's affection of divine power is exercised neither through collaboration with the given Powers (as with Constantine) nor through a hypostatisation of this particular people's logic as something transcendent to other particulars. Against both of these options, the Jeremian logic is an underdetermination of the supposed binary between siding with the dominator or being passively dominated. There is, apart from these two options, the possibility of time, and this is precisely what the Jeremian strategy emphasises – the possibility of exceeding the historically available models of existence through a temporal process of re-writing.

The productive effect of Yoder's underdetermination is a diasporic 'polyglossia'. Expression of divine power becomes inseparable from the divergent expression of worldly particularity. And Yoder leaves no doubt that this divergence is without return, that the value of this divergence does not come from any anticipated re-convergence: 'To be scattered is not an hiatus, after which normalcy will resume.'[63] Divergent scattering, like patience, is not a means to an end but an end unto itself. In Yoder, as in Deleuze, ontology's or particularity's differential divergence (its disaccord without analogy) is not violence. It is, in fact, the possibility of the new. Yoder thus remarks, '"confusion of tongues" is not a punishment or a tragedy but the gift of new beginnings, liberation from a blind alley'.[64] To follow the Jeremian logic is to re-write what is given, to re-express the world from the excess of time.

Notes

1. I would suggest that what Milbank and Hart are doing explicitly is something that is quite frequently done by the post-Christian European philosophical tradition, namely making use of the figure of Christ as a means of mediating the sensible with the supersensible. In this sense, Yoder's account of Jesus, which refuses to make such a move, opens the possibility for a deployment of Christianity that would not participate in this very 'Western' Christological practice. This then raises the question of whether such a deployment would still belong to Christianity (in any recognisable sense of the term).
2. Jacques Derrida, 'On the Gift', in *God, the Gift, and Postmodernism*, ed. John D. Caputo and Michael J. Scanlon (Bloomington and Indianapolis: Indiana University Press), p. 73.
3. Ibid.
4. John Howard Yoder, *The Politics of Jesus: Vicit Agnus Noster* (Grand Rapids: Eerdmans, 1994), p. 138.
5. Ibid.

6. Ibid., p. 141.
7. Ibid.
8. In this sense Yoder's Anabaptist thought might be seen as an heir of Thomas Müntzer's. On Müntzer, see the excellent book by Alberto Toscano, *Fanaticism: On the Uses of an Idea* (London: Verso, 2010).
9. John Howard Yoder, *The Original Revolution: Essays on Christian Pacifism* (Scottsdale, PA: Herald, 2003), p. 28.
10. Yoder, *Politics of Jesus*, p. 145. There is deep problem in the structure of this sentence, which presents Jesus as moving beyond two separate groups – one Jewish, the other Gentile. Obviously Yoder has in mind the 'representatives of Jewish religion', that is, the power structure of established religion, so he is not exactly referring to an entire group of people. That said, the presentation of Jesus (and later of Christianity) as going beyond the duality of Jew and Gentile is still at work in this sentence – and this presentation is at the heart of Christianity's supersessionist logic. It should be noted, furthermore, that Yoder here makes use of a concept of 'religion' that does not exist at this historical moment, given that this concept is produced by Christianity's supersessionism. In other words, Yoder seems, on this point, to be involved in a kind of projective identification: the religion that belongs to Christian supersessionism – certainly *the* example of an established religion, if there ever was one – is attributed to 'Jewish religion', which is positioned as the enemy of a supposedly authentic Christianity.
11. Ibid., p. 145.
12. Ibid.
13. Ibid.
14. Ibid., p. 146; my emphasis.
15. Ibid., pp. 146–7.
16. David Bentley Hart, *The Beauty of the Infinite: The Aesthetics of Christian Truth* (Grand Rapids: Eerdmans, 2003), p. 354.
17. Yoder, *Politics of Jesus*, p. 32.
18. Ibid., p. 33.
19. Ibid., pp. 33, 157.
20. Yoder's stress on the importance of 'nonresistance', and on the limits of 'resistance', can introduce a terminological confusion. When I speak of immanence as 'resistance', I do not mean it in the sense that Yoder does. Yoder's point, after all, is that resistance stays within the given framework, whereas nonresistance breaks with it. The point of resistance, as I have used it elsewhere in the book, is thus in agreement with Yoder's understanding of nonresistance. In order to lessen the terminological confusion, though, in the remainder of this chapter I will use the term 'antagonism' to indicate what I have meant elsewhere by 'resistance'. Antagonism to the coordinates of the given, in fact, is what Yoder's 'nonresistance' and my 'resistance' have in common.

21. Yoder, *Original Revolution*, p. 23.
22. Yoder, *Politics of Jesus*, p. 230.
23. Yoder, *Original Revolution*, p. 15. When Yoder speaks of the secular, I take this in the positive sense of being orientated around this world. The value of the secular is thus the emphasis it gives to the particularity of the world, its complex excessiveness, and its inability to be controlled from above. Too often the name of God has become equivalent with such transcendent control, and Yoder's secularity should be seen as a mode of antagonism against such control. The God of transcendence belongs to the Powers.

    That said, there is something dangerous about Yoder's opposition of the secular to the cultic. It seems quite close to the sort of logic that runs throughout a secularism that defines itself through its opposition to or its regulation of religion. Here, I fear, Yoder's use of 'cult' can stand in for secularism's use of 'religion'. While I want to affirm the secular insofar as it calls for belief in the world, insofar as it stands for the world and against transcendent impositions, I find it necessary to criticise the secular insofar as I find that it is bound up in the colonial project. I have addressed the way this juxtaposition of affirmation and criticism operates – particularly with regard to Yoder's account of the cultic and the secular – in Daniel Colucciello Barber, *On Diaspora: Christianity, Religion, and Secularity* (Eugene, OR: Cascade, 2011), pp. 124–7. For present purposes, it is enough to say that the secular, as it is advanced in my argument here, is meant as an immediate affirmation of the world, one that is indifferent to the imagined opposition between the secular and the religious. The secular that my argument here stands against is the one that generally exists, namely the one that exists through its opposition to religion, and that therefore thinks not about the world but about imposing a certain order *onto* the world.
24. Yoder, *Original Revolution*, pp. 56–7.
25. John Howard Yoder, *Reinhold Niebuhr and Christian Pacifism* (Scottsdale, PA: Herald Press, 1968), p. 8.
26. Yoder, *Original Revolution*, p. 49; my emphasis.
27. John Howard Yoder, 'Armaments and Eschatology', *Studies in Christian Ethics* 1 (1988), p. 58.
28. Gilles Deleuze and Félix Guattari, *A Thousand Plateaus: Capitalism and Schizophrenia*, trans. Brian Massumi (Minneapolis: University of Minnesota Press, 1987), p. 105.
29. John Howard Yoder, *For the Nations: Essays Evangelical and Public* (Grand Rapids: Eerdmans, 1997), p. 3.
30. Yoder, *Original Revolution*, p. 116.
31. Stanley Hauerwas and Chris K. Huebner, 'History, Theory, and Anabaptism', in *The Wisdom of the Cross: Essays in Honor of John*

Howard Yoder, ed. Stanley Hauerwas, Chris K. Huebner, Harry J. Huebner, and Mark Thiessen Nation (Grand Rapids: Eerdmans, 1999), p. 407.

32. John Howard Yoder, *The Christian Witness to the State* (Newton, KS: Faith and Life Press, 1964), p. 18. I understand 'more truly political' not as if there were a standard ideal of the political to which the church accords better than does the state, but rather in terms of mimetic subversion. In other words, I interpret Yoder's move here as an attempt to take a dominant good, the political, and show how its formation by way of the state fails. The church thus enacts something that the state formation claims (but fails) to enact, yet this enactment does not stem from an attempt directly to enact this standard ideal. Thus 'more truly political' is an *observation* about the distinction of the church and state – an observation that presents the church as the antagonist of the state, but that articulates this antagonism in the dominant terms produced by the state. The same sort of move can be seen in Yoder's use of the term 'secular'.

33. Ibid., pp. 17–18.

34. Yoder claims: 'Though the disparagement of the cultic and the priestly elements in the old covenant has gone too far in some recent theology, it does remain true that biblical language about Christ and the church is more political (kingdom, Messiah, New Jerusalem, *politeuma*) than cultic' (*Original Revolution*, p. 18).

35. Ibid., p. 65.

36. Yoder, *Politics of Jesus*, p. 39; my emphasis.

37. Yoder, *Original Revolution*, p. 168.

38. Ibid., p. 171.

39. Ibid.

40. I should indicate my confusion regarding Yoder's apparent willingness to tolerate the role of the state. Nonresistance certainly implies that we do not 'relate' to the state, but does commitment to what is ruled by the state mean we must accord a role to the state? If the only worthy worldliness takes place through social creativity, and if the state, by virtue of its recourse to violence and overdetermination, is hindered from creativity, why not press the sheer nullity of the Powers? Ideally, Yoder says, the state should be a 'sort of delicate balance of essentially destructive forces' (*Original Revolution*, p. 74) – but it seems that constituting the state as a balance of destructive forces cedes too much ground to something without genuine constitutive capacity.

41. Ibid., p. 129.

42. Yoder, *Politics of Jesus*, p. 24.

43. According to Yoder, 'these affirmations of preexistence and creation are not given as new information, revealed for their own sake, but they are the normal, appropriate missionary way to state the priority

of Christ over the preoccupations of pagan faith'. They are made in service of 'the mission of proclamation to the pagan world that presupposes the ultimacy of creation and wants to fit Jesus *within* it'. See John Howard Yoder, *Preface to Theology: Christology and Theological Method* (Grand Rapids: Brazos, 2002), p. 130.

44. John Howard Yoder, *The Priestly Kingdom: Social Ethics as Gospel* (Notre Dame: University of Notre Dame Press, 1984), p. 51; my emphasis.
45. Ibid.
46. Ibid.
47. Yoder, *Preface*, p. 249.
48. Ibid., p. 393.
49. Ibid., p. 276.
50. Ibid.
51. Yoder, *Politics of Jesus*, p. 241; my emphasis.
52. Yoder, *For the Nations*, p. 8.
53. Hauerwas and Huebner, 'History, Theory, and Anabaptism', p. 395.
54. Ibid., p. 395; my emphasis.
55. Ibid.
56. Yoder, *Original Revolution*, p. 79.
57. Stanley Hauerwas, *With the Grain of the Universe* (Grand Rapids: Brazos, 2001), p. 220.
58. Yoder, *For the Nations*, p. 53.
59. Ibid., p. 71.
60. Ibid.
61. Deleuze and Guattari, *Thousand Plateaus*, p. 104.
62. Ibid., p. 105.
63. Yoder, *For the Nations*, p. 52.
64. Ibid., p. 63.

5

Adorno: A Metaphilosophy of Immanence

Our diagnosis of the relation between immanence and theology, now that we have looked not just at Milbank and Hart, but also at Yoder, has enabled us to see that theology, even when it takes the hegemonic form of Christianity, is not necessarily wedded to transcendence. In fact, Yoder's theology is immanent in such a way that it is able to resonate with many of the specific themes in Deleuze's thought – a minoritarian ethics, for instance, or the theory of time as Aion. This means that Deleuze's differential immanence should not be articulated in simply anti-theological terms. The intersection between differential immanence and theology is more complex, and involves affirmative, convergent valences that would be lost by a straightforwardly anti-theological – or by a straightforwardly secular – account of the possibilities opened by Deleuze's thought. We can see, especially after this account of Yoder's immanent theology, that transcendence and the naming of God ought not to be seen as the same thing. This is also to restate that the enemy of immanence is not theology, it is instead transcendence. It is thus all the more important to draw a line within theology, a line that separates theology's tendency toward transcendence from theology's tendency toward immanence. We have modelled precisely such a strategy in the previous two chapters: immanence must become antagonistic toward analogy with the same gesture that it seeks alliance with the sort of theological impulses at work in Yoder.

Part of the reason for pursuing such an alliance is that it allows immanence to disentangle itself from the presupposed opposition between the religious, or the theological, and the secular. Specifically, to ally Deleuze's differential immanence with Yoder's theology is to render it inassimilable to the terms of the debate surrounding the return of religion, or the opposition between theology and the secular. If differential immanence is allied with the theological, then it cannot belong to the secular. What is more, the theology with which it is allied sees itself as always already secular – in this sense, the terms of debate break down not only in the alliance with theology, but also within the theology itself. Along these lines, we must observe that Yoder's theology is secular not because it wants to take theology as something established and in need of secularisation. There is nothing in Yoder's secularity that accords with this developmental narrative. On the contrary, Yoder has claimed that theology is secular from the very beginning, before it was ever something like a theology that could be distinguished from something like the secular. This means that Yoder's strategy of articulating theology as secular is not to bring together two established discourses – much less to separate them, as is the case in the debate over the return of religion – but to insist that they were never separate in the first place. In fact, we can read Yoder as not even committed to the existence of these discourses: if he uses their terms – theology, or religion, and the secular – it is in order to subvert the assumption that these terms refer to discrete registers of existence; if Yoder sees these terms as always already imbricated in one another, and if the meaning of these terms depends on their distinction from one another, then what Yoder has done is insist that these terms have no meaning, or at least that they cannot have anything analogous to the meanings we presume that they have.

Yoder's theology thus calls for something that would be different from what we presently imagine to be possible. In this way, once again, he resonates with the passage of re-expression that emerges from Deleuze's differential immanence. Both Yoder and Deleuze invoke the creation of the new, and they do so through a common refusal of transcendent causality, which actually precludes the change that it claims to enable. It is in this sense, as well, that both Yoder and Deleuze are thinkers of the world. If the new is to be created, it must be created from the world in which we already exist, without reference to something that would be outside the immanence of the world and our thought of the world. Both Yoder and Deleuze invoke the unconditioned – whether in the name of God or the name of virtual intensity – and both insist that the power of the unconditioned must not be separated from the conditions of the world.

This immanence of the unconditioned and the conditioned, however, is a matter that raises certain difficulties, or at least that runs the risk of getting stuck in a paradoxical oscillation. We can say, thus far, that imagination of radical possibility cannot be separated from the present world and its limits of imagination, which means that the naming of the possible emerges in a world limited by its own names. We must say yes to the unconditioned, yes to the capacity of re-expression, but no to the idea that the sheer reality of the unconditioned is found anywhere other than in the world, here and now, to which we must say no. This is to say, furthermore, that even the unconditioned has its conditions, even re-expression begins within what is already expressed. And, finally, we can put this same point in terms of time: while time allows us to exceed the historically determined limits in which we find ourselves, it does not transcend history; time's promise must be sought from within our historical situation.

None of this should be denied. However, all of this should be further articulated. Specifically, we must further articulate the manner in which the unconditioned and the conditioned relate, which is to say that we must begin to articulate the manner in which immanence is a mediation between the unconditioned and the conditioned. The challenge of transcendence was that immanence did nothing more than bless the present state of affairs, and in order to respond to this challenge we have stressed the unconditioned power of immanence. But this unconditioned power, if it is not understood in terms of a mutual mediation with the conditioned, effectively becomes yet another transcendent fantasy: having refused to invoke a transcendent God, we may find ourselves invoking an unconditioned power of immanence that is imagined as if it transcended the conditions in which we find ourselves. What we must now stress, then, is the way that this unconditioned power is itself conditioned – and it is in order to do this that we will address the mediatic character of immanence. In other words, while we have thus far emphasised the capacity of immanence to break with the given, we must now shift registers and focus on the way that immanence – precisely because it is, in fact, immanent, and precisely because it aims to break with the given – cannot be thought outside of the given.

The Mediation of Nonidentity

We can begin by attending to the objective and subjective aspects of immanence. The vexed relation between the simultaneously conditioned and unconditioned nature of immanence can, in other words, be articulated in terms of the relation between object and subject. Immanence, first of all, is objective – in this sense it is more 'real' than 'ideal'. It is always already expressed, and so it exists apart from and prior to any sort of discrete subjectivity. That said, this objective expression cannot be straightforwardly opposed to all modes of subjectivity, for immanence, as it is expressed, sets forth an *operation* of subjectivity. There is subjectivity, but as the upshot or recoil of immanence's objectivity. This is because immanence, in its objective expression, revolves around the virtual, or around difference in itself. Such objectivity, due to its fundamentally differential character, is a matter of disequilibrium. The objective is a problem: it never presents itself as given without also presenting an unstable, problematic pressure that requires, by its very nature, the creation of new modes of existence – and the operation of subjectivity is what responds to this requirement for creation.

We can thus say that the objective is 'first', insofar as one cannot begin from subjectivity, but also that immanence – precisely because of the character of its objectivity – requires the emergence of subjectivity. There is a demand for a subject that becomes capable of re-expressing, and thus creating, immanence. Immanence is thus at once both objective and in need of production. Yet this subject of production is nothing other than an emergence of the given expression of immanence. Subjectivity and objectivity are immanent, but not identical: objectivity produces the subject, not as a discrete entity but instead as an operation of objectivity's own becoming-subject; yet by becoming-subject, the objective is itself created or produced (re-expression). The subject does not exist outside of the objective, yet it nonetheless loops back to create possibilities not already expressed by the objective. So while we can say that objectivity produces the subject, we can say in the same voice that that subject produces the objective.

How, then, are we to think this scenario – where subject and object are both produced by and productive of one another – in a non-circular way? It is time that provides the milieu of this dynamic, but even here we find a similar dynamic of distinction and indiscernibility. Time is an objective attribute of immanence, yet it is that by which the subjective operation, and thus the novel production of immanence, emerges. The subject's affection by time splits or cracks the subject – in fact, the subject is nothing but this crack of the body by time – but, in virtue of this affection, the subject is capable of affecting time. The subject's capacity depends on a pre-subjective temporality (affection or cracking of the subject by time), but, presuming this path is followed, the subject is simultaneously capable of acting upon time (becoming-affector of time, or constructing historical determination through time). We have two distinct moments – the moment of the subject's affection by time, and the moment of time's affection by the subject – that are nonetheless reciprocally constitutive. A relation of coexistence is presupposed by each moment, yet this relation of coexistence is *produced* by, or dependent upon the passage of, the distinct moments. So even when we address the relation of immanence's objective and subjective aspects in the open milieu of time, the same difficulty reoccurs. The immanence that is produced is not the same as an already-existing immanence, yet the latter is what makes the former possible. How can we think this differentiation of the former from and beyond the latter, at the same time that we think this conditioning of the former by the latter?

Here we see the need for mediation – for a mediation that would be completely immanent. In other words, it is only by providing an account of mediation that immanence can avoid getting stuck in the dilemma we have been tracking. If there is no mediation between the conditioned and the unconditioned, between the objective and the subjective, between being affected by and becoming affector of time, then immanence will find itself rather desperately asserting the above paradoxes. Thus we will not truly conceive immanence without a concept of mediation. Right away, though, we should make clear that this mediation has nothing to do with a predicament in which the transcendent is mediated *to* the immanent. Nor is it a matter of mediating something that fully pre-exists to that which is in the process of becoming – for immanence is not something that is somehow already accomplished yet in need of application, it is rather something that itself is in the process of being produced. The mediation that we need to think through is *within* immanence, it is sought in order to account for the relation between, or the middle of, the conditioned and the unconditioned.

In order to make some headway toward an immanent concept of mediation, we can turn to the work of Adorno. This may appear as a strange alliance, due to Adorno's affinity with Hegel, a philosopher who was, for Deleuze, the ultimate enemy. Yet Adorno's affinity with Hegel was a qualified one: what he takes from Hegel, above all, is the dialectic, and I want to argue that the dialectic, when it is understood in a specifically Adornian – and not broadly Hegelian – sense, is one way of thinking immanence.[1] In fact, it is not just one way of thinking immanence, it is precisely the sort of entrance into immanence that we now need, for dialectics, above all, responds to the very real demand for mediation.

We should first observe Adorno's distance from Hegel. While Adorno certainly makes use of an inherited Hegelian conceptual apparatus, what he does with it marks a genuine break with Hegel, rather than something like a modified extension or an internal critique. Adorno's negative dialectic does bear a cosmetic affinity to the Hegelian dialectic insofar as it retains the essential tripartite structure of subject, object, and concept. Yet all three of these terms revolve around what Adorno calls the 'nonidentical', and this is what nullifies any substantive affinity between the Hegelian dialectic and the negative dialectic. More fundamental than the fact that this tripartite structure is maintained is the fact that the way these three parts relate is changed: from identity to nonidentity.

That subject and object are nonidentical means, above all, that they cannot be identified, not even through mediation. Subject and object are differentiated, and mediation has to do with this relation-in-differentiation, but such meditation never has the aim of identifying subject and object. The Hegelian dialectic also feeds off this initial differentiation, for the exteriority of each to the other is what generates dialectical movement. Yet the process occasioned by the mutual exteriority of subject and object moves toward their identification: subject and object reach identity in the concept. Nonidentity, however, insists not only on the awareness that subject and object differ, but also on the essential impossibility of reconciling this differentiation through the mediation of a conceptual identification. Adorno says that the nonidentical, as that which passes between subject and object,

> is not . . . obtainable by a negation of the negative. This negation is not an affirmation itself, as it is to Hegel . . . To equate the negation of negation with positivity is the quintessence of identification; it is the formal principle in its purest form. What thus wins out in the inmost core of dialectics is the anti-dialectical principle: that traditional logic which, *more arithmetico*, takes minus times minus for a plus.[2]

In the Hegelian dialectic, then, the mutual exteriority of subject and object, or their concomitant negation, is captured by identity. Mutual exteriority becomes, under the form of identity, a thing in-itself, functionally transcendent to the dynamism of its movement. Nonidentity, on the other hand, can be understood as a way of expressing the resistance of this mutual exteriority to identity, or to the immobilisation of subject and object in the concept. Let us look more closely at the way nonidentity articulates this resistance.

Initial emphasis must be placed on the object's exteriority to the subject, which Adorno terms the 'primacy of the object'.[3] The reason for first placing the emphasis in this direction is that the general tendency of the dialectic is to drift to the side of the subject. It is because of the implicit connection between conceptual identification and the subject that, when extending the nonidentical stick into the spokes of identity, the lead hand is provided by the primacy of the object. To affirm this primacy is to affirm the logical impossibility of a subjectively driven conceptualisation. In this sense, one can turn the logic of the dialectic against Hegel's own deployment of the dialectic. 'Hegel goes against the intermittent insight of his own logic' insofar as 'positivity springs from the method – not from the thing, as in Hegel's view it should'.[4] Dialectics must keep faith with the exterior 'thing', or object, for the object's exteriority is what occasions the movement of the subject. As with Deleuze's differential immanence, subjectivity emerges out of objectivity.

Hegel, against both Adorno's primacy of the object and Deleuze's differential immanence, makes the thing that matters not the object but the method. He abstracts the method of dialectic from the very objectivity that presses the need for dialectics. Instead of making the method a means of commitment to the thing's exteriority to the subject, he makes this exteriority a moment internal to the subject's process of bringing the method to its goal. The fulfilment of the dialectic is thus conceived not as a turning back out into the object, an encounter with the given expression, but rather as a turning back in on the dialectical logic, as a purely formal operation. Adorno stands against this, observing that 'objects do not go into their concept without leaving a remainder'.[5] The attempt to identify the object with the concept only creates a world littered with cracked objects, or with objective fragments that are too difficult to conceive. This remainder, even in its muteness with respect to conceptual expression, articulates a 'No' in the face of the concept's identification. The object's recalcitrance to identity thus witnesses to the nonidentical, where nonidentity turns the reality of the thing's expression against the desire to transcend, by way of identification, what is given. In this sense, 'the nonidentical would be the thing's own identity against its identifications'.[6]

But it is not just the object that departs from the logic of identity. There must be a corresponding – even if, for the reasons we have mentioned, a secondarily emphasised – departure of the subject. The movement of the subject is occasioned by the exteriority of the object to the subject's conceptual identifications. How then, having asserted the primacy of the object, should we articulate a subjective operation that is also irreducible to identity? What sort of operation of subjectivity might be imagined, such that it would be generated by the primacy of the object? What sort of subjective operation would provide the primacy of the object with a worthy ally in its resistance toward identification? This sort of operation must be located in the *movement* of the mutual exteriority that identity immobilises. The movement is one in which the subject appears not in conceptual triumph over the object, but on the contrary as dispossessed of its imperium by the object. The subject is still there, it is just there as a subjective operation, or as the effect of the object's exteriority.

This is a new kind of subject, one whose essence is not to command an imperium but rather to exercise a strength that thinks against such an imperium. The essence of the subject is not the capacity to adequately cover the otherness of things with the concept, to bring objects under identity; it is the capacity to become adequate to, to think constructively, the movement generated by the object's exteriority. If the object's remainder to identity 'come[s] to contradict the traditional norm of adequacy', then the subject must match the demand this contradiction sets forth by rejecting its own traditional role as conceptual adequator – that is, by refusing the inertia of its presumed role.[7] 'If thinking is to be true' – to be adequate in a new manner – 'it must also be a thinking against itself'.[8] In fact, 'the best energy of thought', Adorno says, 'outstrips . . . the thinker'.[9] Why is this the case? Because it involves the thinker, without reserve, in the object's exteriority. The operation of subjectivity is not to identify the object with its concept, it is to think from the object, or even to think as the object. And this itself requires a new sense of 'objectivity': the fact of the object's exteriority must no longer be understood under a category of objectivity that is opposed to subjectivity; it must be changed from something discretely different from the subject into something that touches on the heart of the subject. Objectivity must be understood as something that affects the subject at a point prior to its own identity with itself. Thinking, the operation of the subject, becomes 'intratemporal, motivated, progressive motion', the mobile thought of the object in the subject. The subject becomes the operation of the object's thought.[10] This means that what the nonidentical names is an immanence of subject and object – that is, a mediation of subject and object that, far from shutting down their immanent movement, actually insists on keeping it open. Dialectical mediation does not immobilise immanence, it maintains its fluidity.

Adorno, against a relation of difference and identity according to the two and the one, claims that subject and object are not simply two, insofar as their mutual exteriority constitutes a movement in which the two are in immanence. But he likewise insists that subject and object are not simply one, since this immanent movement is generated by the exteriority of each to the other. Subject and object 'are neither an ultimate duality nor a screen hiding ultimate unity'.[11] Adorno proposes, instead of a dialectic of two and one, an immanence of differential constitution: subject and object 'constitute one another as much as – by virtue of such constitution – they depart from one another'.[12] Difference is no longer opposed to identity as its inverse. It is rather understood as constitutive of an immanent movement – a movement, moreover, whose immanence, because it is nonidentical rather than purely identical, need not be dialectically opposed to difference.

Yet if nonidentity belongs to an immanence blocked by a discrete duality of subject and object, then why even retain these terms when conceiving the nonidentical? Why not put subject and object out of play and instead speak immediately of their nonidentical immanence? The answer is that the nonidentical, while in excess of subject and object considered as discrete things, is not something simply outside subject and object. Immanence has to do with a *more* of reality, but this more is nonidentical – that is, it is not something immediately apprehended, it is instead something that emerges in the mediation of subject and object. Subject and object are not two discrete poles, they 'are resultant categories of reflection' – indeed, 'they are not positive, primary states of fact but negative throughout, expressing nothing but nonidentity'.[13] This nonidentity, as I take it up, can be understood as naming the mediation of re-expression, the mediation between the given and the production of what would break with the given. From this vantage, subject and object become ways of naming two tendencies within immanence: subjectivity names the operation by which we exceed the given, it names the capacity to re-expressively draw on the power of the unconditioned; objectivity names the priority of the conditioned, the weight of the expression in which we always already find ourselves.

It is in this sense, then, that the dialectic of subject and object speaks to our need for a mediation between the conditioned and the unconditioned. Immanence is nonidentical. Specifically, it is the nonidentity of the unconditioned and the conditioned. What is nonidentical is the excess of the unconditioned over the conditioned and the utter conditionality of this excess. Nonidentity points to that which enables us to pass from one expression to another, to create the new, at the same time that it points to the givenness of our expression. In doing so, it avoids, or negates, two erroneous tendencies: while we would forsake the unconditioned if we were to think solely in terms of the conditioned, the endeavour of thought would also be misbegotten if we were to ignore the conditionality of thought's endeavour to draw on the unconditioned. In other words, while the unconditioned is that which enables thought to resist the given, the production of this resistance must not be abstracted from the given conditions in which this resistance takes place. This point can be framed from an historicist, or perhaps sociological, vantage: the concept of the unconditioned, though it may really be *of the unconditioned*, does not permit us to abstract it from its relation to the historical or social conditions in which it is produced. But the point can also be framed within the terms of immanence itself. While the expression of immanence remains in immanence with its cause, and is thus capable of construction by way of the unconditioned, this construction is always re-expression, it is always said of an already-expressed immanence.

Conceiving the More

But what about the concept? We have seen how the dialectic of subject and object, as nonidentity, mediates the conditioned and unconditioned aspects of immanence, yet we have not addressed the third element of the dialectic structure, that of the concept. This is an extremely important matter, given our concern to name new possibilities of existence. For what does it mean to name if not to conceive? To name a possibility that is not given is to engage in an act of conceptualisation. Concepts can thus become names of the new. So if we do not find a way to conceive – or to conceive from – the nonidentical more, then the novelty of this more cannot be created.

The difficulty with the concept, in Hegel's version of the dialectic, was that it refused the object's primacy. The concept, because it aimed at identity, could not think from the object and thus left behind a remainder, which Adorno calls the 'nonconceptual'.[14] What Adorno is saying is that the concept, insofar as it proceeds according to identity, cuts itself off from what must be thought; what the concept fails to think – that is, the nonconceptual – is the very thing that needs to be conceived. It may be useful to observe what is being done with this term. The nonconceptual can be understood as referring to the primacy of the object, to the objective exteriority that the concept has failed to think. In this sense, the nonconceptual falls on the side of the object. Yet the nonconceptual can also be understood as referring to the concept *in its failure*. This is to say that the nonconceptual is at once exterior to the concept and completely directed toward the concept; it is the mark, at the level of conceptuality, of what is more than the conceptual. Consider, for instance, Adorno's critique of the concept of matter:

> The fact that, just by talking about matter, one endows this matter with form – that is, conceptual form – should not be confused with the meaning of this form itself. The peculiarity of the concept of . . . matter, is that we are here using a concept or speaking of a principle which, by its meaning, refers to something which is not a concept or a principle.[15]

It will not work, when one wishes to conceive matter, just to extend conceptuality to matter, nor even to improve the concept of matter. This is because, with something like matter, conceptuality is trying to think something that is resistant to the form of conceptuality. All one can think here is the failure of the concept, and only by thinking this failure of the concept can one begin to experiment with what remains outside the concept, with different modes of conceptuality, which might emerge from what is outside the given conceptual form. Such tasks are encapsulated in the notion of the nonconceptual, which thus marks the nonidentity between an exteriority of the object and a mode of conceptuality that does not exist, that is lacking in the present. Accordingly, the nonconceptual is at once an insistence on the reality of what remains unconceptualised, a radical refusal of the present mode of conceptualisation, and an invocation of a new kind of conceptuality that would break with the present in the name of that which is unnamed, or unconceptualised.

Attending a bit further to this invocation, we should make clear that it does not involve saying: one version of the concept has failed, let's try another! We cannot just try out a new version of the concept, we must understand the failure of the concept we want to overcome. Since this failure is marked by the nonconceptual, then we should say that invocation for a new kind of concept is one that can emerge only by affirming the nonconceptual, by understanding the failure of the concept. This is to say that while any new version of the concept must think the unconditioned, it must also think the condition we already inhabit, a condition that is shaped by and implicated in the concept we seek to surpass. Therefore it is not that we must give up the search for a new kind of concept. It is just that this concept will be new only if we are first able to grasp the nature of present conceptuality's failure. We need, in other words, a concept of the concept; we need to conceive the failure of the concept. And to do this is to think from that which the old concept denied, that is, the nonconceptual. After all, it is in virtue of the nonconceptual that we say the old concept has failed, and so the measure of a new concept will be its ability to speak from this nonconceptual excess. This is to repeat the impulse behind a minoritarian ethics: only by becoming cracked, only by becoming affected by that which is minor in relation to the regnant standard, are we able to create the new.

We do not break with the given unless we conceive the given form of the concept. This is the critical aspect of mediation. But there is also a constructive aspect of mediation, for the concept of the concept criticises in the name of the need to construct new names. Thus the necessity of mediation by the concept of the concept is inseparable from the task of explicitly attending to the nonconceptual, for the nonconceptual is that which forces us into the 'more' of being. Any sense of the beyond, of that which exceeds the given, must be conceived according to this 'more'. But what, exactly, is meant by the more? Yoder, we should recall, speaks of a 'more', and locates this within the world. It is a more of secularity. And Deleuze, of course, insists on an immanence of the cause of being – which, as unconditioned, is more than the given – and the world's expression of being. Adorno follows suit: 'What is, is more than it is. This "more" is not imposed upon it but remains immanent to it, as that which has been pushed out of it.'[16] What is, is more than what it is, it is excessive to itself. What is, and the more, are nonidentical. The metaphysical dimension of what is, the more, must be conceived in a secular manner. As Adorno says, the 'interpretive eye which sees more in a phenomenon than it is – and solely because of what it is – secularizes metaphysics'.[17] Like Yoder, Adorno's secularity is one that belongs not to given discourse about the world but instead to the emergence of the world precisely where it has not been conceived, where it is nonconceptual and thus unnamed, where it emerges both as what it is and as what is more than we have conceived to be possible.

The more invokes a subjective, conceptual operation, though this operation must not be thought of as coming from beyond the world. Without the more, it would be pointless to speak of a conceptual production; without a new kind of conceptuality, the more will remain outside of thought, as the nonconceptual. Adorno thus imagines a concept that, in its relation to the more as nonidentity, would be capable of bringing forth the more in what is. Such a concept is not propositional; it is not a reflection of what is. On the contrary, a new conceptuality would be one that abandons the demand for correlation with possible objects and involves itself in a tangle with the material. 'Nonconceptuality, inalienable from the concept, disavows the concept's being-in-itself. It changes the concept. The concept of nonconceptuality cannot stay with itself, with epistemology; epistemology obliges philosophy to be substantive.'[18] Such a concept breaks with epistemologically defined possibilities in favour of a reality that is outside of such possibilities; it is not propositional but constructive, it does not accord with possibilities but seeks to produce new ones.

We should not be surprised, given this constructivism, that Deleuze aligns his own account of the concept with Adorno's. Philosophy, he says, must reach 'the nonpropositional form of the concept', which 'is therefore closer to what Adorno called "negative dialectic"'.[19] So it does not matter whether we speak in Deleuzian or Adornian terms, in each case immanence requires a concept that names possibilities into reality, and that does so in the name of what is somehow already there, yet unnamed. Adorno also agrees with Deleuze that such construction is re-expressive. The subjective operation of creation is always *of* what is objective. Thought, Adorno says, must labour 'subjectively according to the demands of the object'.[20] In fact, thought 'must transform the concepts which it, as it were, brings in from outside into those which the object has by itself, into that which the object would itself like to be'.[21] Thus the subject really produces the concept, but this concept must achieve immanence with the desire of the object.

This juxtaposition of a subjective operation that really constructs being with an expressivity that is prior to the subject places a strenuous demand on thought. Adorno recognises this when he says that thought always takes place by way of its 'blind spot'.[22] The cost of thinking a more that is nonconceptual, and of generating rather than reflecting what is, is learning to think with a certain blindness. To locate thought's metaphysical dimension – its capacity to imagine and name that which exceeds the initially presented – in blindness is to turn against the metaphysical tradition as it is conceived within the Platonic patrimony. Blindness is no longer that which one experiences as a result of not seeing the light, or as a result of coming back into the world having already seen the light. Blindness, in other words, is no longer the privation of an already existing light. It is rather that by which one learns to see, it is its own, nonconceptual sight, a sight that does not take its cues from the given form of conceptuality.

One finds a new command: do not seek the light but move into the place of blindness. Such becoming-blind is not without interest, for it opens onto the more of what is. But this more cannot be separated from becoming blind. Deleuze says the same, insofar as it is by way of the crack that we accede to the unconditioned power of time. As with Adorno's more, Deleuze's power of the unconditioned is inseparable from a dispossession of our present sort of health – and this dispossession is inseparable from its risks. And let us not forget Yoder, who locates divine power in a passionate body. The power of immanence does not exist outside the passage of its construction, and this passage requires a capacity and will to be affected, without reserve, without any reservation in the present.

'We lack creation': A Deleuzian Metaphilosophy?

The dialectic of immanence: object and subject, conditioned and unconditioned, conceiving the concept and conceiving the nonconceptual more ... we have seen the various ways that the thought of immanence is a thought of mediation. In each of these instances, mediation concerns the relation between the thought of the given and the thought of the novel. This is also to say that mediation concerns a break with present modes of thought as well as an experimentation with new modes of thought. In this sense, the mediation of immanence does not belong to philosophy, where such belonging would involve characterising immanence as one instance within the broader category of philosophy. For if the mediation of immanence concerns a break with the present mode of thought, and if philosophy belongs to this present mode, then immanence cannot be included within philosophy. On the contrary, immanence must exceed philosophy – and not only as it breaks with the present mode of thought, but also as it experiments with new modes. In order to articulate immanence's excess to philosophy, we can introduce the terms of metaphilosophy and nonphilosophy. Metaphilosophy here refers to immanence's break with the present mode of thought; it is a philosophical practice that attempts to understand philosophy's present failure. Because metaphilosophy insists on the unredeemability of this failure, it is not invested in improving philosophy or getting philosophy back to doing what it is supposed to be doing. Metaphilosophy is thus philosophical only in the sense that it must proceed philosophically in order to comprehend what is called philosophy; its philosophical practice is not meant to correlate to a better, future philosophy, it is instead meant to depart from philosophy.

Nonphilosophy, on the other hand, is that place toward which metaphilosophy enables one to depart.[23] Place, of course, is a difficult term, for the very point of speaking of nonphilosophy is to indicate unrecognisability, or to use the 'non-' as a means of breaking any correlation between the philosophy opposed by metaphilosophy and the nonphilosophy that would emerge. In this sense, it is not quite right to say that nonphilosophy is a place – it is a place only in a utopic manner, it is the nowhere that is freed up by learning to live with the blindness that metaphilosophy reveals. If nonphilosophy is thought in terms of place, then it should be said that it refers to many places, and to places that do not already exist, places that must be made, places that will be made only insofar as one enters a metaphilosophical passage. In short, then, nonphilosophy refers to immanence's experimentation with new modes of thought, modes not reducible to the present mode of thought known as philosophy. This means that while other modes of thought that are defined as other than philosophy – such as art or science – may become forms of nonphilosophy, they are not essential instances of nonphilosophy. What is essential to nonphilosophy is its difference from the present mode of thought. Recalling, then, that metaphilosophy seeks to understand and break with this present mode of thought, we can say that the mediation of immanence may be understood in terms of the mediation between metaphilosophy and nonphilosophy.

Thought is of value only as long as it outstrips itself, as it becomes something else – and this outstripping or becoming takes place in virtue of what is *not* attended to by thought. Nonphilosophy thus names an imperative of immanent practice that makes philosophy open onto the unthought. It affirms that thought must not stop short of the unconditioned. But nonphilosophy, precisely because it is *non*-philosophy, cannot be sought by a simple extension of philosophy as it stands. The practice of thought accedes to the unlimited only by thinking against the limits in which it finds itself; it accedes to the unconditioned only by thinking against its conditions. We cannot move into the nonphilosophical without metaphilosophically understanding and criticising the constellation of concepts that keep us from thinking the unthought. The work of Deleuze, though unparalleled in its attempt to conceive immanence, does not often emphasise this metaphilosophical aspect of immanence. His philosophy, it is often said, is one of affirmation, of excess, of overcoming. Where, in all of this, is there a sense of philosophy's failures and limits? And if, in fact, there is no metaphilosophical sensibility to immanence, at least insofar as Deleuze develops it, does this mean immanence cannot speak to the limits of our existence and the way they affect us, making us sad, frustrated, and hopeless?

Franco 'Bifo' Berardi rightly discerns a shift in Deleuze's work, or more precisely in Deleuze's work with Guattari, where the question of politics is most explicitly posed. He notes that they often answered this question through the invocation of desire, but that as their work continued through the years it became more intensely attentive to finitude, to limitation. According to Berardi, this shift, with its diminution of emphasis placed on desire's directly creative capacity, is on the mark. He states without reservation what they only gesture at:

> Today, the rhetoric of desire – the most important and creative contribution that the authors of *Anti-Oedipus* brought to the movements of hope – seems exhausted to me, waiting for a dimension and a movement capable of renewing it. In their last two books . . . the rhetoric of desire seems already attenuated, if not silenced. What emerges instead is the awareness of the entropy of sense in existential experience and historical perspective, the consciousness of fading, aging and death. This is just what we need today: an awareness of depression that would not be depressing.[24]

What Berardi calls for, and what he discerns Deleuze hinting at, is the basic concern of metaphilosophy. When we live in conditions of depression, it does not suffice to call for an overcoming of depression's limits. That too would be depressing, it would no doubt extend the depression into the future. The way out of depression is to have an 'awareness' of it, to understand why philosophy, as it now stands, has not enabled us to think outside of depression's limits. In order to develop our concept of metaphilosophy, then, let us begin by looking at the degree to which Deleuze enables metaphilosophy to play a role his account of immanence.

Deleuze, in *What is Philosophy?* (one of the later works to which Berardi refers), grants tremendous value to 'the concept'. In fact, the answer to his titular question is 'the creation of concepts'.[25] Deleuze thus provides us with his own concept of the concept. Central for him is the concept's 'autopoetic' character – that is, the manner in which the concept is self-producing. The concept enjoys 'a self-positing of itself' and is a 'philosophical reality'. This reality, as what is produced by the concept, does not exist outside conceptual production; yet insofar as the concept emerges from 'free creative activity', its subjective activity gives rise to an objective reality. The concept, then, 'posits itself to the same extent that it is created'.[26] This power of the concept belongs to the concept by right, it is essential to the concept – and it is this right that Deleuze conceives with his concept of the concept.

Philosophy becomes nothing less than the production of concepts, and this production is simultaneously a production of philosophy itself. Deleuze casts this concept of the concept in terms of 'the image of thought, the image thought gives itself of what it means to think, to make use of thought, to find one's bearings in thought'.[27] For him, there is no image of thought except 'infinite movement or the movement of the infinite'.[28] This movement, which philosophy takes up in the concept, expels every pre-conceived image of what thought must be. Such images are in fact limits set on thought, and the image of infinite movement is not so much another, better image of thought as that which takes up conceptual production, prior to any image. In this sense, there is no image of thought, only the movement of the unthought. To pose infinite movement against every image of thought is actually to pose the intrinsic right of the concept against any image that would measure it, for 'the concept is act of thought, it is thought operating at infinite . . . speed'.[29]

Deleuze's concept of the concept, however, is not metaphilosophical. This is because its concern is not to think the conditions in which such autopoetic philosophical production has been blocked, but rather to demand, in the manner of a manifesto, that philosophy assert – by immediately practising – its intrinsic powers, the capacities that belong to it by right. The exercise of such capacities would open onto nonphilosophy, for they would involve philosophy's constant exceeding of any image of itself. If philosophy is defined by a given image of thought, then it is only by becoming-nonphilosophical that philosophy can realise Deleuze's account of its essence as infinite movement. To define philosophy in terms of the concept is therefore to demand not only the creation of concepts, but also the creation of philosophy itself. As Deleuze puts it here, in his concept of the concept, the point of philosophy is to exceed itself: the essence of philosophy is nonphilosophy. This nonphilosophical aim ought to be affirmed – the problem, however, is the seeming absence of a metaphilosophical tendency. We must ask: what is the relation between this capacity for creation, which belongs to philosophy's nonphilosophical tendency, and the conditions out of which such creation emerges? This is a question posed by metaphilosophy, and Deleuze's own account of the concept cannot respond to it. His account does not concern itself with this question, which indicates the lack of metaphilosophy in Deleuze, at least at this point.

Yet if this metaphilosophical question is here unaddressed, it is raised elsewhere by Deleuze, when he makes the proclamation: 'We lack creation.'[30] That which philosophy has, *by right*, is precisely that which, *in fact*, we lack – a fact that Deleuze emphasises in the following sentence: '*We lack resistance to the present.*' This conjunction of 'lacks' implies that the creation invoked by philosophy bears some kind of relation with resistance to what is. Does Deleuze, apart from this implied conjunction, develop such a relation? There must be some mediation between resistance to what is ('the present') and creation of something else. It is this mediation – between a philosophy against and a philosophy exceeding the present – that raises the question of metaphilosophy. Deleuze, by insisting on the need for resistance, separates creation from what already is; by demanding that philosophy create, he presupposes the capacity to resist. What he does not do, however, is provide a link between the reciprocal yet distinct operations of resistance (thinking against the present) and creation (producing the new).

Let us try to provide this link. On one side, if creation is really possible, then there must be something that exceeds the present, even if only as an intrinsic right of the concept. On the other, if resistance is lacking, then we do not already have, in any meaningful manner, this excess to the present. So while creation requires something that exceeds the present, this excess needs to emerge through resistance. The excess to the present, which enables creation, can emerge only if the present is first resisted. Accordingly, we can say that if creation is lacking, then this is because the excess from which we create is also lacking. And this excess is lacking because we are not resisting. Conceptual creation only has meaning, therefore, against the background of resistance; it does not pre-exist but depends on the act of resistance. This is the link between resistance and creation: only by resisting do we stir up the sort of excess to the present that allows us to create.

If creation depends on resistance, then the constructive moment is mediated by the critical moment; the nonphilosophical tendency depends on the metaphilosophical tendency. But what does this mean for Deleuze's own account of the concept as autopoetic? What does this mean for his claim that philosophy possesses by right, quite apart from any factual conditions, the capacity to create concepts? When Deleuze presents such claims, he fails to consider the conditions from which philosophy emerges. We lack creation, but why? Deleuze tends to ignore this metaphilosophical question, he tends to presume that, if we lack creation, it will suffice simply to invoke the need for creation. Yes, we lack creation, but still . . . philosophy is about the creation of concepts! The concept is autopoetic! Create! This is the sort of immanence Deleuze gives us when he evades metaphilosophy, when he responds to the lack of creation by invoking a manifesto on behalf of creation. There is no mediation here, no question of why we lack creation, nor of how his own account of philosophy – as something with the intrinsic right to create concepts – might be shaped by the very same conditions that produce our lack of creation. If philosophy creates concepts by right, then why is it not, in fact, creating them? Should we just appeal to philosophy to try again, to do better this time? There is something conservative in this – conservative of philosophy, or of our concept of philosophy – when what is needed, on the contrary, is to understand the failure of such philosophy, to break it down, to find places of breakdown.

Of course, there is more to the story. As I have mentioned, Deleuze does insist on the need for resistance to the present, he does gesture toward – but without developing – a metaphilosophical mediation of creation by resistance. It is just that, surrounding this undeveloped gesture, there is another tendency that responds to creation's lack by immediately calling for creation. So while Deleuze calls for philosophy to remake itself anew (to become a different philosophy, a nonphilosophy) and likewise draws attention to the need for criticism of philosophy (a metaphilosophical resistance to the present), he does not think the relation between them. We need nonphilosophy, and we need metaphilosophy, but their mediation is lacking. And it is because this mediation is lacking that the metaphilosophical tendency remains undeveloped in Deleuze. While Deleuze recognises that resistance to the present is lacking, he fails to take this metaphilosophical lack seriously, and this is because he fails to recognise that a *mediation* between nonphilosophical creation and metaphilosophical resistance is lacking.

The confusion this failure produces can be exemplified by his discussion (in *What is Philosophy?*) of chaos. Philosophy, he claims, must turn to chaos in order to surpass its limits. Chaos provides a rejoinder to philosophy's image of itself, it haunts philosophy as that which it has not thought. It is philosophy's nonphilosophical remainder, but it is a remainder that, far from being marginal to philosophy, subverts philosophy's core. This remainder is central to philosophy, which must attain 'an essential relationship with the No that concerns it'.[31] Chaos's 'No' enacts a becoming-nonphilosophical of philosophy: 'nonphilosophy is found where the [immanent philosophical] plane confronts chaos'.[32] And this chaotic motivation or encounter is not occasional, but constant. Philosophy does 'not need the No as beginning, or as the end in which [it] would be called upon to disappear by being realized, but at every moment of [its] becoming or [its] development'.[33] The becoming-nonphilosophical of philosophy, then, requires that philosophy affirm the immanence of thought and chaos. Just as Adorno calls for a thought that proceeds from the nonconceptual, so Deleuze calls for a thought that proceeds from chaos. Nonphilosophy persists in the reality of the chaotic, in excess of the organisation of the present. Chaos is the place one goes in order to create, in order to find what exists in excess of the present. This is why philosophy, as the creation of concepts, must 'plunge into the chaos'.[34]

Yet what philosophy brings out of or extracts from chaos is not the same as the chaos into which it has plunged. In fact, Deleuze continues by saying that the reason philosophy plunges into chaos is, 'We defeat it only at this price.'[35] This tosses us back into an unmediated relation between what already is and what is created. The existence of chaos is what makes possible creation in excess of the present, but what is created is not chaos – indeed, it defeats chaos. If chaos did not exist, there would be no creation, but the effect of creation is to 'defeat' chaos. We are thus left in a confused predicament. Thought's relation to chaos is ambivalent: it must plunge into chaos, but in doing so it must seek to defeat the same chaos.

Why does Deleuze find himself in this predicament? Why is the demand for nonphilosophy tied up with the demand for a prophylactic against – or the defeat of – the same chaos that enables the nonphilosophical? It is because Deleuze approaches chaos solely from the vantage of nonphilosophy; there is no metaphilosophical account of why chaos appears, from the perspective of the present, as both the greatest promise and the greatest danger. Deleuze addresses chaos with the sole concern of articulating how creation may break with the present expression of existence on the basis of something within this expression. Chaos fits this need quite well, for it is already there, in the present expression, but as that which is foreclosed –

rendered 'chaotic' – by the present. Creation can thus take place by pursuing what already exceeds the present order, even if only as chaotic tendency.

Yet this only intensifies the confusion. What, exactly, is the relation between chaos and creation? Is it that chaos is already exceeding the present, and creation takes place by removing whatever limits chaos's excessiveness? Or is it that chaos is ineffectual, or insufficient, unless it is constructed by the concept? On the one hand, the former interpretation seems right, for chaos is what allows us to go beyond the present and must be affirmed as such, in its sheer excess to the present; on the other, the latter interpretation seems right, for the purpose of chaos is not its sheer excess but the occasion it provides, an occasion that also requires defeating chaos (rather than affirming it). If the former interpretation is correct, if chaos is to be affirmed as such, then there is no sense to Deleuze's claim that chaos must also be defeated, that chaos must be rendered consistent with the ordering of the cosmos, so as to give rise to a 'chaosmos'.[36] But if we then side with the latter interpretation, we find another, different problem: if we say that chaos only serves as the material for creation and that the point of this creation is to defeat the material, then in what sense can we agree with Deleuze's insistence on the 'No' of chaos? In such a scenario, the 'No' of chaos is relativised by its relation to philosophical creation, and this would undermine the very affirmation of the 'No', of the nonphilosophical tendency, on which Deleuze insists.

Without metaphilosophical mediation, chaos is both that which enables conceptual creation and that which is defeated by conceptual creation. If, however, we begin to articulate how nonphilosophy is mediated by metaphilosophy, then chaos ceases to play these two antinomical roles. Metaphilosophy, because it addresses the relation between the unconditioned and the conditions from which we conceive the unconditioned, allows us to think about chaos in a more precise way. It allows us to think about chaos not as something immediately exceeding the present, but rather as a concept of something exceeding the present – a concept, furthermore, that emerges from within conditions of the present. With regard to the present in which creation is lacking, chaos provides a way of conceiving a more of what is. To conceive chaos, from the vantage of the present, is to affirm something more than the present. But the concept of chaos, even as it proclaims the more, is also shaped by the conditions of the present. Metaphilosophy then forces us to think not just about chaos but also about the conditions that make us imagine the more *simply in terms of* chaos – in terms of a choice between a limited order (cosmos) and chaos. Presuming these terms, it makes sense to side with the latter, for the latter allows us to move against the present. But if we if leave it in these terms we are in danger of being engulfed by the chaos we choose – hence Deleuze's concern to defeat the chaos into which we plunge. Once again we encounter a binary, now between plunging and defeating, that comes from the lack of metaphilosophy. It comes from a failure to conceive the conditions that force chaos to appear as both promise and peril. If we do not conceive these conditions that oppose the present order to chaos, our attempt to escape them will only invert them.

Shame, Suffering, and Metaphilosophy

The simple demand to create, when there is, as Berardi would put it, a 'depression' of creativity, is itself depressing. If we are to create beyond depression, then we must become aware of depression. Depression, the lack of creation, must itself be conceived. We have so far seen how Deleuze gives us nonphilosophy without any metaphilo-sophical mediation. If this is all there is to immanence, then imma-nence is depressing, precisely because it does not give attention to the depression that now surrounds our lack of creation. We therefore need to find a way to conceive immanence metaphilosophically. We need to construct, within immanence, an awareness of depression, of the wretchedness of our present existence. This, in itself, is resistance, and it is only through such resistance that we can mediate creation of the new. I will proceed along these lines by drawing on Adorno, but only after looking at moments in Deleuze's thought where we find partial indications of a metaphilosophy. My aim is to weave together these indications with certain Adornian insights in order to make immanence metaphilosophical.

We have already seen that Deleuze, when he proclaims that we lack creation, also proclaims that we lack resistance to the present. This lack of resistance, he implies, has a connection to 'shame'. It is shame-ful that philosophy fails to resist the present. Faced with such lack of resistance, the production of resistance now seems to require that philosophy become capable of thinking this shame. Metaphilosophy, as I want to develop it, thus emerges through shame: philosophy's collusion with the present state of affairs gives rise to shame, and any exodus from this collusion requires that we conceive and display critically this collusion. If philosophy is to create, or even to resist, it must conceive its failure to carry out these tasks. Every demand that philosophy open onto the outside is shadowed by an awareness that it fails to do so, an awareness that in this case is felt in the affect of shame. Metaphilosophy, by taking seriously this awareness, turns the shadow into a real condition of thought.

Deleuze's treatment of shame is occasioned by reference to Primo Levi's discussion of 'the shame of being a man'.[37] This very way of putting it reminds us that it is not a matter of simple guilt about a specific event, but rather of being 'sullied' by a 'catastrophe', the effects of which extend beyond the roles of executor and victim, and beyond the specific chronological demarcation from which it stems.[38] Shame refers to the fact that our world is such that we can survive only by 'compromise'.[39] The exercise and pursuit of our existence cannot be abstracted from its conditions, and these conditions are those that govern events such as the Shoah. Shame, then, lies in the fact that our existence accepts, on some basic level, these conditions of existence. For this reason, Deleuze says, it is not

> only in the extreme situations described by Primo Levi that we experience the shame of being human. We also experience it in insignificant conditions, before the meanness and vulgarity of existence that haunts democracies, before the propagation of these modes of existence and of thought-for-the-market, and before the values, ideals, and opinions of our time.[40]

The conditions that governed the Shoah make themselves felt throughout life, even in its everyday practice – and the practice of philosophy does not stand outside the scope of these conditions. Deleuze makes this point by ironising Heidegger's claim to grasp the destiny of thought. The destiny that appears in Heidegger, Deleuze says, is connected to the German philosopher's own collusion with the Nazis: it is 'as if shame had to enter into philosophy itself'.[41] It has, both epochally in Heidegger and everyday in our shame.

Philosophy does not stand outside this compromised existence. Shame has entered the heart of thought – indeed, it is that which calls for thought. The unthought is not just nonphilosophical excess, it is also metaphilosophical shame. The faculty of thought does not enable us to consider this shame from a distance, or to transcend it, for thought is itself ashamed – and it will only increase its shame as long as it attempts to keep a distance. Whatever autonomy thought might have by *right*, no matter how powerful its autopoetic capacities may be, the *fact* is that it too is compromised. Thought does not feel its power immediately. What it feels is shame – shame that it has failed to resist, much less create. Philosophy, the practice that ought to generate possibilities of life, to conceive the new, is struck by its ignoble collusion with the present. 'The ignominy of the possibilities of life that we are offered appears from within. We do not feel ourselves outside of our time but continue to undergo shameful compromises with it.'[42] Philosophy, because it does not stand outside shameful conditions, must be understood as having failed. It is insufficient simply to recommence philosophy; we must critically conceive philosophy's compromises. This is a metaphilosophical task. When philosophy does not stand outside shame, when it is imprisoned by shame, it becomes necessary to conceive shame. When philosophy cannot take a distance from its collusion with the present, it becomes necessary to take a distance from this sort of philosophy. And when philosophy fails to generate new possibilities of life, it becomes necessary to generate new possibilities of thought. As Deleuze says, the 'feeling of shame is one of philosophy's most powerful motifs'.[43] This motif must become a metaphilosophical motive.

Metaphilosophy, as I define the term, is not a *philosophy* about philosophy, for it seeks to make experience, which is often excluded from philosophy, into an essential matter of thought. If metaphilosophy were simply a philosophical account of philosophy, it would lack the capacity to think the sort of affects excluded by the philosophy it aims to resist. If philosophy fails to take seriously the depression that surrounds it, then metaphilosophy, which wants to become aware of such depression, is not merely 'philosophy'. Metaphilosophy becomes resistance to philosophy precisely insofar as it makes central for thought that which pre-existing philosophy has failed to think. If present philosophy is implicated in compromised life, then metaphilosophy must think this compromise, and particularly the way in which our implication in compromised life registers itself affectively.

One finds an important convergence between Deleuze and Adorno around this metaphilosophical awareness of philosophy's fundamental implication in compromised life. For Deleuze, as we have just observed, this failure of philosophy appears affectively (in the feeling of shame) and demands that we become adequate to such an affect. We find the same sort of configuration in Adorno. For Adorno, the conditions of our existence have rendered the classical practice of philosophy inoperative and functionless. Such philosophy never exists except as an alibi, since the maladies of existence have outstripped any philosophical capacity to explain and reconcile their contingency. Philosophy cannot keep pace with the degree and accumulation of the pain, terror, and meanness of our actual experience. Adorno claims that this failure to keep pace puts philosophy in a state of paralysis: 'Our metaphysical faculty is paralyzed because actual events have shattered the basis on which speculative metaphysical thought could be reconciled with experience.'[44]

Adorno, like Deleuze, associates this failure of philosophy with 'Auschwitz', though (also like Deleuze) this historical event is by no means singularly disconnected from generalised conditions of existence shared by all humans and other events. For instance, Adorno notes that even the one who is spared from becoming a victim of Auschwitz can survive only by conforming to the very conditions that governed Auschwitz. 'His mere survival calls for the coldness, the basic principle of bourgeois subjectivity, without which there could have been no Auschwitz.'[45] It is the same phenomenon that Deleuze identified as the source of shame: it becomes impossible to exist without colluding. Of course, the term 'collusion' might give too strong a sense of intentionality, given that the degree and apparent unavoidability of collusion is predicated on the fact that it has become almost entirely involuntary – something like a pre-intentional habit required for survival in a world such as ours. Collusion, it should thus be noted, has less to do with a subject's intentionality than with a generalised production of subjectivity. Our collusion must be understood against the background of a tendency that, in Adorno's terms, seeks to establish 'the absolute controllability of people', and that conditions the 'mass annihilation' seen at Auschwitz and elsewhere.[46] *Collude or perish!*, and *Adapt or perish!*, are said out of the same mouth. We now face a situation, Adorno says, in which 'the process of adaptation to which people are subject is posited as *absolute* – just as torture is an extreme form of adaptation'.[47] This holds not only for explicit threats of violence, but also for the habits of everyday capitalist life. Adorno, echoing Deleuze's lament over the production of thought for the market, and imagining what Yoder calls 'the Powers', emphasises the manner in which capitalism produces collusive subjects by requiring ceaseless and pervasive adaptation. 'Life in the late capitalist era is a constant initiation rite. Everyone must show that he wholly identifies himself with the power which is belaboring him.'[48]

This wretchedness is omnipresent. It involves subjectivities, habits, and historical events, it extends itself into objective horrors such as genocides as well as into the collusion or adaptation of the everyday, and the repetition of this extension and involvement suggests no tendency to abate. All of this signals, for Adorno, another instance in which quantity turns into quality. The quantity of wretched experience is so great that it renders indefensible the notion that metaphysics, or philosophy's tendency to think beyond the present, might provide a meaning to experience. The quality of our experience has mutated, and the mutation is such that it becomes impossible to invoke philosophy as a means of addressing this experience. One cannot resort to a given faculty of thought, for this faculty has itself been engulfed and rendered impotent by the quantity of wretched experience. It has already adapted. A change in sensibility has taken place. Philosophy's failure to resist wretchedness – and, insofar as philosophy continues to search after some hidden, 'metaphysical' meaning to wretchedness, its complicity with this wretchedness – witness to the fact that the failure is not a matter of degree, it is instead the very heart of philosophy.

Philosophy is incapable of granting sense to an existence that is experienced as senseless. To pretend that it is otherwise, to refuse the fundamental necessity of putting philosophy as such under critique (through a metaphilosophical operation), is more senseless than our experience of a senseless existence. It is more depressing than the depression we are given. Indeed, it adds a second-order senselessness to the first-order senselessness of our experience. As Adorno puts it:

> In the face of the experiences we have had, not only through Auschwitz but through the introduction of torture as a permanent institution and through the atomic bomb – all these things form a kind of coherence, a hellish unity – in face of these experiences the assertion that what is has meaning . . . become[s] a mockery . . . For anyone who allows himself to be fobbed off with such meaning moderates in some way the unspeakable and irreparable things which have happened by conceding that somehow, in a secret order of being, all this will have had some kind of purpose.[49]

As long as we continue along the path proscribed by Adorno, philosophical practice colludes with a wretched existence. The fact that philosophy has been incapable of extricating existence from wretchedness does not mean that this wretchedness is necessary and not contingent. It does mean, however, that the production of other possibilities of life has, as its precondition, the production of another practice of thought.

Philosophy fails, the given faculty of thought is incapacitated, but metaphilosophy is capable of conceiving this failure. The failure of philosophy stems in large part from the habit of placing the 'otherness' of history – that is, the capacity of things to be determined otherwise, or what I have called the more of being – prior to history. Where this is the case, historical determination is supposed to converge with, or at least to approach, its 'metaphysical' otherness. And even where historical determination fails to proceed in this ideal manner, convergence or approach remains as a regulative idea, transcendent norm, or analogical distance. In other words, the link between historical determination and metaphysical transcendence, along with the capacity of the latter to measure the former, are kept in place by philosophy even amidst failure. The place one goes for the otherness of historical determination is the metaphysical origin, while the place one goes to realise this otherness is back to history. This moderates the wretchedness of historical determination and relieves us of the task of breaking down philosophy, since the link between historical determination and its otherness is maintained – again, even amidst failure. For Adorno, such a link is the very thing that allows us to adapt to the wretchedness of our present determination. It provides a reservoir of sense in which to bathe and ignore the senselessness of experience.

Because senselessness is that which philosophy cannot think, metaphilosophy demands that we attend to it. If there is a path out of wretchedness, it lies in the act of conceiving senselessness. Here Adorno again converges with Deleuze, who saw in nonsense not the lack of sense, but the capacity to create new sense.[50] Furthermore, just as Deleuze locates the awareness of philosophy's failure in shame, so Adorno locates it in melancholy and suffering. Metaphilosophy must extract the experience of senselessness from philosophy's metaphysical canopy of sense. This means acceding to the melancholy and suffering involved in our wretched existence, acceding to our depressed world. The notion that there is something that transcends the wretchedness of experience must be discarded. It is necessary, Adorno says, 'to work one's way through the darkness without a lamp . . . and to immerse oneself in the darkness as deeply as one possibly can'.[51]

Senseless Animals

To work one's way through the darkness is to expose oneself to suffering. This is valuable, not because of some kind of transcendental masochism nor because there is something sacred about suffering, but rather because it is in suffering that experience exceeds the standard domains of sense. We enter suffering not because it is good but because it is there, in our condition. The present condition produces suffering and wishes not to see it, so to ignore it is to collude with the present. Suffering makes the blind spot of thought appear. If there is otherness to historical determination, then it will be found only by exposing oneself to suffering, yet suffering tends toward the nonsensical. Even when we seek to give it a reason, a sense, such sense will find itself overmatched by the sheer experience of suffering. In fact, it is with suffering that Hume's noted distinction between idea and impression finds its exemplary ground. For Adorno, suffering is an instance in which 'something in reality rebuffs rational knowledge. Suffering remains foreign to knowledge . . . Suffering conceptualized remains mute and inconsequential.'[52] The senselessness of suffering is due to the contingent conditions in which we exist. To expose oneself to suffering's senselessness, then, is to commit oneself not to an ontologically prescribed lack of sense, but rather to the lack of philosophically available sense. 'The smallest trace of senseless suffering in the empirical world belies all the identitarian philosophy that would talk us out of that suffering.'[53] Exposure to suffering is thus tantamount to not being 'talked out' of suffering's senselessness. It is, in short, a commitment to expressing suffering's excess over preexisting canons of sense.

This commitment is a metaphilosophical one, for it resists the configuration presented by philosophy and demands an alliance with the suffering that philosophy has refused to think. Metaphilosophy, in this way, isolates an experience of nonidentity – of something more than what philosophy has conceptualised – from philosophy's form of conceptualisation. The 'metaphysical' desire for otherness must be set within the determinate experience of suffering, or within the horizon opened when the historically determinate is experienced as suffering. This horizon, while determinate, is also open. Senselessness finds autonomy – not only *from* the given sense of philosophy, but also *for* its own production of a new sense, a sense that does not already exist. It is in this context that we must understand Adorno's oft-cited claim that 'The need to lend a voice to suffering is the condition of all truth.'[54] The point is not that we ought to grant an already available sense to suffering's senselessness, as a kind of metaphysical act of charity. It is rather that the only sense worth having, the only sense that will truly be able to stand up, is one that arises *from* and is adequate to this experience of suffering. Deleuze makes a similar point when he says that ethics tells us 'not to be unworthy of what happens to us'.[55]

Furthermore, Adorno's suffering, like Deleuze's crack, is not a fall from the transcendent, but an affection of immanence, of the unconditioned within determinate conditions. Because it is an affection of the unconditioned, it is without a given expression, it is senseless. Adorno says that, in the experience of suffering, we find ourselves in a 'suspended state [that] is nothing but the expression of its inexpressibility'.[56] An exemplary instance of this is found in his remarks on Homer's description of the punishment of prostitutes:

> Homer describes the movement of the nooses and coldly compares the women's appearance as they hang to that of birds caught in a net . . . The passage closes with the information that the feet of the row of suspended women 'kicked for a short while, but not for long' . . . Homer assures himself and his audience . . . that it did not last for long – a moment and then it was all over. But after the 'not for long' the inner flow of the narrative is arrested. *Not for long?* The device poses the question, and belies the author's composure.[57]

It is not as if the agony of the prostitutes is unexpressed, or essentially inexpressible. The agony is undoubtedly expressed. Nonetheless, the expression of this agony is a fissure belying Homer's history, a crack running through its total sense. Does the assurance that though the women kicked, it was 'not for long', adequately make sense of their suffering? Metaphilosophy tells us that it does not. But it does so by following the crack of expression, the senselessness that 'belies' Homer's sense. It makes the suffering of the women a problem for thought.

Suffering, Adorno says, 'is objectivity that weighs upon the subject'.[58] We could say that metaphilosophy makes suffering a problem that outweighs the solutions presented by philosophical practice. What then does it mean to be a subject of this problem, if the problem exists precisely because of the preponderance of objectivity over the subject? The metaphilosophical subject must become like the object, it must think from the vantage of the object. In the context of Homer's history, it means the philosopher must play the role of the women, in the same way a method actor becomes the role or a profane individual becomes a magician.[59] Homer intriguingly attempts to assuage the reader's dismay by creating an analogy between the women and animals. The suffering of the women is given sense by its similarity to the suffering of birds caught in a net. Given this, perhaps the only way to play the role of the women is to also – or to first – play the role of the birds. The way to produce an alternative philosophy, to become-nonphilosophical, is here dictated by a metaphilosophical analysis of what is unthought by philosophy: the animal.

This, in fact, is precisely what Deleuze recommends. Faced with the shame brought about by an existence that compromises with the present, faced with the shame of being human, the exodus from this existence is to practice existing otherwise. As Deleuze says, 'there is no way to escape the ignoble but to play the part of the animal (to growl, burrow, snigger, distort ourselves): thought itself is sometimes closer to an animal that dies than to a living, even democratic, human being'.[60] Any superiority the human – that supposedly thinking animal, the animal that practises philosophy – might have over the supposedly non-thinking animal is compromised by the fact that the thinking animal's practice of thought fails to escape compromise. Philosophy, whatever power it claims to have by right, has not in fact saved humans from being treated like animals, or from believing in the legitimacy and sufficiency of those categories.

Philosophy must be broken down so that thought can be allied with the condition of animality in which we find ourselves, and in which (we) animals have always existed. The practice of the philosopher must be connected not with the human, whose thought attempts to make sense of our wretchedness – who, for example, gives sense to the suffering of the prostitutes by likening them to suffering birds – but with the animal, which exists and dies without any guarantee of sense and without becoming linked to thought. When thought is compromised, and when faithfulness to it only increases our shame, nobility lies in allying oneself with what, we are told, does not think. Perhaps playing the role of the unthinking is the way to find the unthought within thought.

What is at stake here is the connection between the production of philosophy and the production of individual beings. That animals and humans are separated by the lack or presence of thought, that their relation is hierarchical, that they are related analogically rather than interstitially – none of this is necessary. This entire scheme is a contingent expression of being, an expression that is subject to re-expression. The metaphilosophical criticism I am advancing is that philosophy's compromise, its failure to resist and create, is tied up with its implicit commitment to re-express the above scheme.

Concomitantly, the path of resistance and creation – the construction of the new – requires that we constructively re-express the human/animal relation. Indeed, if relations within immanence are interstitially problematic rather than analogically ordered – as I have argued – then the aim is to find the interstitial crack between human and animal, to find something unconditioned amidst the condition of being human or animal.

The fissure between human and animal is often present in suffering. We have seen how Homer makes sense of the suffering of the prostitutes by mediating it through a human/animal analogy. He implies that we ought not crack up over these prostitutes – after all, they were not much different than birds caught in a net, and we don't think too much about that. But why not? Homer's strategy is quite common. Thought often attempts to give sense to the senselessness of suffering by drawing on a distinction between human suffering and animal suffering. Adorno makes this point quite eloquently:

> The possibility of pogroms is decided in the moment when the gaze of a fatally-wounded animal falls on a human being. The defiance with which he repels this gaze – 'after all, it's only an animal' – reappears irresistibly in the cruelties done to human beings, the perpetrators having again and again to reassure themselves that it is 'only an animal', because they could never fully believe this even of animals.[61]

The suffering of humans is given sense by classifying them as animals. But this classification requires that the human is already capable of repelling the gaze of the wounded animal. Metaphilosophy contends that this capacity to repel the wounded animal outside the ambit of thought, to not let it affect thought, is central to philosophy's failure.

I have repeatedly stressed that, in immanence, effects remain in their cause no less than the cause remains in itself. The human and animal are not only equally proximate to (and, in fact, equally *within*) the cause, they are equally capable of drawing on an unconditioned power of re-expression. Yet while this is ontologically true, it is not entirely the case when it comes to the given expression of immanence. Actualised humans possess capacities actualised animals do not, and vice versa. The concern of the beginning of this chapter was to demonstrate the importance of mediation, and mediation can be applied here: while humans and animals share in an unconditioned power of construction, the possibilities of construction are not immediate; unconditioned possibilities must be mediated with the conditions of our given expression. What this means for the human/animal relation is that human power and animal power must be increased by finding cracks within the given expression of immanence, cracks within an order that determines individuals as either humans or animals. *We break with the present by finding the breaks within the present.* Affect is once again central, for shame over the suffering of an animal, or melancholy over the suffering of women likened to animals, is what cracks philosophical sense. Metaphilosophy demands that thought attend to such affects. Thought escapes shame only insofar as it makes the gaze of the wounded animal, or the kicking feet of the suspended women, matter for thought.

Deleuze says we must think 'before' the victim of the conditions with which philosophy has colluded. He makes clear that this does not mean 'for [the victim's] benefit', or 'in their place'.[62] To think before the victim is to make the practice of thought inseparable from the experience of the victim. It is to follow the crack. In Adorno's terms, it would mean to think before suffering, before the objectivity that weighs upon the subject. Thinking-before creates a bond between thought and the experience of wretchedness. Thought cannot separate itself from this wretchedness, but at the same time wretchedness is no longer separated from thought. We might think, for instance, of the titular character of J. M. Coetzee's *Life and Times of Michael K*, who frequently utters statements that link his own human identity with the non-human. These statements – which proceed according to the form, 'I am ...' – should be understood not as literal identifications but rather as attempts to break down the division between human and non-human. The strategy that is manifest in Homer, and criticised by Adorno, is to delink thought from suffering by attributing suffering to the animal, or to that which is seen as distinct from and inferior to the human. To move otherwise, to think before wretchedness, is not to reverse the direction of this attribution, such that the animal becomes thought in terms of the human. It is rather to undo the very division across which attribution moves, to make the suffering of bodies unattributable.

It is precisely this undoing that takes place when Michael K says, 'I am like an ant that does not know where its hole is.'[63] In this moment, it is unclear whether Michael K is human or animal, such that we have an indication of what Deleuze calls 'the zone of exchange between man and animal in which something of one passes into the other'.[64] There is still thought, it is just that this thought cannot be said to belong to one kind of being or another – and if such belonging cannot be provided, then neither can any directional attribution. There is only the zone of exchange, in which the referential capacity provided by distinct identities is dissolved. In fact, the entirety of the sentence reads, 'I am like an ant that does not know where its hole is, he thought.' Coetzee thus makes evident the difference between the movement of thought and the definition of an I's existence. That which can be thought exceeds the limits of any I, with the consequence that it is possible to move the I, by way of thought, into a multitude of relations. To identify thought with the I of the human, or to presume that thinking is necessarily bound to the presupposition, 'I am human', is a contingent expression, one that can be re-expressed in various other directions. It is precisely such re-expression with which Michael K is experimenting. In fact, there is no need even to limit the non-human directions of 'I am . . .' to the animal. We can push further in order to think the I as bound to the vegetal or the atmospheric. We find, for instance, the report: 'Perhaps I am the stony ground, he thought.'[65] And elsewhere we are told:

> I am becoming a different kind of man, he thought . . . If I were cut, he thought, holding his wrists out, looking at his wrists, the blood would no longer gush from me but seep . . . If I were to die here, sitting in the mouth of my cave looking out over the plain with my knees under my chin, I would be dried out by the wind in a day, I would be preserved whole, like someone in the desert drowned in sand.[66]

The I can become everything, for everything can enter thought and crack the I, everything is in immanence. Better yet, everything presses on thought – not just the animal, but also the stony ground, the wind, the cave, the sand, and the decaying body, belong to the objectivity that weighs upon the subject. Michael K thus names an instance of experimentation with the interstice that emerges between the body and every other element. In fact, the body of the supposed human also belongs to such objectivity. What keeps this objectivity from affecting thought is the presumption that thought belongs to the human, which is presumed somehow to belong to something beyond this world, or to a world in which this objectivity no longer exerts such force. All of this objectivity is the world, the world in which we appear not to believe.

Notes

1. There is, it should be noted, something of a contemporary renaissance in the interpretation of Hegel, such that he is shown to be far more

complex than was imagined in the period during which Deleuze wrote. A good survey of these new interpretations of Hegel is Slavoj Žižek, Clayton Crockett, and Creston Davis (eds), *Hegel and the Infinite: Religion, Politics, Dialectic* (New York: Columbia University Press, 2011).

2. Theodor Adorno, *Negative Dialectics*, trans. E. B. Ashton (New York: Continuum, 1973), p. 158.
3. Theodor Adorno, *Aesthetic Theory*, trans. Robert Hullot-Kentor (Minneapolis: University of Minnesota Press, 1997), p. 71.
4. Adorno, *Negative Dialectics*, p. 159.
5. Ibid., p. 5.
6. Ibid.
7. Ibid.
8. Ibid., p. 365.
9. Ibid., p. 128.
10. Ibid., p. 54.
11. Ibid., p. 174.
12. Ibid.
13. Ibid.
14. Adorno refers to this remainder as 'the constitutive character of the nonconceptual in the concept' (ibid., p. 12).
15. Theodor Adorno, *Metaphysics*, trans. Edmund Jephcott (Stanford: Stanford University Press, 2000), p. 67.
16. Adorno, *Negative Dialectics*, p. 161.
17. Ibid., p. 28.
18. Ibid., p. 137.
19. Gilles Deleuze and Félix Guattari, *What is Philosophy?*, trans. Hugh Tomlinson and Graham Burchell (New York: Columbia University Press, 1994), p. 99.
20. Adorno, *Aesthetic Theory*, p. 166.
21. Cited in Gillian Rose, *The Melancholy Science: An Introduction to the Thought of Theodor W. Adorno* (New York: Columbia University Press, 1978), p. 44.
22. Theodor Adorno, *Minima Moralia: Reflections from Damaged Life*, trans. E. F. N. Jephcott (New York: Verso, 1974), p. 151.
23. One cannot, by now, read the term 'nonphilosophy' without thinking of the work of François Laruelle. While I find this work quite powerful and promising, my use of the term in this text should not be understood as an invocation of Laruelle's thought. The nonphilosophy that I am here developing is one that is specific to Deleuze's immanence; my 'Deleuzian' nonphilosophy is distinct from Laruelle's nonphilosophy.
24. Franco 'Bifo' Berardi, *The Soul at Work: From Alienation to Autonomy*, trans. Francesca Cadel (Los Angeles: Semiotext(e), 2009), p. 134.
25. Deleuze and Guattari, *What is Philosophy?*, p. 11.

26. Ibid., p. 11.
27. Ibid., p. 37.
28. Ibid.
29. Ibid., p. 21.
30. Ibid., p. 108.
31. Ibid., p. 218.
32. Ibid., p. 218.
33. Ibid.
34. Ibid., p. 202.
35. Ibid.
36. Ibid., p. 204.
37. Ibid., p. 107.
38. Ibid.
39. Ibid.
40. Ibid.
41. Ibid., p. 108.
42. Ibid., pp. 107–8.
43. Ibid., p. 108.
44. Adorno, *Negative Dialectics*, p. 362.
45. Ibid., p. 363.
46. Adorno, *Metaphysics*, p. 107.
47. Ibid.
48. Theodor Adorno and Max Horkheimer, *Dialectic of Enlightenment*, trans. John Cumming (New York: Continuum, 1997), p. 53.
49. Adorno, *Metaphysics*, p. 104.
50. As Deleuze remarks: 'Nonsense is that which has no sense, and that which, as such and as it enacts the donation of sense, is opposed to the absence of sense.' See *Logic of Sense*, trans. Mark Lester with C. Stivale (New York: Columbia University Press, 1990), p. 71.
51. Adorno, *Metaphysics*, p. 144.
52. Adorno, *Aesthetic Theory*, p. 18.
53. Adorno, *Negative Dialectics*, p. 203.
54. Ibid., pp. 17–18.
55. Deleuze, *The Logic of Sense*, p. 149.
56. Adorno, *Negative Dialectics*, p. 109.
57. Adorno and Horkheimer, *Dialectic of Enlightenment*, p. 79.
58. Adorno, *Negative Dialectics*, p. 18.
59. On the magician as actor, see Marcel Mauss, *A General Theory of Magic*, trans. Robert Brain (New York: Routledge, 1972), p. 118: 'we are not dealing with simple matters of fraud ... The magician then becomes his own dupe, in the same way as an actor when he forgets that he is playing a role.'
60. Deleuze and Guattari, *What is Philosophy?*, p. 108.
61. Adorno, *Minima Moralia*, p. 105.

62. Deleuze and Guattari, *What is Philosophy?*, p. 109.
63. J. M. Coetzee, *The Life and Times of Michael K: A Novel* (New York: Penguin, 1985), p. 83.
64. Deleuze and Guattari, *What is Philosophy?*, p. 109.
65. Coetzee, *Life and Times*, p. 48.
66. Ibid., pp. 67–8.

6

Icons of Immanence: Believe the Now-Here, Fabulate the No-Where

Bleakness and Belief

If immanence turns on a mediation of metaphilosophy and non-philosophy, then it must also be the case that metaphilosophy and nonphilosophy are immanent to one another. The metaphilosophical account of suffering that we have just provided helps fulfil this end, for while suffering puts us in a place of senselessness, such senselessness is the necessary condition for producing something else. There is a productive power in suffering, for suffering binds us to the place where we are, which is to say that it frees us from discourses, from pre-established senses, that would impose themselves on – and thus obscure – this place. If there is to be nonphilosophical production, or creation of something else, then it will be necessary to break with such discourses. Suffering, when metaphilosophically understood, makes this break. In doing so, however, it also enables us to create new possibilities of existence, possibilities made possible only when suffering reveals the impossibility of existence amidst the possibilities we are presently given. Our emphasis on the metaphilosophical character of suffering, however, has foregrounded the break, or the impossibility, rather than the creation of new possibilities. What we must now do, then, is articulate how a metaphilosophy of suffering binds us to a place from which new possibilities may be created. More precisely, we must articulate how this being bound is already a productive act. It is in order to start providing this articulation that we now turn to the question of belief.

The belief I have in mind is an 'immanent belief', which Deleuze invokes as something absent from modernity. It is, he says, a 'modern fact . . . that we no longer believe in this world. We do not even believe in the events which happen to us, love, death, as if they only half concerned us.'[1] The world does not matter to us, it does not matter for thought; thought is not affected by events, not even by suffering, because we have imagined sense as transcending the world in which events happen. This is to say that the lack of belief in the world witnesses to the presence of another belief, namely that thought does not stand or fall on the particular events of the world. A lack of belief in the world, a failure to be bound by the senselessness of what happens, is inseparable from the belief that sense is found apart from its involvement in those events. If the events of the world do not affect thought, it is because thought takes as its aim something that would transcend these events. What is still present, then – even in a supposedly secular modernity – is an implicit philosophical commitment to the idea that the sense of worldly events is provided by a faculty of thought that subsists independently of our conditions.

Deleuze's remark about the present lack of belief in the world is metaphilosophical, as is our discussion of thought's refusal to be affected by experience. This metaphilosophical resistance, however, proceeds in virtue of the very events or affects that remain unbelieved. Metaphilosophy criticises the conditions in which belief is lacking precisely by giving attention to and becoming aware of that in which we do not believe. In other words, metaphilosophy criticises our condition by believing in – or into – our condition.

The resistance enacted by metaphilosophy has a specifically immanent character, for it calls us away from belief in 'another world' or a 'transformed world' and into belief in 'this world, as it is'.[2] Our problem, in fact, is not that we lack belief pure and simple, and that we need therefore to find something to believe in. We lack belief in an immanent sense, but this is due to the fact that we do believe – in another world. In fact, we might say that immanent belief, insofar as it affirms the sort of secularity we saw in Yoder, is able to distinguish such secularity from the regnant discourse of the secular, which believes not in the world but in a project for the world. As Gil Anidjar has pointed out, 'to uphold *secularism* (or, for that matter, religion) as the key word for critical endeavors and projects today is, I am afraid, not to be that worldly. It is to oppose the world rather than that which makes and unmakes it . . . It is to oppose the world and those who inhabit it rather than those who make it unlivable.'[3] Immanent belief, with its demand to be affected by this world and consequently to refuse discourses about the world, thus stands not only against the sort of belief found in analogical theology, but also against the sort of belief found in secularising discourses. In other words, immanent belief is irreducible to the opposition of secular and religious by being opposed to the transcendence involved in both.

Belief in *this* world, as opposed to another world, or a world that would be better than the one in which we live, is an affirmation of immanence, of the constitutive inseparability of thought and world. It restores to thought the reality of what happens and makes particular events into waves that ceaselessly destroy the notion of a fixed boundary between the land of thought and the sea of world. Belief breaks down the barriers thought puts around itself; thought is 'taken over by the exteriority of belief'.[4] As the pop musician Thom Yorke intones over and over, forming an incessant, undulating sonic pedagogy, 'this is really happening, happening'.[5]

What is happening may not make one happy. In fact, it is likely that, because it leads to unhappiness, because it makes suffering, what happens is often not believed. Yet this only intensifies the exigency of turning senselessness, and thus the world, against the discourses of sense that turn us away from the world. We can here call to mind Malcolm X, who took the name 'X' precisely in virtue of this exigency. That the X came about through a religious modality should not obscure the worldly character of its enactment – to think that what emerges in religion cannot simultaneously be worldly is to participate in the discourses that 'make and unmake' the world rather than to encounter the world. If we want to be worldly then we ought to divest ourselves of such discourses, just as Malcolm X did. To get rid of 'the white slavemaster name of "Little"' is to refuse to believe that one's sense in the world comes from a discourse about the world.[6] Malcolm X understood that it is better to be without a name than to have a name that prevents one from being able to believe what is 'really happening', namely slavery, racism, and all the suffering that is too blithely represented by the discourses they name. Better senselessness than the sense that we are given. In fact, it is precisely by affirming senselessness that we reveal the contingency of what is given, the impropriety of the proper name.

Furthermore, what we see in the example of Malcolm X is that to strip oneself of sense, to stop participating in the discourses that give order to the present, is simultaneously to produce a different kind of sense, to create novelty in this world. There is, after all, nothing at all disempowering about Malcolm X's refusal of his proper name. On the contrary, it is precisely by way of the X that he enables himself to imagine new possibilities of existence; the X has a polyvalent potentiality that is otherwise foreclosed. The contrast here with Milbank's romantic orthodoxy, which wants to affirm every image, is telling: only by rejecting the imagination of the past and the present, the archive of images that are supposed to fill the world with sense, does it become possible to take seriously the way the present is disturbed by the suffering happening in the world. For Malcolm X, the divine does not lead to the inclusion of all images, it enables the rejection of every image that would moderate the force of the world's events – and it is only by way of such rejection that a different future becomes imaginable. We can therefore say that it is through the sheer refusal of sense, or through the senseless X, that the world becomes capable of *making* sense. Even better, we can say that the X, precisely as the affirmation of a world that is more than the names already given to and imagined for it, is already the creation of a new sense, of a new way of being worldly. In this manner, the enactment of the X is an instance of what we will later conceive, by way of fabulation, as icons of immanence. For now, it stands as an indication of how to believe in this world.

Immanent belief thus insists on the need to think from within suffering, instead of moderating it in virtue of pre-existing sense. But why is such a strong insistence necessary? Why does not suffering automatically, as it were, force us to break with the canons of sense? It is because of belief. It is our belief in a sense transcendent to the particular events of the world, or our corresponding lack of belief in the world, that prevents suffering from problematising our thought. It is as if transcendent belief provides a protective barrier around sense – no matter what happens to us, the sense that philosophy provides us remains unaffected. Metaphilosophy gives us awareness of this barrier, and calls for immanent belief; immanent belief dissolves this barrier by binding thought to what is objectively there. What is there is what Deleuze terms 'the body before discourses'.[7] Metaphilosophy does not stand against the barrier of transcendent belief without installing a link between thought and what happens to the body. It makes the objectivity that weighs upon the subject matter for thought; it puts thought before the senselessness of our animal body. Metaphilosophy, through immanent belief, isolates this experience of senselessness and locates it *prior* to the discourse of sense. Such immanent belief thus opens a path into nonphilosophy, for it turns that which lies outside the philosophical domain of sense into a motor for the production of novel sense.

When we make the world intervene in thought, we make events of the world intervene as cracks in the state of the present. As Deleuze remarks, 'If you believe in the world you precipitate events . . . that elude control, you engender new space-times.'[8] Metaphilosophy's belief turns particular, mundane events against their resolution within the discourse of the present. Immanent belief turns the events of this world into problems that exceed the coordinates of the present. This excess is produced not by going beyond the world, but by intensifying our connection to the world, even – or precisely – when this connection is senseless.

Badiou criticises Deleuze's immanence on this point, claiming that it cannot ultimately break with the world. There is, he says, too much continuity between thought and world. What is necessary, for Badiou, is 'to render eternal one of those rare fragments of truth that traverse here and there our bleak world'.[9] What he misses, however, is the way this very opposition between 'rare truth' and 'bleak world' makes our world bleak. The bleakness of our world does not call for the remedy of an eternal truth opposed to our everyday world. On the contrary, it is the belief in such a remedy that tends to render our world so bleak. Badiou's approach cannot escape becoming another instance of the philosophical habit that metaphilosophy resists – that of presupposing (and believing in) a sense opposed to the world, which would then come to interrupt and save us from the world.

Thought must break with the present, but not with the world. The world is presently bleak, but this has to do with thought's failure to believe in the events of the world. Rather than break with the world, we must break with the present by believing in the world – especially when it is so bleak. The point, then, is not to break with a bleak world but to make the event of the world's bleakness enter thought. The present makes the world bleak, but to hate the world in the name of such bleakness is to increase bleakness. It is to make depression more depressing. The world may be bleak, but the world is not the present – so to believe in the world is not to bless the given state of affairs, it is to link thought to something unthought by the present. Belief in the world thus breaks down thought by way of non-thought. Metaphilosophy's invocation of an immanent belief opens a non-philosophical terrain.

Intolerability

Belief sets forth an immanent circuit between the labour of thought and the events that befall us. When such events are believed in, we may find that they are too much for us – or that they are, at least, too much for us *at present*. As long as belief in the world is not pursued, the solution to this predicament – where life is too much – is to turn away from these events, to simply not think from them. The immanent circuit between thought and mundane events is then displaced by commitment to a prior conditioning of the terms in circuit. But immanent belief refuses such a prior transcendental condition and takes us beneath and before the given possibilities of existence. Belief does not provide a predetermined accord by which thought and the world are to be resolved. It gives us something less, but also something more – that is, it gives us the unresolved, but nonetheless open, immanence of thought and world. Immanent belief annihilates the present's solution, but this annihilation leaves a problem in its wake. Nihilism with respect to the present's capacity to give sense to what happens is the derivative effect of a prior, affirmative belief in the events that affect us.

Immanent belief encourages and accredits awareness that what happens to us is too much for life as it is presently constituted. This affection of 'too much' can occur in various modalities, running from the ecstatic to the terrible and the depressive (or it might just be the case that we are affected by an apparently insuperable banality). My interest, in other words, lies not in a specific definition of what is too much, but rather in the fact that, throughout these various modalities of affection, we gain awareness that there is something within life that cannot be continued under the present conditions, something, as Deleuze puts it, that is 'intolerable or unbearable'.[10] As immanent belief encourages and accredits this awareness that life is presently intolerable, that it is too much, it also installs the properly problematic nature of thought.

Thought becomes resistance as it actively problematises the intolerable. The nonphilosophical force of the world, excluded by the present, becomes the ally of thought; thought is immersed in the excess of the present so that this excess enters into thought. Thought finds something beyond the limits of the present, but it does so as it is affected by the wretchedness – the shame and the suffering – of life in the present. As Adorno notably lamented, *'Life does not live.'*[11] The world to which belief links us forces us to cry out that the present is intolerable, that it is impossible to continue living this way. Amidst this intense sense of intolerability, one finds oneself hemmed in, on every side, by the problematic. Yet the problematic is not a privation, it is what allows creation to emerge.

Deleuze remarks that it is by 'setting out . . . a problem' that one finds a way of going farther than one previously thought to be possible; a truly creative concept must be 'a response to real problems'.[12] The production of problems is driven by belief's link between thought and world, by the feeling that the present form of accord between these two is intolerable. In this sense, one possesses a right to think only insofar as one invents and gives force to the problematic. The power to think and the power to problematise go only so far as each pushes the other. In order to create, one must resist the given by discovering one's 'own impossibilities'.[13] The possibilities proper to thought are not those already presented to it as possible, but those that are created in confrontation with the impossible and the intolerable: 'Creation takes place in bottlenecks.'[14] In fact, the problem's resistance to the present produces the conditions for creation, which itself produces the future. Present impossibilities, and the impossible intolerability of the present itself, are made into a point of departure for the creation of the future.

There could be no creation from the impossible were it not for the pure and empty form of time, which is capable not only of undoing any form that claims to set the conditions of possibility, but also of becoming a power by which the future is generated. Time presents a more of being. However, if we do not construct this more of being, our suffering and wretchedness will increase in degree. Life is too much to live, and for this reason there must be resistance. Yet in this resistance, the too much might be turned in another, more affirmative direction, a direction that must be constructed. The enemies of this constructive endeavour, Deleuze says, are the 'schemata' that claim to provide the proper accords of life.[15] These schemata are the sovereigns of the present, for they decide on the parameters of sense. They seek to devalorise what is too much for life in the present by 'turning away', 'prompting resignation', or 'assimilating' that which is 'too powerful, too unjust, too beautiful'.[16] But schemata that claim sovereignty are nothing other than sheer *presumptions* about the nature of life.[17] Similarly, for Yoder, the political logic of Jesus is too much for the Powers – and so Jesus reveals the presumptions of the Powers as nothing more than schemata to be opposed. For Deleuze as well as Yoder, then, no deal is to be brokered with these schemata, for they are intolerable.

The Kantian flavour of the term 'schemata' is quite significant, for it reminds us that Deleuze turns Kant's account of time against Kant's account of the schemata. As I have earlier noted, Kant observes that the subject's emergence is a consequence of time. Deleuze, commenting on Kant's observation, says that the subject is 'fractured from one end to the other . . . by the pure and empty form of time'.[18] Time is the generator of subjectivity, such that a logic of the subject cannot condition the logic of time. Time precedes the subject. Yet, despite

Kant's affirmation of temporality with regard to a presumed form of subjectivity, he does seek to hem in the nature of time elsewhere, through his account of schemata. These schemata, Deleuze says, are 'rule[s] of determination for time', rules limiting relations of time to relations of 'logical possibility'.[19]

Kant's concern was to provide some kind of convergence between categories and appearances, which were heterogeneous to one another. Time thus becomes central due to its ability to reconcile these heterogeneous terms through the determination of schemata. What matters for Kant, in the end, is not time's unconditioned nature, but rather its capacity to facilitate the subsumption of appearance – of the particular – under the categories. Time becomes the servant of an operation whereby sensible experience is subjected to rules governing the possibility of meaning. Schemata are thus a function of transcendence: they draw on the categories' forms of logical possibility as a means of imposing order on what temporally appears. Time becomes the material by which the categorial norms realise themselves. If a temporally emerging appearance does not accord with the categories, then it is excluded from the domain of sense. It is, for Deleuze, precisely such exclusion of sheer temporal existence, or of existence by way of the pure and empty form of time, that has become presently intolerable.

Schematic rules, which claim to delineate and govern the conditions of the possible, are quite arbitrary. They are presumptions, and at most reflect – after the fact – the order of that which has already been actualised. Schemata explain what has already been expressed, not what may be expressed. For instance, Kant's schema of the time-series, which determines time as succession of moments, reduces time to the lineaments of the pre-established, or the actualised; it makes time into a frame for continuous yet discrete moments. Time, when determined by schemata, no longer names that which exceeds already-determined sense, rather it becomes the servant of such sense. It is therefore necessary to assert, against Kant's determination of time, that schemata do not govern the possibilities of time as such, they only govern a present cut off from the unconditioned character of time. They govern the old aeon yet are incapable of conditioning the new aeon. What schemata mark as impossible is impossible only with respect to the present, and this says nothing about the future. But if a future can be created through the construction of time, then what is presently impossible is not finally impossible.

Yet even as time exceeds presumptions about logical possibility, alternative possibilities will be brought forth only through a construction of this excess. Furthermore, this excess is not something transcendent, it is found in experience – specifically, the experience in which limits of the present are revealed as such through affection of suffering, shame, wretchedness, or intolerability. So while these rules or forms claim to adequately articulate the possibilities of experience, experience itself is capable of immanently exceeding their supposed governance and thus demonstrating that such articulation is a limit. Simon Jarvis, commenting on Adorno, remarks that 'if categorial forms specified by Kant are the conditions of the possibility of experience, the reverse is equally true: the categorial forms themselves are only made possible by the experience whose conditions of possibility they are supposed to provide'.[20] Experience becomes too much for the conditions of possibility and, rather than accepting this logic of possibility, it reverses the order of conditioning.

This process of reversing the order of conditioning is of absolute importance for the production of the future. The present is not *necessarily* stymied by what exceeds it, since it is capable of capturing and assimilating such excess. For this reason, it is imprecise to see the present as a moment or point in time that is about to be swept away by the now-rumbling future. The present must be understood more broadly, as a kind of governance that, through its schemata of logical possibility, acts constantly to reassert itself (as is the case with the overdetermination-function of the Powers analysed by Yoder, or the Chronic temporality assayed by Deleuze). It is not as if the present is first set aside by the future and must then catch up to the future; it is rather that the present actively sets forth and enforces its own conditions so as to foreclose the emergence of the future. The horizon of the future, in other words, is not immediately given. The present can last a long time ... and there is no guarantee that the future will arise with the dawn of the new day. On the contrary, unless the present is directly resisted, what dawns tomorrow, and each day after tomorrow, is the present of today, even if in a modulated form. It is for this reason that the reversal of conditions – whereby the possible is no longer conditioned by the schemata of the present, but is rather conditioned by the too much of experience – is fundamental. The very future of immanence stands or falls on this reversal. If we do not make the too much of experience, the cracks of the present, mediate the production of the future – the production of immanence – then immanence becomes nothing but a desperate defence of the present.

The Creation of Real Beings

If the future does not immediately emerge, if it is constantly fore-closed by the extension and recapitulation of the present, where then is it 'located'? Where, in other words, does the future take place, or in what does its creation consist? Although the future is not immedi-ately or automatically accessible, and although the schemata of the present seek to overdetermine the horizon of emergence such that genuine novelty is deferred, the future may still be brought about. It is just that, in order for this to take place, there must be a place of the future. This place is found in the products of thought.

Deleuze identifies three kinds of thought, with three correspond-ing products: the functions of science, the sensations (affects and percepts) of art, and the concepts of philosophy. These three are distinct but equivalent in import; they are not hierarchically related. 'Thinking is thought through concepts, or functions, or sensa-tions and no one of these thoughts is better than another, or more fully, completely, or synthetically "thought".'[21] Thought-products, because of the bonds they create, are capable of providing a hinge between the present (including its modulations) and the future. The present, we have seen, can be understood as a resolution of problem-atic difference, or of a differential problematic. It is thus by way of problematising the present that we open up the world in excess of the given solutions. Problems themselves, however, do not determine new relations, but rather pose difference in-itself, which conditions new relations. Accordingly, problematisation's resistance is neces-sary, but creation – as the production of relations stemming *from* the problem – is equally necessary. The problem dissents from the present, but in order for this dissent to achieve genuine antagonism with the present, new relations – relations exceeding the given rules of possibility – must be produced. Only this sort of production of the impossible, as opposed to the reproduction of the present, can be understood as creation. Thought-products are what give these new relations their reality.

These relations are new, yet immanent. This is a contradiction only insofar as immanence is seen as conditioned by the present, rather than as produced by experience of that which is too much for present life. There is a profound senselessness to such experience, but this senselessness is unreal only where one arbitrarily presumes the present's conditions of possibility. If one reverses the order of conditioning, senselessness becomes a condition for the production of a new reality. The experience of senselessness tends toward the pure difference of virtual singularities and away from the present's actualisation of these singularities. Senseless experience thus eviscerates the present state, turning the present inside out by virtue of the singularities that the present claims to condense. This means the path one travels in order to create does not stretch beyond or above the present. It lies, on the contrary, in a scattering of the present that opens in a centrifugal manner. Dispersal thus conditions thought by forcing it to encounter the unthought, but thought's creation prevents this unthought dispersal from evaporating, for it produces new relations out of this dispersal. Thought-products are immanent, then, insofar as the matter of creation is found in dispersal of the present's singularities, but they are new creations insofar as the bonds they set forth do not pre-exist.

This can be seen, for instance, in philosophy's concept and art's sensation. Deleuze's account of the concept begins from the virtual's difference in-itself, but it does not stop there. On the contrary, it prolongs and intensifies singularities into a consistent variation, 'in order to form genuine conceptual blocs'.[22] Philosophical thought constructs virtual difference by bringing forth 'reconnections through a zone of indistinction in the concept'.[23] Artistic thought, for Deleuze, also takes dispersal as a constitutive power for the production of new bonds. The disassociation of the present found in the experience of senselessness becomes the material for the emergence of a new '*bloc of sensation*'.[24] The virtual dispersal of senselessness is composed into a monument of the world, into a compound that can '*stand up on its own*'.[25] In this way, the artist makes senselessness into a new sense. 'The monument does not actualize the virtual event but incorporates or embodies it: it gives it a body, a life, a universe.'[26] Such bonds produced by philosophical and artistic thought are *real beings*. These are neither beings actualised by present conditions of sensibility nor virtual singularities which disperse and render senseless these conditions. They are constructions of these singularities, creations of the novel.

We see the same process in Adorno's account of the artwork. Art, he says, is capable of breaking with the ordering of relations by the present, and it must exercise this capacity by attending to the dispersed. The artwork thus gathers together and gives consistency to the disaccord of the present: it is a 'gravitational force, which gathers around itself its *membra disjecta*, traces of the existing'.[27] What is produced by art is immanent to the world controlled by the present, such that the artwork 'is structured by proportions between what exists, proportions that are themselves defined by what exists, its deficiency, distress, and contradictoriness as well as its potentialities'.[28] The material of the artwork thus exists in the present, but the relations that allow this material to extend beyond the present do not. They must be created, and the artwork is nothing but these novel relations made of material dispersed in the present. Just as, for Yoder, creation belongs to the politics of the world (the matter of determinability) rather than to the origin of the world, so, for Adorno, the artwork is a 'creation out of the created'.[29] It is along these lines that art seeks a thisworldly otherness: 'The elements of this other are present in reality and they require only the most minute displacement into a new constellation to find their right position.'[30] Art produces an immanent relation to the world not by imitating its present configuration, but by dispersing or displacing the configured elements. 'Rather than imitating reality, artworks demonstrate this displacement to reality.'[31]

We find an indication of this in Pier Paolo Pasolini's film, *Teorema*: a stranger enters a bourgeois household, has an intimate encounter with each one of its members, and leaves. The elements of this artwork are mundane, they are taken from the world as it is conditioned, except that they are immanently crossed by an element that cannot be located within the established relations of the household. As a result, these elements are displaced; *Teorema* is the demonstration of this displacement of the conditioned, by the unconditioned, within the conditioned. The 'proportions between what exists' are thus unsettled by the set of encounters, where these encounters can be seen as revealing the interstices immanent to the relations of the household. In short, the household is problematised. While the various responses of its members to this problematisation display a wide range of outcomes, these outcomes are not the only thing that matters. In fact, what matters, first and foremost, is the artwork's problematisation of the given conditions. As Pasolini has remarked about the film, 'a man in a crisis is always better than a man who does not have a problem with his conscience'.[32] Regardless of the outcome, then, what counts is the 'displacement' of reality, a displacement that is not imposed on reality so much as demonstrated in it. *Teorema* does not offer a solution to the given conditions, it demonstrates that they are already problematic.

In fact, even when we move from the artwork's expression of the problematic to its expression of how the problematic is taken up, the refusal to make a move 'beyond' the conditions continues. The father, mother, brother, and sister all suffer some manner of breakdown after the problematising encounter. What *Teorema* refuses, then, is the resolution of the problem by way of the transcendent: the artwork does not mediate a transcendent good to the problematic conditions; instead it immanently mediates the conditions and the problem, making the conditions feel the force of the problem they would like to obscure. However, there is one exception to the sad outcomes, and this is the household servant, who becomes a performer of miracles. If she succeeds, it is because she understands that the other she encountered is in immanence with her, that if, as Adorno remarked, 'the elements of this other are present in reality', then she, as part of that same reality, is already other. Unlike the rest of the household, she does not treat the other as something transcendent, something that comes from beyond in order to save her. Importantly, however, her response to the problematic encounter is but one response among others. The artwork, in other words, presents liberation only as one potentiality within the given conditions. It shows that, and even how, this liberation is possible, but it does not make this liberation the telos of the work. What is instead foregrounded is the problematic character of the conditions, along with the possible ways of experimenting from this problem.

Pasolini thus exemplifies the way in which the form of the artwork – here a dispersal of possibilities that emerge from an encounter with a problem that disperses given relations – is inseparable from displacement. The reality or objectivity of the artwork stems precisely from its expression of immanent displacement. Such immanent displacement constitutes the artwork's form, which resides in its constellation of elements, in the creation of a consistency between the dispersed forces *of* the elements, and not at all by applying something *to* these elements. Aesthetic form 'is the nonviolent synthesis of the diffuse that nevertheless preserves it as what it is in its divergences and contradictions'.[33] Art generates new forms by thinking from the senselessness of dispersal, rather than by imposing forms of coherence upon dispersal. In this sense, 'the essence of [the artwork's] coherence is that it does not cohere'.[34] However, to 'not cohere' is not simply to pose incoherence against coherence. It is to develop consistencies that exceed given schemata. Art's thought-products, its real beings, exceed and thus oppose the form of the present, but they do not transcend it. 'Whereas art opposes society, it is nevertheless unable to take up a position beyond it.'[35] Novel aesthetic forms are developed by discovering and following the cracks between the present's formal possibilities; thought opens onto a more of what is, and it does so by inhabiting the interstices of what is. 'Artworks say what is more than the existing, and they do this exclusively by making a constellation of how it is, "Comment c'est".'[36] Thought breaks with the present by displaying and then constellatively creating a real being out of the present's senselessness. In true minoritarian fashion, the artwork 'achieves opposition only through identification with that against which it remonstrates'.[37]

We are able to similarly appreciate Adorno's philosophical method of parataxis, which Gillian Rose eloquently describes as 'placing propositions one after the other without indicating relations of co-ordination or subordination between them'.[38] What is produced in a paratactical operation cannot be discerned through deductive or inductive movement, for there is no order to the propositions. The propositions form a non-hierarchical set, an open constellation of equals. But neither is the product of parataxis a synthetic association of propositions. The paratactical product does not reside in an addition of its propositional elements; it resides in the interstices of these elements. To say that the paratactical product is not associative is not to say that its elements fail to construct something. There is, in fact, a construction of thought in parataxis, it is just that what is constructed is not the same as what is propositionally said. What is constructed is a non- or extra-propositional movement between the propositions. It is for this reason that parataxis is capable of speaking the language of the present without accepting the present forms of sensibility. While the propositions are not foreign to the present language – they display 'how it is' – they can, because of the way they constellate this language, enter into its interstitial cracks. The product is not directly posited, it exists more precisely as the non-coordinated relations that emerge, interstitially, from the propositions that are said. The force of parataxis, or the product that it forms, thus resides in its movement rather than in the present sense of the propositions it constellates.

It is just such a paratactical dynamic that one finds in the artwork. When the artwork 'preserves' the 'divergences and contradictions' of the world, it does so by juxtaposing elements already given in the world. The aesthetic form that is produced thus consists of the relations that develop in between the diverging elements, and in the chiasms that dawn between contradictory elements. One could see the artwork as a dramatisation of the bottleneck brought about by the pressure, on one side, from an excessively restricted form, and on the other, from a threat of chaotic divergence. This artistic process of dramatisation, however, provides a mediation that refuses either side. It does so not by stepping beyond these two pressures of form and divergence, but by dramatising them and thus generating a movement in between them. The elements or parts of the artwork develop 'centers of energy' that exceed the pre-formed, but that are nonetheless not simply formless.[39] The paratactically-related elements generate a mobile product, a consistent disequilibrium. As Fredric Jameson remarks, Adorno's artwork is 'a force-field and a thing all at once'.[40]

Consider, for instance, Steve Reich's 'Different Trains'. The strings seem to be based on the recorded speech melodies, such that one can hear them mimicking the voices. At the same time, this mimicry does not preclude our continuing awareness of the distinction between the sound of the voices and the sound of the strings. The same may be said of the way in which the strings mimic the tone of the trains that are recorded. Trains, voices, and strings are at once implicated in and inassimilable to each other. They are, we might say, in immanence, and differentially so; they are inseparable from one another, and yet they do not admit a vantage according to which they could be perceived in terms of unity. On the contrary, any point of unity – such as trains, voices, or strings – is mimicked in a direction that diverges, even as this divergence remains mimetically linked to that from which it diverged. This piece thus provides a differential immanence of sound, where sound is too immanent to be divided up and yet too differential to escape the sense of disequilibrium.

These diverging elements of immanent consistency can be addressed not only at the level of sound but also at the level of world. In other words, just as the strings differentially re-express the recorded voices within the piece, so the piece as a whole, or the artwork as such, re-expresses events of the world. We can see that this is the case by noting that the title refers, on the one hand, to the American trains that took Reich, as a young boy travelling between the homes of his divorced parents, between New York and Los Angeles, and on the other, to the German trains that took Jews to the concentration camps. Had Reich been living under German rule, he would have been on a different train; since he was in the United States, he was on a train different from the one on which he could otherwise have been. The piece thus addresses the immanence of these trains, precisely by thinking through their difference. The divergent mimesis of train, voice, and string sounds, within the piece, is connected to the divergent mimesis of the different trains within the world. What is the nature of the connection? It is itself one of divergent mimesis: the nature of the artwork mimes the nature of the world, and yet the very fact that it is art rather than world marks a divergence. The divergence between American and German trains becomes immanent with the divergence between the world's trains and the artwork's trains, but all these divergences are thinkable precisely through their mimesis. Because of its divergence, the artwork does not represent the world, but because of its mimesis, the artwork does not transcend the world. In fact, one cannot hear *Different Trains* without thinking of the suffering it expresses, of the objectivity of history that weighs on and sounds through the piece. Yet even as the disequilibrium of historical experience, with all of its senselessness, shapes the artwork, the artwork still emerges as something in excess of this senselessness. Something different is produced in *Different Trains*, something new emerges in the work it names, and yet this novelty has nothing to do with an attempt to endow the world's senselessness with meaning.[41]

Deleuze's concepts and blocs of sensation, Adorno's artworks and paratactical constellations – each and all of these indicate products of thought. Thought creates the new, and it does so through the creation of products. It draws on the senselessness of the present in order to produce things of the future – or to produce the future in things. These things are products of an interstitial immanence, such that their consistency is inseparable from disequilibrium. Yet such disequilibrium is the mark of their immanence with the world, which makes them real beings. The disequilibrium of the world, its differential re-expression, enables the displacement of the world from its present equilibrium and into these real beings of thought. It is in these real beings that the future takes place. This is also to say that the future does not simply happen due to the passing of time – for time, though unconditioned, is empty. If we do not construct it then it will be filled by what is already present. Time, when it is not given a name through the creation of real beings, will disperse into emptiness; it will be filled in by the present, again and again. Immanence does not guarantee novelty – no, the new must be immanently produced in real beings. Without the creation of real beings, the coordinates of the present will expand and reoccur, the present will last forever, it will become as if eternal.

Against Communication

The central importance of real beings to the creation of the future is further demonstrated when we take a look at our contemporary predicament. One could, after all, argue that our particular present is deeply committed to dispersal. Our particular present, after all, seems to require continuous adaptation to various styles of labour, geographical mobility, constant expansion of social-informational networks, and a generic sense of fluidity. Is this not an affirmation of dispersal? And what, one might ask, is the value of calling for the production of the new when we seem to be daily inundated with the novel? Or, similarly, what is the value of emphasising creation, when 'creativity' is such a highly prized attribute in the contemporary marketplace? How, in such a predicament, can creation have anything to do with resisting the present?

We can begin to respond by observing that all of this fluid productivity, or all of these phenomena of dispersal and creativity that mark the present moment, are not without a certain schema, a certain governing logic of possibility. Our particular present appears to call for a very large quantity of mobility and innovation, but this call is ultimately determined by the logic of communication.[42] The historical emergence of communicative schemata marks the passing of a present that proceeded by discipline – which posed relatively stable norms with which we were expected to accord – and the rise of a present that proceeds by control.[43] It is no longer a matter of apparent opposition between broadly uniform standards and a fluidity that opposes the ensuing restrictions. Fluidity has triumphed, but the present remains. The present, by becoming fluid, or communicative, has rendered itself eternal in a way that discipline could never imagine.

It is therefore correct to assert that communication encourages fluidity, as long as we do not pass over the more consequential fact that it is an ultimately limited sort of fluidity. The aim of communication is not the prevention or disciplining of fluidity but the control of fluidity. If we do not grasp this, we will be unable to resist – for we will have misrecognised the basic nature of the present's limits. Don DeLillo, addressing the dawn of a post-Cold War communicative globalism, highlights the paradoxical character of a disinhibited, unleashed desire that is nonetheless deeply invested in limitation and control.

This is what desire seems to demand. A method of production that will custom-cater to cultural and personal needs, not to cold war ideologies of massive uniformity. And the system pretends to go along, to become more supple and resourceful, less dependent on rigid categories. But even as desire tends to specialize, going silky and intimate, the force of converging markets produces an instantaneous capital that shoots across horizons at the speed of light, making for a certain furtive sameness, a planing away of particulars that affects everything from architecture to leisure time to the way people eat and sleep and dream.[44]

It is as if the break with one particular present, which was marked by its reliance on 'rigid categories', simultaneously produces another particular present, marked by a flattening of the possibilities it appears to welcome. Here we see just how long the present can last.

How then are we to explain this scenario whereby the affirmation of possibility becomes indiscernible from the control of possibility? We already possess the resources to respond: the language of possibility itself is schematically overdetermined, such that the possibilities to be affirmed are possibilities conditioned by the present. But we must be more precise, insofar as our particular present is not one in which a relatively stable form conditions the realm of the possible. While this may have been the case for a disciplinary regime, it is most definitely not the case for a regime of control. With control we face a self-consciously fluid schema, a schema that, in a reflexive manner, seems to make fluidity as such its object. The task of resisting this present requires that we articulate the logic of communication's schematic fluidity and make this the determinate object of resistance.

It is in view of this task that we turn to the distinction between interstitial and associative logics. We have already seen how interstitial logic motivates Adorno's paratactical conceptual construction and account of the artwork as dramatised force-field, as well as Deleuze's theory of the concept as bonds of differential singularities and of the bloc of sensation created from dispersal's senselessness. Common to these is an operation whereby the present order is dispersed or dissolved through its interstices. Interstitial difference then provides the becoming by which new relations, or the bonds constituting new beings, may be created. So how does this sort of operation depart from that of communication's fluidity? The creation of real beings can be separated from communicative fluidity in virtue of the distinction between the interstitial and the dissociative. While creation stems from interstitiality, communication stems from dissociation.

This distinction can be elaborated by resorting to the classical terminology of parts and whole. In fact, the advance provided by the interstitial operation is that it refuses each side of this terminological opposition: the product is constituted neither through the gathering of parts by the whole nor through the reduction of the whole to its parts. Everything turns on the character of the relations between parts. It is through the interstices of parts that new relations, and thus new beings, are created. This is the lesson of both Deleuze's composition of the differential and Adorno's paratactical constellation of elements. What is intriguing about communication, however, is that it too, in its own manner, seems to generate relations that bypass a reduction either to the parts or to the whole. Yet these relations follow an associative logic.

If, for instance, we imagine a whole that is composed of parts, then communication proceeds by constantly reassociating elements, or by associating new elements with old elements. It dissociates the whole into its constituent parts in order then to reassociate these parts – again and again. This ceaseless process of association and reassociation enables communication to discard previous forms – inherited wholes of associated parts – in favour of new associations. For the same reason, communication can permit (and in fact often requires) dissociation of pre-existing forms of existence. But this dispersal is not interstitial. It does not, in other words, seek to think from the difference between parts, it does not address the bottleneck of the problem. On the contrary, communication seeks *as a given course* to dissociate and reassociate, over and over. There is, in this scenario, no construction of real beings, for real beings require form – a fluid form, or a consistency of divergence, but nonetheless some kind of form. Communication does not find in dispersal the possibility of creating real beings, or novel forms of existence that could stand up against the present. It instead makes fluidity into its own, eternally present form. For communication, dispersal is not the condition of interstitial production but rather the dissociative conduit between associations. Dispersal becomes the given condition. But this does not mean we need to suddenly foreswear dispersal, or the disaccord it occasions, it just means that we must – metaphilosophically – understand it. And to understand the disaccord we presently encounter is to distinguish between dissociative dispersal and interstitial dispersal.

While it is therefore correct to locate the problematic within disaccord, within that which does not accord with the present, communication forces us to nuance this observation. Disaccord is no longer simply disciplined, it is controlled by being put to work. The aim of our particular present is to ceaselessly modulate accord and disaccord, such that disaccord is always communicable, always capable of provoking a new association. This means that disaccord, which exerts pressure on the present configuration by invoking a differential problematic in excess of the present's solution, is granted a release valve. Association cannot ultimately abolish disaccord, or the problematicity presented by disaccord, but it can lessen the pressure that disaccord exerts. The intolerability of present sense can be moderated by a reassociation of the present. This capacity to absorb the differential force of the problematic through (re)association is the benefit communication accrues for itself by making association as such, rather than a particular form of association, its object. Communication does not limit the problematic excess so much as absorb it. That is, instead of just delimiting interstitial production through the governance of forms of logical possibility, it stifles interstitial production through the equation of possibility with associative logic.

The associative logic of communication proceeds, like the temporality of Chronos, by encompassing and incorporating that which dissents from and breaks with the present. The present is quickly *associated* with that which might resist it. In this sense, the present is ceaselessly recast and reconfigured, but never expelled. Cracks in the present may begin to emerge, but they are filled in and plastered over by communication. Let us recall Deleuze's claim: 'Creating has always been something different from communicating. The key thing may be to create vacuoles of noncommunication, circuit breakers, so we can elude control.'[45] It becomes necessary, from this vantage, to resist the possibilities of communication, to refuse to make use of our supposed communicative faculty, and to think by way of the interstitial problem, of the crack, that communication wants to render non-existent.

Adorno saw the stakes of thought in a similar manner. Faced with capitalism's tendency toward integration, Adorno, according to Rose, asserted 'that the increasing concentration of capital has made everyone into a function of capital'.[46] The individuated being lacks the capacity to resist integration, insofar as it has been integrated. Communication aids this integration by supplying it with fluidity, with a flexible field of association. Accordingly, the path of resistance lies not in a better association, but in a refusal of association itself. Adorno conceived this resistance as 'commitment', which 'is not simply out to correct unpleasant situations'.[47] It 'aims at the transformation of the preconditions of situations, not at merely making recommendations'.[48] The 'precondition' of the situations schematised by our particular present is the logic of association, which promotes integration. Only by creating vacuoles of nonassociation do we break with, rather than offer recommendations for, presently existing society; only in this way do we create real beings.

Utopia

Communication, now that we have conceived it metaphilosophically, can be understood as the expansion of the present rather than as the creation of the future. Communication renders the present eternal. It is a permissive transcendence that listens to everything in order to put itself everywhere. Communication saturates every place, it leaves nothing outside itself. It works hard in order to make every place say yes, so much so that no place says no. Yet if we are to create, then there must be a 'No'. There is no nonphilosophy without a 'No' to thought. And it is with this problem in mind that we turn to the concept of utopia.

The function of this concept, according to Deleuze, is to articulate the force that the movement of difference exerts on any territory schematised by the present. This force tends to 'deterritorialise' such a territory, or to disperse even its associations. 'Utopia does not split off from infinite movement: etymologically it stands for absolute deterritorialization but always at the critical point at which it is connected with the present relative milieu, and especially with the forces stifled by this milieu.'[49] In this sense, utopia concerns the production of immanence, or the politics of immanence. That is, it does not simply pose virtual difference against the actualised present, it also conceives the link between differential excess and those elements that, while within the present, resist this present. Utopia thus names the connection between disassociated elements and virtual difference – the interstice – without mediating this connection through a logic of association. In virtue of this connection, Deleuze claims that 'utopia is what links philosophy with its own epoch'.[50] The concept of utopia concerns not immanence as such, but rather the unconditioned power of immanence in connection with resistance to a particular present. Accordingly, 'it is with utopia that philosophy becomes political and takes the criticism of its own time to its highest point'.[51]

Etymologically, the concept of utopia speaks of a 'no place' or a 'non-place' – that is, a place that is not. This has special relevance for our contemporary moment in which communication is everywhere. If every place is in communication, if there is no place that is not open to (re)association, then the import of utopia is its capacity to affirm the force of the place that is not. It affirms, in other words, the place that does not communicate, the place that says no. And this has nothing to do with a negative transcendence. Utopia is immanent, it is just that its place is not a given place – its 'non-place' is the interstice, which says no to every given place.

Deleuze draws on this etymological connotation by borrowing Samuel Butler's translation of utopia as 'Erewhon', which has the double meaning of no-where and now-here.[52] Utopia is no-where: it is not a future place nor a better place nor a transcendent place. Yet this does not mean it is simply a lack of place, for utopia is now-here, in the present. Still, we must not equate utopia with the present, for even if it is now-here, it is in the here and now *as* the no-where. In short, utopia does not transcend the present, but neither is it equivalent to the present. It is, apart from these two alternatives, the interstitial space, or the non-place, that persists in the cracks of the present. It is by being both no-where and now-here that utopia is able to connect the power of the unconditioned with the conditioned.

Deleuze explicitly relates his discussion of utopia to Adorno's. Deleuze's own understanding of conceptual production, he says, is akin 'to what the Frankfurt School called "utopian"'.[53] Adorno's interest in the concept of utopia, and especially its iconoclastic character, is well known. Materialism, Adorno says, brings 'the theological ban on images . . . into secular form by not permitting Utopia to be positively pictured'.[54] A common interpretation of this ban is that it calls us to see utopia as something that can be invoked but not produced, or something that can be produced only in a negative mode. But this is to overlook another tendency at work in Adorno's concept of utopia, one that points in the direction I have been moving and that concerns the productive character of philosophy and art. When this productive character is emphasised, it becomes possible to move beyond the binaristic choice between utopia as referent (as in the image of utopia that Adorno bans) and utopia as sheer negativity. This is possible because, as I have argued, what emerges in Adornian intellectual production always does so indirectly. The product has a 'para-' character, and consists in the novel relations produced through interstices. Thought's utopic dimension thus cannot be identified with the propositions of a concept or the content of an artwork. But this does not mean that it exists only negatively. Even though the utopic dimension cannot be placed in these manners, this does not mean the utopic is the sheer negation of place. Its place is interstitial – that is, it consists in what arises in the interstitial non-place, in what Deleuze calls the no-where of the now-here. Therefore utopia belongs not to the content of the artwork but to the formal drama of apparent divergence and contradiction, and not to the propositions of the concept but to their paratactical constellation.

Yet even if Adorno's utopia conceives the nature of the paratactical and dramatic interstices by which production proceeds, it does not seem to conceive the nature of the product itself.[55] There is, in fact, a certain weakness in the concept of utopia as such, and it concerns the role of the thought-product, or the creation of real beings. Utopia holds open the possibility of interstitial creation, it allows us to distinguish the incessant yes of communication from immanence, which concerns what says no to the given. Utopia allows us to think beyond communication without resorting to transcendence; it immanently liberates us from association through its nihilising interstice. When we feel that the place of the present comes to nothing and cannot accept the cheap promise of a place beyond, we find ourselves in utopia; when the communication of global capitalism leaves no place outside of itself, utopia deterritorialises it. So utopia is a radically political resistance, it frees thought by banning the images that we are given, the clichés with which we communicate. But, having said all of this, we must also admit that utopia does not produce real beings. It annihilates the ever-expanding present, it mocks communication's presumption of eternity, but it does not yet create the future.

The Fabulation of Icons

Deleuze helps us address this lack, though he does so with the concept of fabulation rather than utopia. Fabulation names the capacity to tell a story that outstrips the criteria that would decide on its truth or falsity. While Deleuze speaks of fabulation on various occasions, he offers an especially important indication of the concept's force while addressing the relation between story and reality in Pierre Perrault's 'cinema of the lived', which focuses on the colonisation of Quebec. Of particular relevance is that the real is defined not in opposition to story-telling as such, but in opposition to a fiction that is already presumed to be real. Deleuze comments that 'when Perrault criticizes all fiction, it is in the sense that it forms a model of pre-established truth'.[56] However, one resists this fiction not by casting one's lot with the real, since the real – at least when it is defined in stark opposition to the fictive – is the effect of a presumed fiction. For this reason, 'When Perrault is addressing his real characters of Quebec, it is not simply to eliminate fiction but to free it from the model of truth which penetrates it.'[57] And one frees the real from the pre-established fiction not by refusing the fabulous, but rather by 'rediscover[ing] the pure and simple *story-telling function*'.[58] Deleuze's point is that one resists the fiction of the present by producing another story – or, more precisely, by turning the power of fabulation against the fictions that present themselves as the truth. 'What is opposed to fiction is not the real . . . it is the story-telling function of the poor, in so far as it gives the false the power which makes it into a memory, a legend, a monster.'[59]

The opposition between the true and the false is thus crossed by the necessity of telling a story, and excessively so. In other words, to tell a story is to exceed the given coordinates of truth and falsity. This means that the basic opposition is not between true and false, it is not even between fiction and reality. It is rather between a fiction that imposes a 'model of truth' and the 'pure and simple' function of telling a story. Fabulation is thus distinguished from fiction that resembles what actually is, for fabulation does not refer to the conditions presumed by the present; fabulation is likewise distinguished from fiction that accepts the status of being purely untruthful or unreal, for fabulation does wish to express something real. We are, in fact, able to see the fable as proceeding from utopia: the now-here provides the elements of the fable, while the no-where provides a field for fabricating 'false' relations between these elements. But again, these relations are not false in a classical sense. They are false not because they lack truth; they are false because they depart from the fictive truth of the present, from the place known as the present. They are false only in the sense that they refuse the truth-conditions provided by the present, and affirm the interstitial field of the no-where. Thus, while utopia dissolves the place coordinated by the present's fiction, revealing its falsity, fabulation constructs a new story out of utopia's dissolved elements. In doing so, fabulation constructs a place for the future.

The sense of the fable emerges through a construction of the senselessness of experience. It is for this reason that a suffering people will often enter into resistance through fabulation. In this regard, Deleuze notes the example of Palestinian resistance.

> Was there ever a Palestinian people? Israel says no. Of course there was, but that's not the point. The thing is, that once the Palestinians have been thrown out of their territory, then to the extent that they resist they enter the process of creating a people. It corresponds to . . . the act of telling tales. It's how any people is constituted.[60]

The immense value of fabulation lies in the fact that it exceeds any correlational model of truth. One says, making use of Deleuze's example, that there is no Palestinian people. How is the truth of such a proposition decided? It cannot be decided by reference, for the field of reference is itself decided by present conditions of possibility. And if one wishes to refute the decision of the present, it does not suffice to refer to past history, for the present is certainly able to provide its own narration of the historical past. Indeed, in order to resist the present by way of the historical past, we must follow the example Yoder sets with his 'legendary' account of Jeremiah. As with Deleuze's fabulation, the elements of Yoder's legend are not ahistorical – that is, they are not *opposed* to historical reference – but neither are they merely referential. One does not refer to them without telling a story about them. Just as Deleuze counters the historical fiction of the present through 'the story-telling function of the poor', so Yoder counters it through an historical legend of a minority that refused to emulate the majority. In each case, one resists the conditions of the present by fabricating a new story, by telling a tale. Fabulation, then, does not aim to correlate with the present or with the history told by the present. It opposes the presently associated elements through the creation of new relations, which supplant the preconditions of correlation. Fabulation, because it creates such relations, produces real beings.

But if the truth of the fable is not derived from correlation with the present, which determines fabulation's tale as simply lacking in truth, then in what sense can we insist on the truth of fabulation? Or, perhaps more importantly, how are we to conceive the reality of the fable such that it exceeds correlation with the present conditions of possibility? We must, in view of these questions, return to the utopic conjuncture, for the material of the fable emerges through the connection of the no-where and the now-here. Were the fable simply no-where, it would lack the consistency of being; were it simply now-here, it would never break with the present. What is central, then, is that the fable addresses the elements of the here and now, but that it does so in relation to the dispersal of the no-where. It is due to the reality of the differential, virtual field of singularities that the fable can produce a new reality.

In this regard, let us recall that Yoder's Jeremian legend is about polyglossia, or the dispersal of language itself. Therefore the Jeremian legend is something like a legend of legends, for one practises this legend only by affirming a continual scattering of language or sense. The Jeremian legend is not once for all. It does not fabulate a unified telos of history. Rather, it fabulates the demand to re-fabulate – that is, to tell the story of divergence, ever anew, against the totalising teleology of the 'right' history (which is provided by the Constantinian legend). Similarly, Deleuze calls not for a unitary fable, but instead for a constant multiplication of fables in virtue of the story-telling function of the poor, those elements that are minor, or even 'false', in relation to the coordinates of the present. The fable, then, is a construction of divergent singularities – or, more precisely, it is a construction of new relations between these singularities. Because they draw on this differential dispersal, on the no-where, the relations produced – which constitute the fable – do not need to resemble the present's resolution of difference, yet can still claim to be real.

Consider, for instance, the emergence of the Occupy Wall Street movement. It was often said that this movement, despite the energy it displayed, was limited by its lack of clarity regarding its demands, or even by its sheer refusal to present demands. At some point – so went this line of thought – it was going to have to get involved in the reality of political negotiation. But such refusal does not stem from the kind of naiveté supposed by its critics; on the contrary, Occupy's refusal stems from a strong awareness of what takes place when demands are presented. The presentation of demands strips away the power of senselessness, it renders the movement sensible within the present, it makes the movement take place in the present. Occupy, of course, is not without place, and for a good while it quite explicitly placed itself in Zuccotti Park. But what kind of place is Zuccotti, or what takes place in Zuccotti? Such a place is certainly utopic: it is a place that refuses to accept the schemata of the present, or a place constituted by those who desire this refusal, who desire to experiment with modes of relation exceeding the present's schemata. Such a place is unrecognisable within the present, and this unrecognisability is what gives rise to the scenario in which it is criticised for lacking demands. From the vantage of such critics, the refusal to present demands is necessarily a lack, for the movement, as long as it lacks demands, cannot be placed. Yet this is precisely the point, since the lack of demands is a lack only insofar as one presumes that it is necessary to participate in the present. It is precisely this presumption that Occupy refuses, and utopically so.

At the same time – and in order to observe the passage from utopia to fabulation – this refusal was not without production. Zuccotti becomes utopic, but in doing so it creates new possibilities of existence. By becoming a nowhere with regard to the present, a nowhere that nonetheless *is* taking place here and now, it creates a new space-time, or a space-time in which the experimentation with new possibilities of existence takes place. Even better, we might say that such experimentation is what constitutes the new space-time – and this experimentation includes not only the projects of Occupy but also the interactions that take place in Zuccotti, or that make it into a different kind of place. Zuccotti may thus be understood as a fabulation, for it makes reality irreducible to what is called reality in the present. Take, for instance, the proclamation, 'we are unstoppable, another world is possible'. What matters for such a proclamation is not correlation with the present order of things, and yet this refusal of correlation does not thereby leave reality to the present. On the contrary, it asserts that reality includes possibilities exceeding the present, and that the expression of such possibilities requires their fabulation. We can also say, along these lines, that Zuccotti, or the Occupy movement more broadly, becomes an icon: it is a real being, but its reality does not stem from a recognisable demand, or even from a presentation of identity; its reality is named, but the name is nothing more than the mark of a differentially dispersed consistency, of a reality that is all the more real because the relations that constitute it do not correlate with the possible relations of the present.

In fact, if 'another world is possible', then this world is already being enacted in the fabulation of its possibility. Its otherness resides not in transcendence but in the novel relations that emerge in the icon of 'Zuccotti', in the interstices that constitute its fabulation. This is to say that the fable does not come from above but instead is made up of the senseless elements of the present, of the elements so dissatisfied or disturbed with the present that they do not present a demand to the present. The truth of the fable lies not in the attribution of a higher reality, but in the interstitial creation of an immanent reality, in the constellation that sets forth novel inter-elemental relations – as is the case with Yoder's affirmation of Babel. We could say that what changes is not the quantity of elements, but their quality. Deleuze, commenting on the role of fabulation in literary characters, observes:

> It is of little importance whether these characters *are* mediocre: they *become* giants . . . without ceasing to be what they are. It is by dint of mediocrity, even of stupidity or infamy, that they are able to become not simple (they are never simple) but gigantic. Even dwarves and cripples will do: all fabulation is the fabrication of giants.[61]

The animal body that suffers does not leave behind its body, but the senselessness of its suffering achieves a new quality, it creates a new, more powerful sense from its infirmity.

Utopia's break with the present gives way to fabulation's creation of the future. In this sense, *the mediation of utopia and fabulation is the mediation of metaphilosophy and nonphilosophy*. It is not just that utopia exerts force on the present, it is also that fabulation, by drawing on the utopic, creates products that exceed the present. The utopic conjuncture provides the conditions for a truthful fable, or a fable whose reality exceeds the reality supposed and imposed by the present. But the fable itself, as a thought-product, a construction of reality, is not utopia. It is not that it falls short of utopia as a result of having created an image of utopia. On the contrary, it has created an extra-utopic real. Utopia ceaselessly haunts the present, for it maintains a connection between any present and the no-where that disperses it. Yet even as the no-where deterritorialises the present in this manner, the present may still reterritorialise through its communicative schemata. Fabulation, however, injects something else into this potentially chronic back-and-forth. The fable does not simply deterritorialise the present. It requires deterritorialisation's dispersal, but it also names what is created in virtue of this dispersal.

Fabulation thus supplies the connection between utopia and the political creation of new possibilities of existence. Deleuze himself remarks, in a discussion of thought's political function, 'Utopia isn't the right concept: it's more a question of a "fabulation" in which a people and art both share.'[62] Fabulation, one could say, adds labour to utopia, thus creating products that stand out beyond both the present and its dispersal. Fabulation, he remarks, involves a 'tendency to project . . . an image . . . so intense that it *has a life of its own*: an image that is always stitched together, patched up, continually growing along the way'.[63] Thus, if fabulation has a referent, it is utopia, and yet even here we refuse correlation, for the fable is an *autonomous* product: it responds to utopia's excess by creating a real being out of this excess. Fabulation creates real beings in which the future takes place. It produces a reality that gives the future a life of its own.

Fabulation also calls attention to the fact that we cannot speak of immanence without speaking of the production of immanence, or of the creation of immanent products. It is, in fact, possible to see a shift toward production, or toward the construction of products, in the trajectory of Deleuze's thought. While his work initially emphasises the manner in which immanence in-itself can be turned against every *image of thought* – every presupposed model of the nature of thought and the form of truth – it later begins to pursue another path, which lies in *the production of thought-images*.[64] The emphasis shifts from the senseless, immanent excess of (non-)sense to the creation of an autonomously existing multitude of new senses. In other words, value begins to be placed not simply on the unconditioned immanence that undoes every limit of thought, but also on the creation of thought-products that this unconditioned immanence makes possible.

Let us push this tendency even further than Deleuze does by calling for an iconic immanence.[65] Thought-products – such as Coetzee's Michael K, Pasolini's *Teorema*, Reich's 'Different Trains', Malcolm X's self-creation, or Occupy's 'Zuccotti' – are icons of immanence. Right away, though, we must make a qualification. The term 'icon' is associated with theology, and so it might be imagined that an iconic immanence re-introduces something along the lines of analogy. But this is not the case. Iconic immanence has nothing to do with a supposed analogy between a particular being and its transcendent source. The icon, as I conceive it, is not an immanent opening onto the transcendent. On the contrary, we should understand immanence as nothing outside of its icons. The icon does not even incarnate immanence. The immanence that belongs to the icon does not pre-exist the icon, it is instead produced by the icon; the icon expresses the power of the unconditioned in and as a particular thought-product.

This means, furthermore, that an icon of immanence is not equivalent to Deleuze's concept of the crystal, which renders the actual and the virtual indiscernible or immanent to one another. To remain within the crystal, we demonstrated, is to remain within a paradox: does the crystal set forth an already established immanence, or does it create a novel form of immanence? The icon, however, does something different – its aim is not to establish a circuit of immanence that is given but not perceived, it is instead to produce immanence. Though the icon draws on the unconditioned power of immanence, the immanence it installs does not pre-exist it. The icon, then, is not a particular that participates in the unconditioned, it is a particular that creatively re-expresses or constructs immanence. Immanence involves a mediation between the conditioned and the unconditioned, but the aim of this mediation is to create – as a kind of fabulation – icons that produce immanence by giving reality to a different immanence, the only immanence there is.

One finds a key indication of this iconic convergence between the unconditioned and the particular in Deleuze's account of film's time-image. Once again, it is his account of cinema that leads him to emphasise the thought-product. Film's time-image allows us to see neither history, nor 'the purely empirical succession of time – past-present-future', but rather time itself.[66] Time, '"a little time in the pure state" . . . rises up to the surface of the screen'.[67] It is thus unnecessary to divide unconditioned time – that which allows us to expel the present and produce a future – from the image, for the image now achieves a relation with time itself. Indeed, film's image becomes an icon of time. What is noteworthy, however, is not only that the unconditioned nature of time finds a productive relation with particular thought-products (in this case, the time-image). Also intriguing is Deleuze's realisation that these particular images must be created. Cinema finds itself capable of 'making visible . . . relationships of time', but it does so precisely through creation – these relationships of time 'can only appear in a *creation* of the image'.[68]

Film's time-image, then, is iconic not only in the sense that it makes the unconditioned and the particular converge, or renders them inseparable, but also insofar as it makes the unconditioned nature of time turn on the *creation* of particular images. Generalising this, we can say that the power of immanence becomes inseparable from the creation of icons, such that the concept of immanence itself becomes inseparable from the iconic production of immanence. In other words, the concept of immanence is generated *by* the creation of icons, it is named by their production. An immanent politics of being thus advances from the no-place of utopia to the many places of polytopia, which is composed by the fabulation of a multitude of icons.

I insist on the iconic character of immanence, on the necessity of an iconic production of immanence, in order to separate immanence from any totality or any unity of the given. Immanence consists neither in a simple circulation of what is given, nor even in a utopic excess to the present. It consists in the production of icons, which do not just exceed the present but actually create the future. Real beings, the icons of immanence, construct a reality that breaks with the present – not with the particular moment of the present, but with the extension of the present that can last a long time. We resist this present by producing from the edge, by populating the edge with icons. If we do not do so, we satisfy the present, which then encompasses the edge. If we 'put off writing until tomorrow', tomorrow will not arrive.[69] Or, more exactly, tomorrow will arrive but the future will not. In the absence of iconic production, the present remains. Deleuze, citing Nietzsche, speaks of 'acting counter to our time and thereby acting on our time and, let us hope, for the benefit of a time to come'.[70] This is possible because the products of thought are real beings – iconic creations of the real. To 'benefit' a time to come has nothing to do with waiting for or even anticipating more favourable conditions. It concerns the creation of such conditions, here and now, through the fabulation of icons. Deleuze says that 'writers generate real bodies', and this point may be applied to thought in general.[71] The aim of thought is to create real beings that iconically put the future in place.

Notes

1. Gilles Deleuze, *Cinema 2: The Time-Image*, trans. Hugh Tomlinson and Robert Galeta (Minneapolis: University of Minnesota Press, 1989), p. 171.
2. Ibid., p. 172.
3. Gil Anidjar, *Semites: Race, Religion, Literature* (Stanford: Stanford University Press, 2008), p. 50.
4. Ibid., p. 175.
5. 'Idioteque', *Kid A*, CD, Radiohead (London: Parlophone, 2000).
6. Malcolm X, *The Autobiography of Malcolm X* (New York: Ballantine Books, 1964), p. 203.
7. Deleuze, *Cinema 2*, p. 172.
8. Gilles Deleuze, *Negotiations*, trans. Martin Joughin (New York: Columbia University Press, 1995), p. 176.
9. Alain Badiou, *Deleuze: The Clamor of Being*, trans. Louise Burchill (Minneapolis: University of Minnesota Press, 2000), p. 92.
10. Deleuze, *Cinema 2*, p. 17.
11. Theodor Adorno, *Minima Moralia: Reflections from Damaged Life*, trans. E. F. N. Jephcott (London: Verso, 1974), p. 19.
12. Deleuze, *Negotiations*, pp. 127, 136.

13. Ibid., p. 133.
14. Ibid.
15. Deleuze, *Cinema 2*, p. 20.
16. Ibid.
17. Discussing François Châtelet, Deleuze remarks: 'Toutes les transcendences, toutes les croyances en un monde autre, il les appelle «outre-cuidances».' See Gilles Deleuze, *Périclès et Verdi. La Philosophie de François Châtelet* (Paris: Les Éditions de Minuit, 1988), p. 7.
18. Gilles Deleuze, *Difference and Repetition*, trans. Paul Patton (New York: Columbia University Press, 1994), p. 86.
19. Ibid., p. 218.
20. Simon Jarvis, *Adorno: A Critical Introduction* (New York: Routledge, 1998), p. 156.
21. Gilles Deleuze and Félix Guattari, *What is Philosophy?*, trans. Hugh Tomlinson and Graham Burchell (New York: Columbia University Press, 1994), p. 198.
22. Ibid., p. 208.
23. Ibid., p. 202.
24. Ibid., p. 164.
25. Ibid.
26. Ibid., p. 177.
27. Theodor Adorno, *Aesthetic Theory*, trans. Robert Hullot-Kentor (Minneapolis: University of Minnesota Press, 1997), p. 7.
28. Ibid.
29. Ibid., p. 143.
30. Ibid., p. 132.
31. Ibid.
32. Cited in Guy Flatley, 'The Atheist Who Was Obsessed With God', available at <http://www.moviecrazed.com/outpast/pasolini.html> (last accessed 18 February 2013).
33. Adorno, *Aesthetic Theory*, p. 143.
34. Ibid.
35. Ibid., p. 133.
36. Ibid.
37. Ibid.
38. Gillian Rose, *The Melancholy Science: An Introduction to the Thought of Theodor W. Adorno* (New York: Columbia University Press, 1978), p. 13.
39. Adorno, *Aesthetic Theory*, p. 178.
40. Fredric Jameson, *Late Marxism: Adorno; Or, The Persistence of the Dialectic* (New York: Verso, 1996), p. 186. Adorno's account of the artwork, according to Jameson, 'is a process essentially in the relation of its whole and parts. Without being reducible to one side or the other, it is the relation itself that is a process of becoming' (p. 178). The

becoming of this relation is interstitial, it is driven by what emerges in between the elements, such that otherness is materially embedded. Adorno here echoes Deleuze, who remarked that 'sensory becoming is otherness caught in a matter of expression' (*What is Philosophy?*, p. 177). Art is able to widen the bottleneck by dramatising the failures and intolerability of the possible, or by, as Deleuze says, 'exhausting the possible'. See Gilles Deleuze, *Essays Critical and Clinical*, trans. Daniel W. Smith and Michael A. Greco (Minneapolis: University of Minnesota Press, 1997), p. 154.

41. Regarding this account of Reich, I am indebted to discussions with Zeynep Bulut.

42. For an account of how such a logic of communication functions within recent American politics, see Jodi Dean, *Democracy and Other Neoliberal Fantasies: Communicative Capitalism and Left Politics* (Durham, NC: Duke University Press, 2009).

43. I am observing here the movement from a disciplinary society to a control society. Deleuze's most explicit account of this shift, which depends on his interpretation of Foucault, may be found in *Negotiations*, pp. 177–82. For more on this subject, see Maurizio Lazzarato, 'Life and the Living in the Societies of Control', in *Deleuze and the Social*, ed. Martin Fuglsang and Bent Meier Sørensen (Edinburgh: Edinburgh University Press, 2006).

44. Don DeLillo, *Underworld* (New York: Simon & Schuster, 1997), pp. 785–6.

45. Deleuze, *Negotiations*, p. 175.

46. Rose, *Melancholy Science*, p. 88.

47. Adorno, *Aesthetic Theory*, p. 246.

48. Ibid.

49. Deleuze and Guattari, *What is Philosophy?*, pp. 99–100.

50. Ibid., p. 99.

51. Ibid.

52. Ibid., p. 100.

53. Ibid., p. 99.

54. Theodor Adorno, *Negative Dialectics*, trans. E. B. Ashton (New York: Continuum, 1973), p. 207.

55. It is in this precise sense that those who discern a retreat from the political in Adorno have a point. The weakness of Adorno's thought lies not in the failure to provide a specified political program so much as in the failure to explicitly conceive the connection between the utopic dimension of production and the political – that is, the being-making – dimension of production. For instance, Adorno is right to assert that the 'immanence of society in the artwork is the essential social relation of art, not the immanence of art in society' (*Aesthetic Theory*, p. 232). It is by refusing the conditions of society that thought finds the capacity

to evade the pre-conditions of society. Furthermore, the conditions that the thought-product (in this case, the artwork) sets forth derive from the utopic and the interstitial, rather than from the present possibilities of association. What is lacking at this point, however, is any conception of how the bonds created by the artwork act back upon society. Or, to put it more generally, what is lacking is a conception of how the process of producing thought-products does not simply gesture toward the utopic, but actually draws upon it in order to create the real.

56. Deleuze, *Cinema 2*, p. 150.
57. Ibid.
58. Ibid.
59. Ibid.
60. Deleuze, *Negotiations*, p. 126.
61. Deleuze and Guattari, *What is Philosophy?*, p. 171.
62. Deleuze, *Negotiations*, p. 174.
63. Deleuze, *Essays*, pp. 117–8.
64. On this shift, see Paola Marrati's excellent book, *Gilles Deleuze. Philosophie et cinema* (Paris: P.U.F., 2003).
65. I am, with regard to the relation between the concept of immanence and the concept of the icon, indebted to conversations with Anthony Paul Smith and Erin Yerby.
66. Deleuze, *Cinema 2*, p. xii.
67. Ibid., p. xi.
68. Ibid., p. xii; my emphasis.
69. Deleuze, *Difference and Repetition*, p. xi.
70. Ibid., p. xi.
71. Deleuze, *Negotiations*, p. 134.

Conclusion: The Future of Immanence

Let us return once more to Nietzsche's proclamation. We observed, when first looking at it, that it was motivated by a decisive insight about the connection between imagination and the world. The world we imagine is the world we will get. This insight concerns not just the immanence of thought and world, but also the way that the future of immanence turns on our imagination of it. By way of conclusion, then, we must insist on the importance of continuing to conceive immanence. This is to say that immanence is not given. When we speak of immanence we are not speaking of something that is there regardless of the way we conceive it. This might be an adequate way of talking about a transcendent God, but it has no value for the articulation of immanence. On the contrary, if we do not conceive of the future of immanence, then the possibilities of immanent existence will not emerge. It is in view of this fact that I now offer three theses for the future of conceiving immanence.

Immanent Belief: Immanence must adopt a radically critical perspective on the secular. We have seen how the claim issued by theological transcendence – that immanence cannot provide the sort of 'outside' necessary for a break with the given and an invocation of new possibilities of existence – falls flat. Immanence is able to do precisely what such transcendence claims it cannot. Yet if theological transcendence is bankrupt, this does not mean we must, by way of inversion, advocate a straightforwardly secular immanence. This is because immanence can converge in interesting ways with theological discourse. We have seen this with Yoder, who presented a theology that was not only immanent, but also secular. This means that two presumed oppositions miss the mark: the opposition between theology and immanence, as well as the opposition between theology, or religion, and the secular. Immanence, when it poses itself against transcendence, must not assume transcendence's oppositions. That is, it must not surrender theology to transcendence, nor must it assume that the affirmation of theology requires opposition to the

212

secular. Immanence can be theological, but it can simultaneously be secular; in being both, it breaks down their opposition as well as their ability to identify registers of reality.

It is by refusing these oppositions that immanence criticises the secular: the secular means, from the vantage of immanence, nothing but affirmation of the thisworldly. The secular, in its proper sense, amounts to a rigorously immanent affirmation of the world, however it may emerge. And this is what allows immanence to adopt a radically critical perspective on the secular. If the secular is defined in terms of its opposition to religion, then this is not the sort of secular that immanence demands. Or if the secular is defined in terms of its relation to Christianity, then this is likewise not what immanence means by the secular. Sadly, from the perspective of immanence, it is the presence of these two oppositions that overdetermines contemporary theories of the secular. Immanence proceeds by opposing these oppositions. It underdetermines them, and it does so centrally through its belief in this world. *Immanent belief* concerns the very emergence of this world, it links us to the senselessness of experience that is prior to the oppositional discourse of secularism versus religion.

Immanent belief may be imagined as secular, but this has nothing to do with modernity's developmentalist opposition between the religious and the secular. The modern secular is caught up in its need to liberate itself from religion and thus render itself superior to its supposedly religious others. It is too bewitched by a spell of its own casting to become capable of establishing a genuinely immanent relation with the world. In this respect, the future of immanence requires the rejection of every presumption that equates immanence with the secular. If there is a secularity intrinsic to immanence, then it is one that has little to do with the modern secular's desire to oppose itself to religion. On the contrary, immanence supplies the conceptual clarity by which we can advance a radical critique of the modern secular. Only in this way can we refuse the limits imposed *onto* the world while simultaneously entering *into* the world.

Metaphilosophy: Immanence must actively refuse every tendency that would reduce it to 'affirmation' or 'positivity'. The concept of immanence, when it is taken up by contemporary philosophy, is generally imagined as a call for affirmation, or as a critique of negative thought. This is no doubt due to Deleuze's own manifesto-like style of writing. He constantly presents immanence as pure affirmation and thus as the critique of all negativity. But this can, as Berardi observed, itself be a mode of depression. To present immanence as a manifesto for affirmation not only keeps us from encountering the problem of depression, it also diverts attention from the still indeterminate way that immanence is conceived, even in Deleuze. Christian Kerslake rightly contends that '"immanence", despite appearing to connote philosophical transparency, is in fact a problem for Deleuze; indeed perhaps it is the problem inspiring his work'.[1] Accordingly, to respond to Deleuze's concept of immanence by simply calling for affirmation is to treat his concept as a solution, as something given (a fact of 'philosophical transparency') rather than as a contingent response to a real, and very live, problem – a problem that continues even in Deleuze's own articulation of immanence.

I have reversed the tendency toward affirmation by moving from the presumed resolution of Deleuze's immanence back into the problematic of immanence that inspires, but also remains not finally addressed by, Deleuze's thought. This reversal is most explicit in my construction of the concept of *metaphilosophy*. If Deleuze's concept of immanence is depressing, if it is less a solution than something that indicates a more fundamental problematic, then this can be seen most notably in his ambivalence regarding the relation between creation of the new and resistance to the present. The difficulty with Deleuze's thought, in this respect, is its overcommitment – perhaps as overcompensation for anxiety about the depressive senselessness of present experience? – to affirmation, or to the positivity of creation. Deleuze was ultimately unable to think the connection between philosophy's capacity to create and its failure to do so. Even when he addressed the fact of philosophy's failure, he did not conceive the way in which the potency and demand for creation must be mediated by critical awareness of such failure. It is at this juncture that it becomes necessary to think immanence through the concept of metaphilosophy. Only in this way do we prevent immanence from turning into another version of transcendence, where what is affirmed is imagined as existing above and beyond the conditions that, here and now, make us depressed.

Immanence does, of course, involve the capacity to create the new. But if this capacity is going to be truly immanent then it cannot separate the unconditioned from the conditions in which we seek to re-express the unconditioned. Immanence will have a future only if it is able to take seriously its implication in the present; it will exceed the given practice of philosophy only if it is able to conceive philosophy's complicity with the present's failure. This is something that Deleuze failed to do; to respond to this failure by doubling down on affirmation only exacerbates the problem. Deleuze's conception of immanence does not solve the problem, though it can return us to the problem – which is metaphilosophical.

Fabulation: Immanence cannot be conceived apart from its production of icons. Immanence, because it insists on the pure relationality of all things, such that no term of relation is prior to any other term, is often imagined in terms of 'oneness'. While this image is not without some truth, it keeps us from attending to an essential aspect of immanence. An emphasis on 'oneness' misses the productive capacity of immanence, and specifically the way that this capacity is inseparable from the creation of products – which I have spoken of as real beings, or as *icons of immanence*. In other words, the production of immanence is not just a matter of a generic power, it also has to do with the creation of particular products. Like a film's flicker, which quickly, almost imperceptibly flashes in between frames, immanence emerges as the cracks of the present. The concept of immanence must articulate this cracked, flickering horizon, but it must also articulate the thought-products that may be created from the interstice's flicker.

Too much emphasis has been given to immanence's concern for imperceptibility and deterritorialisation. To conceive immanence in this way is to accommodate the present reign of communication, which prizes process over product and the maintenance of continuous malleability over the creation of real beings that, because of the roughness and density of their particular constellation of existence (the sheer 'thisness' of their character as products), might render themselves incommunicable within the present. This is to insist on the political character of immanence, or on the politics of conceiving immanence. It is not enough simply to have immanence name possibilities beyond the perceptible, possibilities that deterritorialise our received ways of orienting ourselves in space; the present, overdetermined as it is by communication (also a kind of 'oneness'), wants the very same thing. It becomes necessary to dial down the celebration of generic possibility and to focus on the creation of new perceptions and new territories.

This is why we must assert that there is no immanence outside the production of its icons. It is by way of icons that the concept of immanence evades the lure of all-pervasive connectivity and affirms instead the right to difference – that is, the power to produce particular realities that differ from the ever-expanding continuity of the present. This has nothing to do with the conservative 'defence' of particular identities, for these are part of the present. They form one end of the spectrum within which we communicate; they are 'part of the dialogue'. It has to do instead with *fabulation*, with the constructive imagination of particular realities that are excluded from present communication. Immanence must not be imagined as a kind of 'oneness' that is hindered by the particularity of perceptions and territories. It should instead be seen as the creation of a multitude of icons that, in their own respective manners, give reality to differing modes of existence. When the possibilities of life itself seem to be already encompassed by an eternal present, the future will arrive only when we create it. It is not enough to say that the future is 'to-come'. We must give the future a place – indeed, as many places as we can imagine. We must fabulate the future into existence, here and now, through the creation of icons.

Note

1. Christian Kerslake, 'The Vertigo of Philosophy: Deleuze and the Problem of Immanence', *Radical Philosophy* 113 (2002), p. 10.

Index

Index